# TOWARD
# 2012

JEREMY P. TARCHER/PENGUIN

*a member of Penguin Group (USA) Inc.*

*New York*

# TOWARD
# 2012

*Perspectives on the Next Age*

EDITED BY

*Daniel Pinchbeck & Ken Jordan*

JEREMY P. TARCHER/PENGUIN
Published by the Penguin Group
Penguin Group (USA) Inc., 375 Hudson Street, New York, New York 10014, USA • Penguin Group (Canada),
90 Eglinton Avenue East, Suite 700, Toronto, Ontario M4P 2Y3, Canada (a division of Pearson Canada Inc.) •
Penguin Books Ltd, 80 Strand, London WC2R 0RL, England • Penguin Ireland, 25 St Stephen's Green, Dublin 2,
Ireland (a division of Penguin Books Ltd) • Penguin Group (Australia), 250 Camberwell Road, Camberwell,
Victoria 3124, Australia (a division of Pearson Australia Group Pty Ltd) • Penguin Books India Pvt Ltd,
11 Community Centre, Panchsheel Park, New Delhi–110 017, India • Penguin Group (NZ), 67 Apollo Drive,
Rosedale, North Shore 0632, New Zealand (a division of Pearson New Zealand Ltd) • Penguin Books (South Africa)
(Pty) Ltd, 24 Sturdee Avenue, Rosebank, Johannesburg 2196, South Africa

Penguin Books Ltd, Registered Offices: 80 Strand, London WC2R 0RL, England

ISBN-13: 978-1-58542-700-0

Printed in the United States of America

BOOK DESIGN BY NICOLE LAROCHE

Neither the publisher nor the authors are engaged in rendering professional advice or services to the individual reader. The
ideas, procedures, and suggestions contained in this book are not intended as a substitute for consulting with a physician.
All matters regarding your health require medical supervision. Neither the authors nor the publisher shall be liable or
responsible for any loss or damage allegedly arising from any information or suggestion in this book.

While the authors have made every effort to provide accurate telephone numbers and Internet addresses at the time of
publication, neither the publisher nor the authors assume any responsibility for errors, or for changes that occur after
publication. Further, the publisher does not have any control over and does not assume any responsibility for author or
third-party websites or their content.

# CONTENTS

# VI. COMMUNITY

# INTRODUCTION

## *Daniel Pinchbeck*

Along time ago, Karl Marx realized that modernity was based on
successive revolutions in which "all that is solid melts into air," as
the force of capitalism reshapes society and tears apart ecosystems. In
our time, this process of melting down and vaporizing has reached a new
level of speed and violence. When we face the future, there seems to be
nothing we can grasp with certainty. Not only our economic system and
the future of our civilization, but the integrity of our environment and
the continuity of the human species—along with most other species who
share this planet with us—are immediately endangered. At such a threshold, everything is up for grabs, and all beliefs are open for questioning.

In *2012: The Return of Quetzalcoatl*, I proposed that our Western
knowledge system was severely limited because it denied the value of
intuition, visionary, and psychic experience. I sought to assemble an alternative paradigm, encompassing older ways of knowing and mystical
thought, without denying the validity of the modern scientific method.
I suggested we might take indigenous people seriously in their prophetic
views of this current era, since they preserved access to those dimensions
of the psyche that our society has systematically suppressed.

Around the world, many traditional cultures see this time as an ep-
och of transformation—the shift from the Fourth World to the Fifth
World, according to the oral foretelling of the Hopi in Arizona. In the
Yucatán area of Mexico from the second to ninth century AD, the Classic
Maya developed an advanced civilization, with a system of knowledge

based on study of astronomical cycles and exploration of nonordinary states of awareness. Mayan monuments indicate that they denoted a rare eclipse of the galactic center by the Winter Solstice sun on December 21, 2012, as the transition between world ages. Even if you are not inclined to give credence to ancient prophesies, it is clear that humanity faces grave threats to its existence, and society must change or life on the planet may be at risk.

I do not pretend to know what will happen on that date, or in the years ahead of us leading up to it. I hope that nothing drastic will take place, for, if the hypothesis is correct, our world may undergo severe cataclysms and immense suffering in the immediate future—the current slew of droughts, deluges, forest fires, hunger riots, and mortgage foreclosures being only a faint indicator of what is in store for us. The severity of the crises may be devastating for modern people, who believed their technology had shielded them from brute survival. Some, perhaps many, will not survive.

In my book, I argued that personal and global change are inseparable, concluding with the Hopi that "We are the ones we've been waiting for." For me personally, writing my own work no longer seemed enough of a way to contribute to the larger process of transformation. After an initial effort to start a company with collaborators in Los Angeles, I joined forces with Ken Jordan, a digital media expert and an old friend of mine from New York, to launch *Reality Sandwich* as a web magazine and think tank for ideas and projects related to this current period of accelerating intensity. We found a magnificent designer, Michael Robinson, to be our creative director, and chose Jonathan Phillips, a radical activist turned Gnostic visionary, as our community director. Our team has followed up *Reality Sandwich* with the release of Evolver.net, a social network designed to facilitate collaboration and community development, and the Evolver Exchange, an online marketplace for artisanal products and tools that support sustainable living.

Ken and I chose the name "Reality Sandwich" from an Allen Ginsberg poem, as an homage to the shared elements in our personal backgrounds. Ken's father, Fred Jordan, was editor in chief of avant-garde publisher Grove Press and edited its magazine *Evergreen Review,* a major force in the counterculture of the fifties and sixties. My mother, Joyce Johnson, was involved with the Beat Generation as a young woman, writing about her relationship with Jack Kerouac in her memoir, *Minor Characters*. My mother was also a book editor in the 1960s, publishing Abbie Hoffman, Kerouac, and others. We hoped that *Reality Sandwich* would follow in this legacy of countercultural media of the past, developing a new forum for the present.

The 1960s counterculture brought together separate scenes that realized the connection between individual awareness and social change: the Beats, LSD proponents, Black Power radicals, Buddhists, environmental activists, sex liberationists, feminists, the gay rights movement, the American Indian Movement, John Cage avant-gardists, popular rock bands, hippies, and Yippies!, among many groups. The Vietnam War incited a populist effort to force the government to withdraw U.S. troops, and the antiwar movement gave the counterculture great social significance and influence. A similar mixing of diverse subcultures seems to be happening in America today.

We intended *Reality Sandwich* to mesh together a number of aligned but separate tribes that have been developing for years: permaculture activists, Burning Man hedonists, shamanic candidates, cultural creatives, open-source programmers, yogis, anarchist puppeteers, DJs, design scientists, tantric practitioners, and urban homesteaders, among others. These disparate interest groups share an awareness of the critical state of our planet. In their own way, all of them seek to engage with current events. The endless Iraq War and, above all, the dire environmental crisis are this generation's wake-up call, intensifying the global stakes.

Our initial results exceeded our expectations, as the volume of article submissions and enthusiastic outpouring of support were almost more than we could handle. Over the first year, our audience grew to fifty thousand unique visitors a month—without any marketing or promotion on our part, outside of our speaking engagements and a few events. We had created a vital hub for a large number of writers to pursue a range of interests—from environmental design to alternative relationship models, visionary technologies to spiritual practices—at a level of depth beyond what the mainstream media allows. At the same time, writers could explore edgy subjects such as crop circles, UFOs, and psychedelic shamanism that were often dismissed and disregarded by the cultural gatekeepers.

Unlike the one-directional approach of traditional media, where the author is the "authority" who imparts knowledge to the ignorant masses, our website encourages engagement between writers and readers, leading to many extraordinary exchanges in the "comments" sections that follow the pieces. Writers will comment on articles by other writers, blurring the line between editorial voice and audience. This form of dialogue has great promise. The collaborative infrastructure of "Web 2.0" points toward an open forum in which a community can sharpen its wits and discover its values and principles through public discourse, creating a foundation for cooperating and collaborating. In a sense, this type of forum revives the Ancient Greek concept of the polis, creating a public space, albeit a virtual one, for individuals to come together freely and discover where their interests intersect. The capacity for new media technologies to support the rapid emergence and self-organization of collective intelligence may be one of the ways that the prophetic time frame of 2012 could bring about a truly cooperative and sustainable global society.

Through *Reality Sandwich,* Ken and I discovered many brilliant and inspiring writers who explore the current processes of spiritual and material transformation in their work, usually outside of the mainstream. We are truly delighted to be presenting their essays to you here, and hope that you will learn from them, as we have. When I wrote my books, I often felt isolated from a larger community of thinkers pursuing similar ideas. Now it seems that *Reality Sandwich* is helping to unify and define this global network.

Joseph Campbell described the phases of shamanic initiation as "separation, initiation, and return." Since the 1960s, several generations of modern seekers embarked on initiatory paths, but they lacked ways to bring the knowledge they gleaned from their personal quests back into the larger society. 2012 may represent the completion of an initiation process for the modern psyche. Over thousands of years, the modern mind separated itself from the natural world, individuated, and made inquiries into the essence of matter. Completing the circle, we can now overcome our alienation and materialism through conscious reintegration with a holistic worldview, accepting the limits of human knowing and the many dimensions of being that exist beyond the range of our physical senses.

I believe that the only way we can avoid or at least mitigate the likely effects of imminent cataclysm is through a rapid evolution of collective intelligence. My hope is that the extraordinary ideas and initiatives presented by *Reality Sandwich* writers help to build a solid foundation for a practical—and visionary—alternative to the current system. The design scientist Buckminster Fuller liked to say that you do not change a system by criticizing it: If you really want to change things, you find ways to make the old model obsolete. The perspectives presented in the essays that follow could make the old practices of our greed-driven corporate culture obsolete, and begin to indicate a new path for humanity.

# I

# INITIATION

# MEETING THE SPIRITS

## Daniel Pinchbeck

All through my childhood, I felt certain that something extraordinary—absolutely amazing and out of the ordinary—was going to happen to me. The world seemed bursting with a secret that nobody would divulge, and someday this tremendous mystery would be revealed. Simply because they were older, I assumed that all adults had passed through this portal into the miraculous essence of existence, although they never spoke about it. As I approached adolescence, I began to suspect that my deepest hopes were going to be unfulfilled. By the time I went to college, I had realized, to my horror, that "maturity" meant accepting constraints and being bound to a limited career path, rather than blossoming into a deeper dimension of possibility and wonder. This was a painful shock.

I now suspect that what I felt is a nearly universal disappointment for young people in our world: I was yearning for initiation into a culture that had abandoned it. Initiatory techniques and rituals have been an essential part of human cultures for tens of thousands of years. In tribal and aboriginal societies, initiations serve a number of different purposes. On one level, rites of passage create a threshold between childhood and adulthood, marking a major life boundary. They are also a time when the elders pass on oral traditions and knowledge to the young. But most importantly, the traditional process of initiation involves a disciplined training in extrasensory perception and nonordinary states of consciousness—

learning to communicate with the spirit worlds that lie beyond the limits of our physical senses.

While our modern secular culture denies the existence of a spiritual dimension to life, many of our popular postsecular movements of mysticism still refuse to address the question of spirits. Philosophers such as Ken Wilber tend to reduce them to psychological tropes or delusions. Based on my own experiences, I strongly suspect we need to attain a more sophisticated understanding of how spirits may operate, as well as a set of techniques for dealing with them, before we can approach higher states and stages of development. We cannot have "Spirit" without spirits.

For many indigenous cultures, it is a high priority to stay on good terms with the ancestor spirits, who can wreak havoc if they are not given respect. The living and the dead maintain a reciprocal relationship. For the indigenous Maya, if the dead are not handled properly, their ghosts hang around, inflicting neuroses, addictive patterns, and depressions upon their descendants. Such a perspective does not conflict with modern psychology, but adds a deeper dimension to it. As Amit Goswami explores in *The Self-Aware Universe,* quantum physics offers the possibility that incorporeal patterns of thinking, feeling, and action might continue and have effects in the world, even without a physical reference point in a living organism.

One way we could consider our current situation in the U.S., perhaps, is as a case of spirit possession on a mass scale. Since we dismiss spirits as nonexistent, we have no defenses against the forces that prey upon us. When a college student guns down his classmates, when a soldier tortures a defenseless victim, when corporate officers avoid facing the environmental consequences of their profit-making, we might be looking at situations in which unappeased demons and aggrieved ancestor spirits are overtaking people, entering their psyches in states of detachment and disconnection. Such a situation cannot be solved through rational means alone, but calls for shamanic techniques such as soul retrieval and banishment.

Personally, my youthful sense of being cheated of some deeper potential melted away once I discovered shamanic practices as an adult, and explored visionary states of consciousness in traditional ceremonies in South America, West Africa, and the U.S. Through this work, I restored the primordial connection to the sacred that I had lost after my childhood, as well as my original sense of wonder, and this was tremendously healing and empowering. Through my own shamanic journeys, I realized that modern culture was facing an initiatory crisis on a global scale. We have created a planet of "kidults," perpetual adolescents trapped by material desires, with no access to higher realms and little sense of purpose or moral responsibility.

Despite the best efforts of people like Robert Bly and Malidoma Some, we are not going to institute a new culture of initiation in the next few years. As Westerners, each of us has to follow a personal path to recover the numinous for ourselves, shedding our self-limiting beliefs and narcissistic complexes in the process. In tribal cultures, initiation is ultimately a public process that requires an act of witnessing from the collective before it is complete. The visionary knowledge gained through initiatory discipline only becomes meaningful when it is integrated into the community through storytelling, dance, and pageant. In our postmodern world, those who undergo initiation may need to create a shared cultural context to impart the wisdom they have gained from their ordeals. Such knowledge is both a gift and a responsibility: Indeed, if frenzied spirits and sneaky demons are attacking us from beyond the margins of our interpreted world, we may require a revival of shamanic practices to reveal and release them.

# *HOMO LUMINUS:* YOU WITH WINGS

*Stella Osorojos*

Recently, I asked the Vermont-based Shaman Jeffrey Triplatt what he knows about the Inka prophecy of *Homo luminus*. This might have been a mistake, I realized, when Jeffrey's initial response was to sink deep into his sinuses, affect his nerdiest voice, and say, "There's this gay guy and he's holding a lightbulb . . ."

Then again, in this case, levity probably makes sense.

Before I get around to explaining, let me backtrack a bit. About two years ago, in the midst of pursuing a master's degree in Traditional Chinese Medicine, I started seeing an acupuncturist who has written a lot about sacred geometry and methods for aligning the body with the Earth's energetic grids. At the time, I didn't understand half of what he talked about, though I loved getting his needles and listening to him patter on about triangles, light frequencies, and "It's all about the heart, it's all about the heart." When he suggested that, while I meditate, I should activate a pattern of acupuncture points on my back and ask for "The Wingmaker Frequency," I didn't hesitate to comply, though I didn't know to whom I was making my supplication nor what the "wingmaker" anything was.

The first couple of times I meditated in this manner, I noticed a gentle lifting occur through my spine, as if that string that yoga teachers are always talking about was suddenly being activated by some cosmic pulley system. It felt pretty good and I didn't think too much about it until some weeks later, during a weekly meditation group I host at my house.

There were four of us present that night. We sat facing one another and began. I silently activated the pattern and asked for The Wingmaker Frequency. The now-familiar lifting sensation ensued and then, about fifteen minutes into the meditation, I felt a sharp kick between my shoulder blades and was thrown forward off my meditation cushion. I blurted out, "Excuse me!" and looked around. Everybody was still meditating quietly, though I did see one friend stifle a giggle, no doubt assuming that I'd fallen asleep on my cushion.

Not knowing what to think, I shook my head, sat back up, and tried to resume meditating. But the second I returned to the upright position, another astonishing thing happened: Wings sprouted from my back, I shit you not. Feathers as white and strong as bleached turkey quills sprouted from my shoulder blades and my ears filled with a special effects sound track of crunching, grinding, and flapping as these *things* filled the space behind me, growing enormous. On the one hand, I knew that this wasn't actually happening, that people don't grow wings. On the other hand, I wasn't so sure; the episode was that tangible.

Thinking that I might have hit some extraordinary sweet spot that would vanish as soon as I emerged from meditation, I balanced as quietly as I could, enjoying the miraculous weight I felt on my back as well as the feeling of being bathed in light. When the iPod gong rang and our allotted thirty minutes was up, I opened my eyes reluctantly, entirely expecting the sensations to vanish as my lids lifted. To my surprise, however, the "wings" did not disappear. In fact, they stayed with me all through the subsequent walking meditation and postsit chitchat. I was dying to ask someone what they could see, but it was just too crazy a question to pose. *Excuse me, but do I have wings? Could you commit me now or should I make the call for you?*

After everybody had left, I managed to screw up enough courage to ask my husband what he saw. He assured me that he could not see anything atypical, though I did look clear and bright, perhaps more than usual after a meditation. As we talked, I surmised a connection between my experience and The Wingmaker Frequency for which I'd been asking and I vowed to grill my acupuncturist about it the next time I saw him.

As synchronicity would have it, the next time I saw him was the following day. I walked onto the campus and there he was, talking with the school's president about teaching an elective. I rushed over, wrested a moment alone, and started to chide him for not telling me that The Wingmaker Frequency meditation would make me "grow wings." To my surprise, the good doctor claimed to have no idea what I was talking about. In fact, he looked at me quite skeptically, apparently suspicious of my sanity. Let me tell you that when a man who claims to have gotten his treatment patterns from little green men thinks *you're* crazy, the knees, they do shake.

But once I slowed down and repeated the whole thing, beginning with the kick to my shoulder blades, something seemed to click. This time, he nodded sagely and smiled a little. He shifted his eyes in that way that allows him to see energy and looked me over. "I don't see wings, but I do see a lot of energy back there," he said.

That was all he could say?

Yep, that was all.

I was busy with exams and clinic shifts, so I put aside the experience until, trolling the Web some months later, it occurred to me to type in "wingmaker" and see what I could uncover. I found this: www .wingmakers.co.nz, which probably should have done nothing to dispel fears about my sanity, though it did. If someone else sees the pink elephant in the room, you just might be at the circus.

The creator of this website calls himself Darren Murphy and writes that "The term Wingmaker comes from the opening of wings technique developed in the year 1979 by wingmaker 732 . . . [and means] a person who moves with spiritual wings upon the physical plain of existence. . . ." He has put up meditations that are meant to open our "wings," as well as tools for working with them, and lots of other far-out energetic techniques. The material is badly in need of a copy editor and seems to shift geographically with each click-through. I once found a section that admitted that the difficulty in navigating and comprehending the website was intentional, designed for protection, though I would be hard-pressed to find that paragraph again.

All this primed me, in the way these things do, for my first encounter with Jeffrey Triplatt, whom I met when he visited a mutual friend last June. After training at Alberto Villoldo's Four Winds program, Jeffrey said, he had become friendly with a shaman in Peru who had initiated him in the Altomisayok tradition, a lineage of so-called Celestial Shamans who work with, among other energies, the Angelic Realms.

Up until that point, I'd never heard anybody talk about the Angelic Realms as if they were real, though I suppose it *was* implied in the Catholic schools I attended as a girl. And I really hadn't connected my meditation experience with angels, probably because the prospect slightly mortified me. On occasion, my mother has sent me angel paraphernalia—a coin with an angel-shaped cutout, a bookmark with cherubs and a scrolling font, like that. The saccharine whiff of grannydom that accompanied those stuffed envelopes always sent a shiver through my DNA, so I suppose it was natural that I resisted the most obvious link.

Nevertheless, upon hearing Jeffrey's words, I knew the man had information for me. With hands shaking, I asked him if he had any idea what The Wingmaker Frequency was. He didn't, but he did listen to a recounting of my meditation incident without betraying any hint of surprise. When I was done, he said he could see wings on my back, though they were folded down. If I wanted, he could help me pull them out in ceremony.

Jeffrey linked my experience to an idea he first learned from Dr. Villoldo, that we are in the process of evolving from *Homo sapiens* to *Homo luminus,* though he didn't say exactly what that meant. Nor would he answer the millions of new questions that sprung up: Was he saying that *Homo luminus* would have wings? Was my experience part or all of the process? Was I done then? I could go back to bed because I'm all evolved?

Would my New Year's henceforth be spent with Shirley MacLaine and Dennis Kucinich? Because normally I hate New Year's, but that could be cool.

Typical for a shaman, Jeffrey wouldn't say much beyond the few hints he'd already dropped, though he did say that everyone has wings. Later, when he was working on us all around the fire, I saw him moving behind other peoples' backs, digging his hands into their shoulder blades, and unfurling giant, invisible, wing-shaped sails that he articulated with his fingers, raking the smoky night air.

When I finally had the time to do a bit of research about *Homo luminus,* the go-to guy was obviously Villoldo. In the epilogue of *Shaman, Healer, Sage* (Harmony Books, 2000), he writes about the teachings he received from his mentor, Don Antonio, about the Inka *pachacuti,* or time of upheaval, which has supposedly already begun and will last until the year 2012:

> Although the prophecies mention the possibility of annihilation, they actually promise the dawn of a millennium of peace, beginning after this period of turmoil. Even more important for the shamans, the prophecies speak about a tear in the fabric of time itself, a window into the future through which a new human species will emerge. Don Antonio used to say that *Homo sapiens* has perished, and that a new human, *Homo luminus,* is being born this very instant on our planet. Interestingly, my mentor believed that evolution happens within generations, not in between generations, as biology believes. This means that *we* are that new human. We are the ones that we've been waiting for.

Curious, I checked these ideas with an evolutionary biologist. Jerry Coyne, a professor of evolutionary biology in the University of Chicago's Department of Ecology and Evolution, has this to say: "Everything in this is hogwash. No evidence of a new species of human emerging. And evolution happens between generations, not within generations. This is just all New Age garbage!"

Given Coyne's position, I decided not to ask about the other page I marked in Villoldo's book, within a section titled, "Death, Dying, and Beyond." In it, Villoldo describes five levels of an after-death domain in which a life review process happens. He says that the fourth level is where we meet our ancestors and families, but it's the fifth level that snagged my attention:

> The fifth world is the domain of luminous beings dedicated to assisting all humankind. Shamans who have mastered the journey beyond death return to this level. Long ago, when the shamanic death rites were first developed, this was a difficult level to attain. Today it is much more accessible. Trails have been blazed by the courageous men and women who have come before us. The prophecies of the Hopi and the Inka speak about our entire planet emerging into the fifth world. They refer to our entering the domains of angels.

To me, this suggests that *Homo luminus* could be angelic, or at least take an angelic form. I wanted to ask Villoldo what he thought about this idea, but he didn't respond to my e-mail.

Jeffrey did talk to me, though, starting with that untoward lightbulb crack. Then he got serious, saying that *Homo luminus* is the next phase of our evolution, in which we develop our light body, the shamanic envisioning of our energetic anatomy. This process he described as moving "from the mind-center of our knowledge into our heart." Wings, he suggested, are "a metaphor of [this] ascension," in that they, quite literally, "point the way to being more centered in the heart."

Lisa Renee, a self-described Galactic Emissary with an "ascension" practice in Santa Monica (you gotta love L.A.), had much more definite ideas about my "wings." She said that wings are a human's birthright, part of the original, twelve-dimensional design, and that "the clipping of our wings is an enslavement program." Who might be doing this enslaving she, naturally, wouldn't much elaborate on. Does the opening of my "wings" therefore imply that I'm evolutionarily cooked? Jerry Coyne would say no, but I believe it suggests that I'm on the way.

And so, perhaps, are you. Consider the prevalence of angel-related messages that permeate our culture. From TV shows, to movies, jewelry, greeting cards, and untold numbers of trinkets, angels abound. Sometimes they're cloying; sometimes they're sinister, as in a recent *Nip/Tuck* billboard campaign showing an angel with her wings surgically removed. Perhaps they're all whispering about the aspirations of not only our souls, but also our very genes.

# A NEW UNDERSTANDING
# OF THE PSYCHE

## Stanislav Grof

*Stanislav Grof, M.D., renowned researcher into nonordinary states of consciousness, was honored in 2007 as the recipient of the Vision 97 Award at a ceremony in Prague. Below is a description of the award, in the words of its founder, former Czech president Václav Havel, followed by Doctor Grof's acceptance speech:*

> *To thinkers whose scientific work returns science into the framework of general culture, transcends the dominant concepts of knowledge and being, reveals unknown, surprising, or overlooked connections, and touches in a new way the mysteries of the universe and of life. It is thus an Award by which we would like to bring the attention of the public to spiritual achievements, which in the best sense of the word do not meet the criteria of the established ways of exploring of reality.*

Dear Mrs. Havel, dear President Havel, ladies and gentlemen,

It is a great pleasure for me to return to Prague, where I was born, spent my childhood, grew up, and received my basic training. An even greater source of pleasure than my visit to this city that I love so much are the extraordinary circumstances that brought me to Prague this time. I would like to thank wholeheartedly President Havel, Mrs. Havel, and the board of consultants of the Dagmar and Václav Havel Foundation for granting me the prestigious Vision 97 Award for my work in the area of research of consciousness and the human psyche. It is for me an immense honor and also a great surprise after fifty years of struggle with the "public anonym" in science, described in such an articulate way by professor Vopenka in his 2004 acceptance speech, after he himself received the Vision 97 Award.

An important reason why the Vision 97 Award means so much to me is my profound admiration and respect for President Havel as an artist, philosopher, and statesman with a broad spiritual vision, and as a man of extraordinary personal values. My admiration is shared by many of my American friends, who have repeatedly expressed to me their wish to have in the present difficult situation a president with the intellectual, moral, and spiritual qualities of Václav Havel. And during my journeys to different countries, I have often had the opportunity to find out that similar feelings are shared by many people all over the world. I cannot imagine another appreciation of my work that would be for me personally more meaningful. Today's ceremony falls on President Havel's birthday, and I would like to use this opportunity to congratulate him on this important anniversary and wish him much happiness, inner peace, personal satisfaction, and good health in the years to come.

It seems to be my destiny—or karma, if you wish—to be involved in research of areas that are subjects of great controversy in science and society. My unconventional professional career started here in Prague more than fifty years ago when I volunteered as a beginning psychiatrist for a session with LSD-25, diethylamide of lysergic acid. My preceptor, Docent Roubicek, received this fascinating experimental substance from the Swiss pharmaceutical company Sandoz. The incredibly powerful psychedelic effects of this ergot alkaloid had been discovered by Dr. Albert Hofmann, who accidentally intoxicated himself while working on its synthesis.

The research project of Docent Roubicek required a combination of the pharmacological effect of LSD with exposure to a powerful stroboscopic light oscillating at various frequencies. This combination evoked in me a powerful mystical experience that has radically changed my personal and professional life. It had such a profound effect on me that research of the heuristic, therapeutic, transformative, and evolutionary potential of nonordinary states of consciousness has become my profession, vocation, and personal passion for the rest of my life.

During approximately half of this period, my interest focused on clinical research of psychedelic substances, first at the Psychiatric Research Institute in Prague-Bohnice and later at the Maryland Psychiatric Research Center in Baltimore where I headed for several years the last surviving official psychedelic research in the United States. During the second half of this period, my wife, Christina, and I developed jointly the method of holotropic breathwork, which induces deep nonordinary states of consciousness with the use of very simple means, such as accelerated breathing, evocative music, and a certain kind of bodywork. Over the years, we have also worked with many people undergoing spontaneous episodes of nonordinary states of consciousness—psychospiritual crises or "spiritual emergencies" as we call them.

Research of nonordinary states of consciousness (or their important subgroup, for which I coined the term *holotropic*) has been for me a source of countless surprises and conceptual shocks, requiring radical changes in understanding consciousness, the human psyche, and the nature of reality. After many years of daily encounters with "anomalous phenomena," which contemporary science was unable to explain and the existence of which was in conflict with its fundamental metaphysical assumptions, I came to the conclusion that careful study of holotropic states and various phenomena which are associated with them, such as statistically highly improbable meaningful coincidences (Jung's "synchronicities"), shows the inevitability of a radical revision of thinking in psychology and psychiatry.

Conceptual changes required in these disciplines would in their nature, depth, and scope resemble the revolution which the physicists experienced in the first three decades of the twentieth century, when they had to move from Newtonian mechanics to theories of relativity and later to quantum physics. It is even possible to say that, in a certain sense, this conceptual revolution would be a logical completion of the radical changes which many years ago already occurred in physics.

The changes in the understanding of consciousness and of the human psyche in health and disease that naturally follow from the research of holotropic states fall into several categories. This research has shown the necessity to expand the traditional model of the psyche, limited to postnatal biography and the Freudian individual unconscious by two vast areas—perinatal (which has a close connection with the memories of biological birth) and transpersonal (mediating experiences of identification with other people, animals, and the botanical realm, and with human and animal ancestors, as well as experiences of the historical and archetypal collective unconscious, as described by C. G. Jung). Traditional psychiatry sees the beginnings of "psychogenic" disorders—those that do not have any demonstrable biological causes—in infancy and childhood. The work with holotropic states shows clearly that these disorders have additional deep roots in the perinatal and transpersonal realms of the unconscious. This finding might seem in and of itself very pessimistic, but it is outweighed by the discovery of new effective therapeutic mechanisms which operate on these deep levels of the unconscious.

The goal in traditional psychotherapies is to reach an intellectual understanding of how the human psyche functions—what are its basic motivating forces, why do symptoms develop and what is their meaning. This understanding then forms the basis for the development of techniques that psychotherapists use for the treatment of their clients. A serious problem associated with this strategy is a striking lack of agreement among psychologists and psychiatrists concerning the most fundamental theoretical problems and, consequently, an astonishing number of competing schools of psychotherapy. The work with holotropic states offers a surprising radical alternative—mobilization of deep inner healing intelligence of the clients that is capable to govern the process of healing and transformation.

Materialistic science does not have a place for any form of spirituality and considers it to be essentially incompatible with the scientific worldview. It perceives any form of spirituality as an indication of lack of education, superstition, gullibility, primitive magical thinking, or a serious psychopathological condition. Modern consciousness research shows that spirituality is a natural and legitimate dimension of the human psyche and of the universal order of things. However, it is important to emphasize that this statement refers to direct authentic spirituality based on personal experience and not to the ideology and dogmas of organized religions.

New observations show that consciousness is not an epiphenomenon of matter—a product of complex neurophysiological processes in the brain—but a fundamental primary attribute of existence, as it is described in the great spiritual philosophies of the East. As suggested by the Swiss psychiatrist C. G. Jung, the psyche is not enclosed in the human skull and brain, but permeates all of existence (as anima mundi). The individual human psyche is an integral part of this cosmic matrix and can under certain circumstances experientially identify with its various aspects.

This new understanding of the human psyche has important sociopolitical implications. Medical anthropologists have shown that the striking physical differences between various human groups disappear when the scientific research of *Homo sapiens* penetrates the thin layers of the epidermis; the basic anatomical, physiological, and biochemical characteristics are shared by all of humanity. Modern consciousness research complemented this observation by similar findings related to the human psyche. On the postnatal biographical level exist large individual and cultural differences; the conditions of life differ radically from person to person, from family to family, and from culture to culture.

However, these differences begin to disappear as soon as experiential self-exploration in holotropic states of consciousness reaches the perinatal level. All members of the human species share the experiences of prenatal life and birth; the differences in this area are interindividual rather than specific for various racial groups. And when the process of deep experiential probing reaches the transpersonal level, all differences disappear.

Our observations have shown that people from all human groups with whom Christina and I have worked in various parts of the world—in Europe; India; Japan; Taiwan; Australia; South, Central, and North America; and Polynesia—had in their holotropic experiences access to the entire collective unconscious as described by C. G. Jung, both in its historical and archetypal-mythological realms, without regard to their own racial, national, and cultural background. These experiences have even frequently bridged gender differences; many karmic, ancestral, and racial experiences contained convincing identification with members of the opposite sex. Equally frequent were identifications with representatives of other animal species. Observations of this kind provide strong evidence for something that traditional materialistic scientists would consider impossible and utterly absurd—that the entire history of humanity and life on this planet are permanently recorded in an immaterial field to which each of us has under certain circumstances experiential access. The Hungarian/Italian system theorist Ervin Laszlo has been able to define scientifically such a field and gave it the name the "psi field"; more recently, he renamed it as the "akashic field" by linking it explicitly to the spiritual traditions.

Perinatal and transpersonal experiences have profound psychological implications. When the content of the perinatal level of the unconscious surfaces into consciousness and is adequately processed and integrated, it results in a radical personality change. The individual experiences a considerable decrease of aggressive tendencies and becomes more tolerant and compassionate toward others. The experience of psychospiritual death and rebirth and conscious connection with positive postnatal and prenatal memories reduces irrational ambitions and urges and increases élan vital and joi d'vivre—the ability to enjoy life and draw satisfaction from simple situations such as everyday activity, eating, lovemaking, nature, and music.

The process of spiritual opening and transformation typically deepens further as a result of transpersonal experiences. Feelings of oneness with the universe and its creative principle lead to identification with all sentient beings and bring a sense of awe, wonder, love, compassion, and inner peace. Spirituality that results from this process is universal, all-encompassing, transcending all organized religions; it resembles the attitude to the Cosmos found in the mystics of all ages. It is extremely authentic and convincing, because it is based on deep personal experience. It is therefore capable to compete successfully with the dogmas of organized religions, as well as the monistic-materialistic worldview of Western science.

People who are experientially connected with the transpersonal dimensions have a tendency to appreciate existence and feel reverence for all creation. One of the most remarkable consequences of various forms of transpersonal experience is the spontaneous emergence and development of genuine humanitarian and ecological interests, and the need to take part in activities aimed at peaceful coexistence and well-being of humanity. This is based on an almost cellular understanding that any boundaries in the Cosmos are relative and arbitrary, and that each of us is, in the last analysis, identical and commeasurable with the entire fabric of existence. As a result of these experiences, individuals tend to develop feelings that they are planetary citizens and members of the human family before belonging to a particular country or a specific racial, social, ideological, political, or religious group. It seems obvious that transformation of this kind could significantly increase our chances of survival if it could occur on a sufficiently large scale.

It seems that we are involved in a dramatic race for time which has no parallel in human history. What is at stake is nothing less than the future of humanity and the fate of life on our planet. If we continue using the old strategies that have caused the current global crisis, and which are in their consequences destructive and self-destructive, it might lead to annihilation of modern civilization and possibly even the human species. However, if a sufficient number of people undergoes a process of inner psychospiritual transformation and attain a higher level of awareness, we might in the future reach a situation where we will deserve the name which we have so proudly given to our species: *Homo sapiens sapiens*.

In closing I would like to express my deep gratitude to Christina, my wife, best friend, and coworker for everything that she contributed over the years to the research, which has today received such an extraordinary appreciation.

# EXORCISING CHRIST FROM CHRISTIANITY

## Adam Elenbaas

Recently, much of the Bible-centered, evangelical Christianity in the United States has been charged with playing politics from the pulpit. Evangelicals have commonly associated themselves with a Christian/moral agenda that they believe to be present in the Republican Party. In this niche, the military might of the United States is equated with the evangelism of the Christian Gospel. Accordingly, the Middle East becomes like a pagan, as was Vietnam before it, and the church has to bring the light of the gospel (which is the United States and its military power) to the lost sheep.

Some Christian pastors have spoken out against the politicization of the gospel. Perhaps the most popular of these right now is the Baptist pastor, author, and biblical scholar Greg Boyd. His recent book, *The Myth of a Christian Nation: How the Quest for Political Power is Destroying the Church,* has been big news in evangelical communities around the world. In his writing, Boyd explains a new, "counter-cultural" understanding of the Christian Gospel and the life of Christ. This view is called the "Christus Victor" theory of the atonement.

After the book's publication and a series of sermons that refused to equate the gospel of Jesus with the Bush regime, Boyd lost over one thousand of the five thousand members of his Baptist church in St. Paul, Minnesota. *The New York Times* recently quoted Boyd as saying in one of his particularly controversial sermons: "I am sorry to tell you that

America is not the light of the world and the hope of the world. The light of the world and the hope of the world is Jesus Christ." Boyd's mega-church quickly gained more members than it had lost. The new members largely came from minority communities.

The *Times* interview with Boyd summarized the event: "Mr. Boyd lambasted the 'hypocrisy and pettiness' of Christians who focus on 'sexual issues' like homosexuality, abortion or Janet Jackson's breast-revealing performance at the Super Bowl halftime show. Boyd said Christians these days were constantly outraged about sex and perceived violations of their rights to display their faith in public. 'Those are the two buttons to push if you want to get Christians to act,' he said. 'And those are the two buttons Jesus never pushed.'"

Sounds like progressive theology for an evangelical Christian, right?

During my undergraduate years at Bethel College in St. Paul, Minnesota, I was a Christian evangelical. However, a secret cannabis habit was slowly dissolving my more extreme views of Jesus and the Gospels into a broader understanding of the divine mystery. Each semester, my theology was becoming more and more liberal. During that period of dissolution at Bethel College, Greg Boyd was my favorite theology professor.

In the classroom one day he told a story about an LSD trip that he'd been on as a teenager, before becoming a Christian. It was the first time I'd ever heard a Christian pastor talk about psychedelics. He said that he felt he had become one with the universe while looking into a Christmas tree. He recalled that he wrote a treatise that night about the ultimate meaning of life. But, Boyd told the class, he quickly discounted this acid-inspired revelation. He said that he realized the very next day that his experience was meaningless.

Recently, in an article from the *Star Tribune* in Minneapolis, Boyd recalled the LSD trip again. When he read his treatise, after the trip had ended, he couldn't understand anything he'd written. "It was incomprehensible," he said. In my theology class, he also concluded that "If everything is 'one,' then we would have to throw logic away." We would slide into a vortex of meaninglessness.

After years of working in ayahuasca ceremonies, it occurs to me that while Greg Boyd is one of the most progressive theologians and pastors in the evangelical community, and refuses to equate the gospel with politics and evangelism with imperialism, he is still operating under an assumption about the life of Christ that I have come to disagree with.

The Good News of the Gospel, in my opinion, is that oneness or void, emptiness or even meaninglessness, perhaps paradoxically are not always negative or undesirable states of being. This understanding started with my first vision of Christ, in Peru during an ayahuasca ceremony.

After using cannabis for years during and after college, and then attempting to be a Christian youth pastor for a year in Chicago, and resigning, I finally left the Christian church altogether. I began experimenting with more drugs. During my experimental phase I eventually tried mushrooms, which shifted my attention from party drugs like cocaine, ecstasy, opiates, liquor, and cigarettes to entheogens, shamanic literature, drum circles, sweat lodges, lucid dreaming, and creative writing.

The visionary experience of psychedelics was not, after all, completely dissimilar from the ecstasy of the pentecostal lifestyle I had been a part of for some time during my exploration of Christianity. In fact, it was through my experiences with psychedelics that I began to see it was possible to be "Christ-like" without being a "Christian."

After reading about ayahuasca shamanism, I traveled to Peru to drink the magical vine of the spirits. I decided that I wanted a visionary experience that was a part of an ancient medicinal and spiritual tradition. In my first ceremony, downriver from Iquitos, a jungle outpost city in northern Peru, I drank a strong cup of ayahuasca medicine and entered into a deconditioning sequence. The ceremony cleansed me of an unhealthy relationship to Jesus.

I was cleansed of evangelical Christianity like many people who drink ayahuasca find themselves purging drug addictions. The fear-based pathology of my days as an evangelical had left residual scar tissue throughout my body and mind. Christian culture, for me, was like a drug. I had been using it to medicate my own confusion and fear, my own insecurity. The first healing of my evangelical dis-ease came an hour into my first ceremony, when I had my first real conversation with Jesus.

It was raining in the jungle. Thunder clapped over the mesa, which was on the top of a hill, tucked in against the bank of a shady, green lagoon. Bullfrogs croaked and birds called, strangely, back and forth. Cicadas buzzed loudly, like an electric fence, and larger sentinels crashed in the distance. The jungle was alive, and an hour into the ceremony I felt the pulsing of the universe.

I could no longer sense where my skin and bones ended and the rest of the universe began. I dissolved into bliss. I laughed and cried with joy. I listened to the rain and the whistling of the magical icaros. I stretched out like a cat, and felt as though my body was unwinding from years of tightly held stress. My nostrils opened, and I could smell the lush plants of the jungle.

I heard the small yawn of a sleeping dog outside of the mesa, protected from the downpour by the awning of the roof. My muscles relaxed, and I began to float out of my body.

I found myself knee-deep in water, standing in a grid of Greek columns. I saw Jesus walking toward me in the water. He looked strong, like a carpenter. His skin was dark, not white like the portraits from the walls of my childhood churches. His eyes were fierce and powerful, but he looked like he had a sense of humor, like he knew how to laugh. His humanity startled me. Then I was afraid.

Fear welled up from my stomach, I began bubbling like a fountain, saying "thank you." I doubled over clutching my stomach, feeling like I would vomit.

I couldn't stop saying "thank you." When he finally reached me, I would not lift my head to look into his eyes. And my "thank yous" poured out of my mouth, faster and faster, until it was clear to me that the language was a vessel for a deeper communication. I might have been saying "thank you," but the sounds of my words actually said things like, "I am not good enough. I am afraid. I am alone."

It instantly occurred to me that most of the words I had ever said to people about Jesus when I was an evangelist had been filled with fear, anger, jealousy, insecurity, and sadness. It occurred to me that I rarely ever meant what I said. I saw that my words often betrayed my feelings.

While lying on the floor of the mesa, I felt as though a sinister witch doctor, and not an emissary of light, had been speaking through me during my Christian days. The dog outside of the mesa began snarling protectively. The wind began to blow hard through the treetops.

The "thank yous" were coming out of my mouth like liquid, a golden oil. The oil formed into a statuesque calf, trembling and undulating on the surface of the water. The rain blew sideways in sheets against the side of the mesa. Through mosquito netting on the windows, I could feel the humid spray of the jungle, alive, pulsing, swallowing me whole.

Then, in my vision, Jesus lifted me up onto the water. I was looking into his eyes.

The "thank yous" stopped. He touched the golden calf, and it dissolved. Then he looked at me and we shared silence. I held eye contact with him, and it felt wonderful to see the man's proportions, his skin, to look into the cracks and lines of his forehead and cheeks. He was human, like me.

Then he spoke.

"Adam. Love me. But do not make me into an idol." He held my shoulder in his palms, gently.

The rain was settling in the jungle. Outside of the mesa, I heard the dog sigh deeply and lie down again.

Looking into the eyes of Jesus and hearing the dog adjust its body to sleep, it occurred to me that all of life is an intelligent web, infinitely connected. I began to cry. My tears felt like bricks, crumbling away, my face crackling open, white light shining through, so bright it could blind the sun.

He continued, "Our father is the only one who has the right to judge anything." He pointed up. And the sky opened above me. There were stars twinkling in the rafters of the mesa. "And he never does. He never judges *anything*."

So now, years later, why do I have this bone to pick with my old theology professor? I suppose I challenge Boyd's theology because I believe that it is becoming increasingly important for the universal spiritual communities to engage in healthy dialogue with liberal evangelicals, those who are countercultural but still see Christianity as separate and essentially "the best."

We should seek a spirited debate with evangelicals as we attempt to create a more unified spiritual community on our planet—a community that includes all of the many avatars that have walked the earth, not just Jesus.

I picked Greg Boyd because he is a new kind of evangelical, one that is coming closer and closer to a more universal understanding of the divine mystery. Because it turns out that the evolution of consciousness is happening everywhere.

Boyd recently outlined his evangelical theory in a sermon at his mega-church. Angering some of his members again, he said that it was good to see a black man, Barack Obama, and a woman, Hillary Clinton, running for president. "It's about time we realize that all people are created equal, regardless of whether you like their politics or not," Boyd declared. He then outlined his Christus Victor theory, annotating a passage from Matthew as he went.

But in order to understand Boyd's Christus Victor theory of atonement, and why it's making such a splash in evangelical communities, it's important to first understand its classic theological rival: the "penal substitution" view.

This view is the common understanding of the cross, where Jesus came to be the sacrificial lamb that would appease God, the judge, for man's sins. In the penal substitution view, Jesus takes the place of the sinner, and if we say a prayer, join a church, or become a "Christian," then we sign into the contract that was made between God and Man, via his son Jesus. Of course, by doing so we also avoid hell and damnation, which is the alternative to the contract.

Boyd's view is different—it's far more liberal. In his understanding, Christ did not come to take the place of sinners but came to free Christians from the shackles of the strong man: Satan. His theory is comparatively progressive because the emphasis of the cross translates to social action more than imperialistic evangelism. Its primary thrust is not the fear of hell but the need for change and healing.

Jesus came to heal the world, and it was by healing the world (not by paying the debt of our sins) that he saved us. Jesus came to remove the blinders of hatred and to enlighten human beings to a more peaceful way of life. By dying on the cross, according to Boyd's Christus Victor theory, Jesus conquered the Kingdom of Satan once and for all. Now, since his departure from the earth, we're supposed to mimic his lifestyle until he returns to establish the new kingdom.

Oppressing those we perceive as different is not a part of this gospel. Neither is war or violence or aggression. The world needs love, and Christ was the turning point in the battle.

In his sermon elucidating the Christus Victor understanding of the atonement, Greg delves into the book of Matthew, chapter 12, using this passage to highlight his theology:

*22 Then was brought unto him one possessed with a devil, blind, and dumb: and he healed him, insomuch that the blind and dumb both spake and saw. 23 And all the people were amazed, and said, is not this the son of David? 24 But when the Pharisees heard it they said, This fellow doth not cast out devils, but by Beelzebub the prince of the devils. 25 And Jesus knew their thoughts, and said unto them, Every kingdom divided against itself is brought to desolation; and every city or house divided against itself shall not stand. 26 And if Satan cast out Satan, he is divided against himself; how shall then his kingdom stand. 27 And if I by Beelzebub cast out devils, by whom do your children cast them out? Therefore they shall be your judges. 28 But if I cast out devils by the Spirit of God, then the kingdom of God is come unto you. 29 Or else how can one enter into a strong man's house, and spoil his goods, except he first bind the strong man? And then he will spoil his house. 30 He that is not with me is against me; and he that gathereth not with me scattereth abroad.*

Boyd notes it was astonishing that Christ exorcised a "mute" demon because mute demons were impossible to exorcise, according to Jewish history. They were tricky because you couldn't get their name, and getting a demon's name was important to pulling it out of a patient's body. He went on to cite verse 25, where Christ rebukes the Pharisees using what Boyd calls "good logic."

By saying that a kingdom cannot stand "divided against itself," Boyd suggests that Christ was proving, logically, that he was casting out demons by the power of God and not by the power of Satan (because it would be logically impossible to cast out Satan by Satan).

He then goes on to say that the "binding of the strong man" and the "spoils" of the strong man's house represent the idea that Christ came to free people from the grand illusion that Satan had cast over the planet. The final deathblow to Satan's Kingdom was dealt on the cross, according to Boyd.

While this view is progressive, it is still exclusive. The Buddha is excluded. Krishna has nothing to add. It was Jesus, not anybody else, who took home the largest spiritual victory in the history of the planet. This is what was accomplished on the cross, and this is why Christianity is the truest religion on the planet, in Boyd's view.

In his sermon, Boyd proclaims, "War is not acceptable, America! Hatred of gays is not the gospel! That's what Christ conquered. Our walk with Jesus is about social action and being 'counter cultural,' not political."

This view speaks to the majority of the liberal and countercultural evangelicals in our nation. (It's important that we recognize that not all Christians are conservative.) But even then, I cannot subscribe to any religion that attempts to assert itself as the only path to God.

I believe there may be a deeper way to read the passage from Matthew—one that perhaps reveals Christ's esoteric teachings, and a more rounded, more universal understanding of the Gospel.

I'm not a biblical scholar, but I'll give it a shot in the hopes that my reading might spark good conversation.

In order to fully understand how the Christ energy worked in the exorcism of the mute demon in the book of Matthew, one should have experience with exorcisms of mute demons. This past December I experienced demonic possession in an ayahuasca ceremony in Peru, my twelfth ceremony since my first vision of Christ in the jungle. The possession involved, specifically, my old evangelical fear of hell and the devil.

It was my third year of working with ayahuasca, and the lodge I first drank at had been rebuilt outside of Iquitos. Instead of a twenty-four-hour boat ride downriver, I took an hour bus ride to the new jungle camp.

There were thirty of us in the mesa instead of the mere six that had been there when I had first drank. The number of Westerners seeking medicinal ayahuasca healing has grown exponentially in recent years, and I have met many people seeking healing from years of religious confusion spawned from evangelical Christianity.

As I scanned the mesa before the ceremony, I thought to myself, "All of you are going to be healed by the ayahuasca." I could feel a bit of the old evangelical in me, thinking something pious like, "Ayahuasca will save you all . . . you just wait and see."

There was a full moon. It shone brightly and illuminated the ceremonial circle. As one of the shamans, Don Alberto, whistled an icaro into my cup of medicine, I began to feel queasy. I began to remember my fear of hell. My fear of damnation, both personal and collective. I drew a deep breath. I knew that Christianity was going to come up again in the ceremony, but I had no idea how deep the teaching would be.

An hour into the ceremony, I was seeing snakes and jaguars, vines and plants. I could see the icaros, the medicine songs, floating in the air like serpentine bubbles decorated with stars and diamonds. Then I saw the sky open above me. I saw the blackness painted purple, like a king or queen, and I saw an angel of death. It beckoned to me, as if to say, "die little one, let go." I tried to vomit into my bucket to get rid of the vision, but nothing came up. I pounded my fists on the ground, trying to make the fear go away. I spat. I tried to walk to the toilet, but I fell to the ground.

My body was possessed with fear. I could hear people all throughout the mesa crying and vomiting, some screaming. I could not speak. How long had it been since I last had a voice?

The scent of vomit wafted through the air, mingling with Alberto's mupacho smoke.

As I struggled on the floor, losing touch with physical reality, my joints moved in and out of their sockets. I saw shadow-wraiths moving through my limbs in the shadows cast through the mesa by the light of the moon. I was losing all sense of my body and my mind. I could not control my thoughts or my physical actions. Then I saw the death-angel fly into my stomach.

I began to seizure on the floor. My body was shaking so hard that I was propelling myself off the wooden floorboards like a live wire. In my head, like a hailstorm, I saw memories of hell, sermons on hell, sinners in the hands of an angry god, images of fire, explosions, and black holes. I was scolding myself, scolding others, burning my secular music collection. Every memory swarmed around the fear that all of my best efforts, all of anyone's best efforts, might not be enough. In the end, damnation would take us. My fate was hell.

While I shook on the floor, a strange glossolalia released from my stomach. My voice, usually a tenor, became a bass, and I grunted in strange rhythms. I could not cry out for help. My voice was gone.

Alberto walked casually to where I struggled on the floor. He began performing a healing on me. He shook his chakapa in a circle around my head and anointed my crown with smoke.

Another shaman, Hamilton, said, "You must know fear so that you will not be afraid of it. You must know confusion so you will not be confused by it. These are your demons, Adam. You have to own them, and then you'll come back to your body."

I was not there to respond in that moment. Though I heard the words of the shamans, I was lost. I didn't know who I was or what was happening inside of me. I had no voice, and my normal sense of self was forgotten.

Finally, Alberto sang an icaro that forced me to vomit several times, at which point the energies subsided.

Then, almost instantly, the craft of the healing was revealed in a teaching vision that came to me. I felt cradled. I could feel my body again, my muscles, my joints, my face. I remembered my name again— Adam. *Here I am again.*

Alberto sang a song calling in the "Christo" energy. I saw rainbow-colored dragonflies and golden moths descend from the rafters of the mesa. A temple filled with light manifested in front of me. And I understood that the demonic inside of me was being integrated, transformed, built into a beautiful temple of spirit. It had not been simply "cast out."

What had felt demonic inside of me did not feel "gone," but instead embraced and understood, able to be held in a new energetic space within my body. The demonic was not "bad" or "good." It was more like a birth canal, and it was fueled by the contractions of my fear, my resistance to change. It occurred to me that God is everything and that fear and spirit are one and the same thing. It turned out that there was nothing at stake, the whole time. The mute demon inside of me had an identity, after all.

From the top of the golden temple there was a tube of rainbow colors shooting up like an arrow into space. And, like my first vision, I saw stars twinkling above. This time I did not see Jesus, but I felt his energy.

I understood that the Christ energy is all about saying "yes" to fear. Because what we say yes to can never be the actual fear. When we say yes to fear, we are only saying yes to integration, transformation, and new life. This is why Christ took to the cross, and while he was on the cross, cried out, "Father, why have you forsaken me?" And then, "It is finished."

I sat near a lantern after the ceremony was over, until the sun came up the next morning. And while I sat, looking into the light of a tiny, steady flame, I saw myself more fully than ever. It turns out that my true name, like the true name of everything, is really simple: Here I am.

Returning to the exorcism from the book of Matthew: I recognize that there are other passages in the synoptic Gospels where Christ directly casts demons out of people, as in the book of Matthew where he casts demons out of two men and into a herd of pigs—but my point should still be heard.

This point is not to say that all understandings of the shadow or the demonic are only internal. It is to suggest that there is room for both internal and external understandings of the demonic and also Satan, or evil.

In the passage from Matthew that involves the mute demon, I believe Christ was revealing one of his more esoteric teachings about the craft of a particular kind of healing.

Greg Boyd sees the kingdom of Satan as something in complete opposition to the kingdom of God, but perhaps my old theology professor did not read the passage from Matthew with the appropriate assumption about the Kingdom of God. What if the Kingdom of God is omnipresent and unified already, in and outside of time? What if, in one sense, there is no division in reality at all?

Perhaps Jesus understood a deeper level of logic: That dualism itself, in order to be consistent, must exist within a relationship to nondualism. When Christ said that "every kingdom divided against itself will fall," maybe he was speaking esoterically. He could have been speaking to the Pharisees about the nature of exorcising a mute demon like mine.

Imagine that Jesus was saying that God, in "one" sense, is *never both* divided, and neither is his kingdom, which is all of reality. This implies that the mute demon from the book of Matthew was not "bad" or "good" but simply a divided state of consciousness that is *both* illusory and painful, real and false, simultaneously.

Christ then went on to say, "If I cast out the devil by the devil, then who do your people cast demons out by? They will be your judges." In other words, if Christ was casting out the devil by the devil, then he was performing quite the miracle, since it was a logical impossibility (according to the time-bound and dualistic logic of the Pharisees).

According to the Pharisees' logic, Christ's healing was more impressive than the exorcisms that they were performing. The Pharisees couldn't get the name of the mute demon because their logic didn't allow for it.

In the infinite sense of dualism and its inherent paradox, the Pharisees were only able to perform healings through the dualistic side of dualism and nondualism. In his response to the Pharisees, maybe Christ was dishing out a mystical and rhetorical smack-down about the infinite, self-enfolding nature of dualism.

Bam! Take that Pharisees.

Christ proclaims, "But if I cast out the devil by the spirit of God, then his kingdom has come upon you." In other words, in my own colloquial take, "I am naming the mute demon after my big Dad in the sky. Because that's how you handle mute demons. You integrate them instead of casting them out."

Then Jesus says, "Or else how can one enter into a strong man's house, and spoil his goods, except he first bind the strong man? And then he will spoil his house."

Maybe Jesus was saying that there is good in the devil, there are spoils within the kingdom of the devil (there are treasures to be found in Satan's house), but first you have to bind the extreme idea that Satan and God stand in complete opposition to each other, entirely separate.

Only when this illusion is bound can the goods in the kingdom of Satan be distributed. I believe this was Jesus' most esoteric teaching on the nature of exorcising a mute demon. He was teaching people about the craft of healing and medicine. I believe this to be true because the demons that were exorcised from my body were not cast out. They were integrated after the shamans named them. They named the demonic pure Christos, the anointed one within.

Once you see Christos energy in a mute demon, you have the true name of the demon, because you have the true name of the eternal self, the great "I AM."

Greg Boyd assumes that Christ came to assassinate Satan, as if Satan is an evil entity who exists in complete opposition to God. But by making this heavy-handed distinction the underpinning of Christ's death on the cross, I believe that Boyd places too much emphasis on the power of the crucifixion as a "once and for all" destruction of the kingdom of the devil (which stands entirely separate from God's kingdom).

In this sense, Boyd might be idolizing the historical person of Christ. He might be idolizing the cross, when perhaps Christ's most powerful message was to remind us that we are all Christ, we are all anointed ones, and we all have a cross to bear—even if you're not a "Christian" (or Jew).

We can easily remember that Christ did not teach Peter to bow down to him. Jesus didn't instruct Peter to use the canonical Bible (which wasn't even around) to logically demonstrate the dualistic nature of Satan versus God in order to perform miracles or exorcisms. Instead, he told Peter to see that there was no division between his feet and the water. He taught Peter to walk on water. And if Peter really got up and walked on water, then maybe Peter sank when he began to see himself as separate again. In that sense, maybe Peter was incarnating the dualistic side of dualism and nondualism, so he sank.

Sometimes it's good to just come right out and say it . . . so I will. I appreciate the biblical texts. I know it's not popular, but I do. And I wonder if the biblical texts are shunned because of the way they, too, like Christ and the cross, have been largely idolized in the evangelical churches? Evangelicals claim that the Bible is infallible. But the Bible is not an infallible book. It is a collection of sixty-six books by over forty different authors on three different continents, written over fifteen hundred years ago and in three different languages.

As powerful as Christ's message was, I feel as though he'd be the first to say that many "Christs" came before him, and many would come after him whose power would be equal to or greater than his own. Should we even assume that Christ would be a Christian today?

Before he left the planet, Christ suggested in the book of John that "You will do greater things than I have done in my name." Lest we forget that his true name was not Jesus, but "I am."

Of course, when I heard Boyd's sermon about Satan and his idea of the "Christus Victor" theory of atonement, the old evangelical inside of me leapt up into the air. *Finally!*, I thought, *someone in the Christian community is taking a leap of faith. Finally the evolution of consciousness is coming to the church.*

Moving away from the penal substitution view is a large theological step, and we should be happy that evangelicals are opening up to new readings of the gospels. Christianity, according to Boyd and Christus Victor, is no longer about saying a simple prayer and being "saved" from your sins. We should appreciate that there are evolutions of consciousness happening in the evangelical community. And I admire that he preached against the politicization of the Gospel. I admire that he lost those angry members, yet gained a new flock.

But if I could go back and say one thing to my old professor, as an adult man having experienced an exorcism, having drank ayahuasca, and having felt the Christ energy in the visionary space, I would ask if perhaps Christ's last desire, after his death and rebirth, now, today, would be to have his historical persona exorcised from Christianity, to have Christianity itself crucified.

I wonder if Jesus wouldn't have seen a "mute demon" in the evangelical church that's been set up in his name.

But, then, what's in a name anyway?

How many members would someone like my old theology professor lose if he drank ayahuasca, or crucified his Christianity, and who would come in the doors afterward?

# THE WOUNDED HEALER

*Paul Levy*

O ne of the deeper, underlying archetypal patterns which is being
constellated in the human psyche that is playing itself out collectively on the world stage is the archetype of the "wounded healer." To
quote Kerenyi, a colleague of Jung who elucidated this archetype, the
wounded healer refers psychologically to the capacity "to be at home in
the darkness of suffering and there to find germs of light and recovery
with which, as though by enchantment, to bring forth Asclepius, the
sunlike healer." The archetype of the wounded healer reveals to us that
it is only by being willing to face, consciously experience, and go through
our wound do we receive its blessing. To go through our wound is to
embrace, assent, and say "yes" to the mysteriously painful new place in
ourselves where the wound is leading us. Going through our wound, we
can allow ourselves to be re-created by the wound. Our wound is not a
static entity, but rather a continually unfolding dynamic process that
manifests, reveals, and incarnates itself through us, which is to say that
our wound is teaching us something about ourselves. Going through our
wound means realizing we will never again be the same when we get to
the other side of this initiatory process. Going through our wound is
a genuine death experience, as our old self "dies" in the process, while
a new, more expansive and empowered part of ourselves is potentially
born.

Going through and embracing our wound as a part of ourselves is
radically different than circumnavigating and going around (avoiding),

or getting stuck in and endlessly, obsessively re-creating (being taken over by) our wound. The event of our wounding is simultaneously catalyzing a deeper (potential) healing process which requires our active engagement, thus "wedding" us to a deeper level of our being. Jung's closest colleague, Marie Louise Von Franz, said "the wounded healer is the archetype of the Self [our wholeness, the God within] . . . and is at the bottom of all genuine healing procedures."

An encounter with something greater than our limited ego, what Jung calls the Self, is always a wounding experience for the ego. This is symbolically represented when the mythic Jacob, after making it to daybreak in his fight with the angel of God (who was clearly the more powerful of the two), becomes wounded on the hip by the angel's touch. The event of our wounding is initiatory, as our wounding originated in and potentially introduces us to "something greater than ourselves." At the same time that something greater than ourselves wounds us, something greater than ourselves enters us as a result of our wounding, setting in motion a deeper dynamic of psychic reorganization and potential transformation. In the myth, the angel then changes Jacob's name to "Israel," "he who has wrestled with God," which symbolizes that Jacob's identity has been changed in the process of his encounter with the numinosum. Our wounding is a "numinous" event, in that its source is transpersonal and archetypal, which is to say that our wound is the very way by which the divine is making contact with us. The origin of both our wounding and the healing that precipitates out of our wound comes from beyond ourselves, as it is beyond our own personal contrivance. Our wounding activates a deeper, transpersonal process of potential healing and illumination that we could not have initiated by ourselves.

It should be noted that Jacob was wrestling with the angel in the first place because he would have been killed otherwise. The more powerful archetypal forces that wound us and become activated in us through our wounding literally challenge us to the core of our being to connect with, become intimately acquainted with, and step into more empowered aspects of ourselves, or else. Talking about his own personal experience of living out this deeper, archetypal pattern, Jung said, "I would wrestle with the dark angel until he dislocated my hip. For he is also the light and the blue sky which he withholds from me." The dark angel who wounds us is at the same time the Luciferian agent who is the bringer of the light. There is a secret tie between the powers that wound us by seemingly obstructing our true nature and the very true nature that they appear to be obstructing.

Through our wound we become introduced to the realization that we are participating and playing a role in what Jung calls "a divine drama of incarnation," in which we step out of identifying ourselves in a personal way that is separate from others, and we step into, as if stepping into new clothes that are custom-tailored just for us, a "novel" role which requires a more all-embracing and expansive identity. We realize we are all sharing in and playing roles for each other in a deeper, mythic, archetypal process that is revealing itself to us as it acts itself out through us. We find ourselves instruments being moved by a greater, invisible hand, as if something vast, with more volume than our previously imagined selves is incarnating through us. To recognize this is to have a more open-ended and expansive sense of who we think we are, and who we imagine others are in relation to us. The wound is not only a personal experience, but rather it is a doorway, a hyperdimensional portal into the transpersonal/archetypal realm, which is a higher order (in terms of freedom) of our being.

The wounded healer only becomes able to heal and help others (which is to simultaneously be healing and helping him/herself again and again in the form of seeming "others"), when instead of being resentful, bitter, and feeling victimized by their wound, he or she recognizes their wound as a numinous event, an archetypal moment that seeks to make them participants in a divine, eternal happening.

## OUR WOUND IS THE WOUND

Just like a dream, the situation in our outer world is reflecting back to us what is happening deep inside of us. There is a nonlocal correlation between the violence that we see playing out in the outside world and the wound that we feel inside of ourselves. This is a holographic universe in the sense that, just like a hologram, every minute part of the universe— such as ourselves—contains, reflects, and expresses the whole. The microcosm and the macrocosm are mirrored reflections of each other, as if they are different dimensional, fractal-like iterations of the same underlying dynamic. What we are suffering from individually within ourselves is the doorway through which we can more deeply relate to and become engaged with the suffering in the outer world in a way that helps alleviate both the suffering in the outer world as well as within ourselves.

There is a transformative and healing effect when we recognize how our individual suffering is a personalized reflection or instantiation of the collective suffering that pervades the entire field of consciousness. Our personal wound is, in condensed and crystallized form, the footprint and signature of the collective wound in which we all share and participate. It is liberating and healing to step out of pathologizing ourselves and recontextualize our personal conflicts, problems, and wounds as part of a wider transpersonal pattern enfolded throughout the global field of human experience. The outer, personalized guise of our wound is the particularized form in which the underlying, eternal mythological motif incarnates itself in linear time and makes itself felt in our personal life. We are like psychic organs who individually "process" the unresolved, unconscious shadow and wound in the collective field. We are each simultaneously reflecting, creating, and affected by what is happening in the very universe in which we are embedded and of which we are an expression.

It is important to note that this is not a linear, one-way process, but is circular and reciprocally co-arising. The unconscious in the greater body politic of the seemingly outer world affects us, stimulating a reso-nant unconscious energy within ourselves, while at the same time, our unconscious is contributing to and being nonlocally expressed by events in the seemingly outer world in a mutually reinforcing feedback loop. The point is that we begin to see the true nature of the situation we are in when we recognize that, just like a dream, there is a synchronistic co-respondence and fundamental inseparability between what is going on within our psyche and what is happening in the seemingly outer world, as if they are mirrored reflex-ions of each other. This recognition of what has always been the case is itself the very expansion of consciousness which is required—make that demanded—for us to be effective, trans-formative, bodhisattvic agents of positive change in our world.

To realize that each one of us is uncannily embodying and acting out in our personal process (with all of our problems, symptoms, relation-ship conflicts, traumas, etc.) what is at the same time playing out in the outside world is to step out of identifying ourselves as isolated, discrete entities who are separate from the universe. Contrary to being "alien" to this universe, we find ourselves intimate expressions of it. It should be noted, however, that the way to this realization is not through bypassing the personal dimension of our experience and artificially identifying with the mythic/archetypal level in a contrived and fabricated way, but rather by entering the mythic/archetypal dimension by fully incarnat-ing, in a full-bodied way, our personal process in our life. The deeper, mythic/archetypal dimension "clothes" itself in our personal process, which is to say that our personal process is the doorway which intro-duces us to the deeper archetypal dimension of our being.

In this expansion of consciousness, we step out of interpreting our experience personally and reductively, based solely on cause and effect and the past, and step into experiencing the mythlike, timeless dimen-sion of our situation. Interpreting our experience through a personal and reductive lens is an expression of a naive, uninitiated, and ego-centered consciousness that knows no psychic center other than its own. Being linear and time-bound, it is a limited viewpoint that can only lead to depression, despair, resignation, disillusionment, and meaningless and hopeless suffering, as our soul feels seemingly destroyed in the process.

When we expand our consciousness and interpret our experience transpersonally, however, we step out of linear time into synchronic time, a dimension of our being in which the past, our wound, the world, and ourselves do not literally, concretely, and objectively exist in and over time in the way we had previously imagined. Realizing the impermanence and fluidity of our situation, we do not have to make our wound "real" and grant it an unwarranted solidity or invest it with an apparently substantial, independent existence. We can awaken to the fact that the situation we find ourselves in is malleable, is fundamentally characterized by open-ended potentiality, and is infinitely and effortlessly creative if we simply allow it to be.

Talking about this moment of recognizing that our wound is the (archetypal) wound, to quote Jung, is to see that our "suffering is archetypal and collective, it can be taken as a sign that [we are] no longer suffering from [ourselves], but rather from the spirit of the age." Jung continues that we are suffering from an "impersonal cause, from [our] collective unconscious which [we have] in common with all [humanity]" [words in brackets have been changed from singular, masculine to gender neutral]. If we are able to channel and creatively express the spirit of the age from which we are suffering with consciousness, however, we become the "medium" through which the spirit of the age reveals itself to us so as to potentially transform itself, the world around us, as well as ourselves.

As wounded healers, we become transformed when we recognize that our wound is completely personal and uniquely our own, while simultaneously being a universal, impersonal process in which everyone is participating. It is this shared felt sense that deeply connects us with one another. This is the paradox: An experience of our wholeness, what Jung calls the Self, is both personal and archetypal/transpersonal (beyond the personal) at the same time. To experience this contradiction consciously is itself the expansion of consciousness that initiates a transformation in ourselves, and by extension, the world around us. This is to paradoxically step into being a genuinely autonomous, independent being while at the same time realizing our interconnectedness, interdependence, unity, and ultimate inseparability from the world and one another. The energetic expression of this realization is compassion.

What is playing out in the world theater is not separate from, but is intimately correlated to, an expression of what is happening inside of ourselves. This is significant in that it reveals to us that a way to gain more traction to effectively deal with the pervasive destructiveness that is happening in the outside world is to become intimately acquainted with what it constellates inside of us. The unconscious, mad, violent, destructive, evil, wounded, and wounding energies in the outer world nonlocally reflect and activate, trigger and express themselves in similar, resonant processes within ourselves. The dynamic unfolding in the outer world "translates" itself through the organ of our psyche, thereby giving shape and form to our subjective experience of our wound, our world, and ourselves.

Our wound introduces and connects us with the transpersonal dimension of our being, whose realization, amazingly enough, initiates the transformation and potential healing of our wound. Simultaneously containing both the pathology and its own medicine, our wound is a higher-dimensional event which has manifested in the flatland of our third dimensional life. Symbolically encoded in the wound, uniquely tailored to our exact sensibility and aesthetic, is both the seeming "problem" and its own re-solution cojoined in a state of open-ended and boundless, indwelling potentiality.

Our wound is a genuine quantum phenomenon: Will it destroy us or wake us up? Is it a wave or a particle? Answer: It depends upon how we dream it. Our wound is not separate from the psyche that is experiencing it. This means that the way we interpret our wound, the meaning we place on it, and the story we tell ourselves about it, and thereby ourselves, has an actual effect on how our wound, ourselves, and by extension the world manifests in this very moment.

## OUR WOUND IS INITIATORY

Through our wound we become introduced to the part of ourselves that is not wounded, just as we would never notice the mirror if it were not for its reflections. The reflections are indistinguishable from the mirror while simultaneously "not" being the mirror. Paradoxically, the reflections in the mirror reveal what is not a reflection. Similarly, our wound reveals to us the part of ourselves that is free of our wound. The reflections in the mirror help us recognize the underlying mirror which embraces, contains, and is fundamentally unaffected by whatever it reflects. Our wound doesn't affect our mirror-like nature, just as a mirage of water in the desert doesn't make the grains of sand wet. We won't notice the underlying mirror, however, if we become entranced by, fixated on, absorbed into, and identified with the reflections.

The reflections in the mirror are the inseparable, indivisible, unmediated expression of the mirror, as we never have reflections without a mirror, or a mirror without reflections. Similarly, the wound is, in disguised form, a manifestation of the part of us that is not wounded.

Until we became wounded, however, we were unaware of the part of ourselves that is invulnerable to being wounded, as we were unconsciously identical with this part of ourselves, which is to say we were not relating to it as an object of our knowledge, i.e., it wasn't conscious. From the dreaming point of view—where the inner process of the dreamer plays itself out in the seemingly outer theater of the dream so as to become conscious of itself—the deeper part of ourselves dreamed up our wound so as to make us conscious of the part of ourselves that is transcendent to the wound—i.e., "healed." The wound itself is the very instrument through which our intrinsic wholeness prior to our wounding becomes consciously realized in time—the present moment—the only "place" where our wholeness can be realized.

To realize this is to have an expansion of consciousness, in which the opposites such as being wounded and not being wounded lose their previous sense of distinctive meaning relative to each other. Of course, on the relative level of reality, being wounded is different than not being wounded. To expand our consciousness, however, is to be introduced to the absolute level of reality, a state which simultaneously includes the relative, and yet embraces and transcends it in a higher synthesis. It is only our conceptual mind which "thinks" of the opposites as being separate. To recognize the relativity and, hence, the identity of the opposites is to realize what Jung calls the "Self" (which he described as a union of opposites). One of the deeper meanings of the Buddhist word *nirvana* is to be free from the opposites. In alchemy, the philosophers stone is found and the "gold" (which is none other than an expansion of consciousness) is made when the "greater conjunction" is accomplished, which is when the opposites are united.

To recognize the union of opposites is to connect with and remember our intrinsic wholeness, which is the ultimate healing, as we become "one piece" with ourselves (and can create "one peace" with one another). This is "as though by enchantment, to bring forth Asclepius, the sunlike healer," who symbolizes the healing power and hidden theophany latent in the wound that is invoked by the light of consciousness. When enough of us recognize the healing that our wound is revealing to us, the healing aspect of our wound becomes constellated collectively, writ large on the world stage.

As a wounded healer, we are continually deepening the healing of the disassociation in our world. Healing our internal disassociation from ourselves nonlocally impacts and is correspondingly reflected back by the seemingly outer world, as we reassociate with one another (the powers-that-be's worst nightmare), remembering who we are with regards to both

ourselves and one another. We can help one another to step out of a hierarchical universe based on fear, power, and separation, and step into our
deeper, coequal identities as wounded healers and spiritual friends who
ultimately depend upon and care about one another. We are interdependent parts of a greater, all-embracing whole and holy being. Realizing
our interconnectedness, we can collaboratively put our lucidity together,
becoming empowered agents of healing in the world.

It could not be more crystal clear that it is only through an expansion
of consciousness that we will be able to transform our world crisis.
Maybe all that is needed in this moment is for any one of us to wake up,
as all the great enlightened teachers throughout the ages have said that
when any one person wakes up and realizes the union of the opposites
within their own selves, the entire universe wakes up with them.

From this deeper, more expansive point of view, our wound, instead
of obstructing our wholeness, is actually an expression of it, as without
our wound we wouldn't have been introduced to the part of us that is
free, healed, whole, liberated, and awake. Our true nature can never be
obscured, just as the clouds in the sky seemingly obscure the sun, but
from the sun's point of view, it is always radiantly shining, even on the
cloudiest of days.

# II

# THE SHAMANIC

# JAGUAR MEDICINE

*Alberto Villoldo*

U ntil 1971, it was thought that the Nile was the longest river in the world. That year, National Geographic explorer Loren McIntyre, along with a local Indian guide and a friend who owned a pickup truck, set out to discover the source of the Amazon. On October 15, 1971, McIntyre and his party reached a summit 18,200 feet in altitude, an icy ridge called Choquecorao from which they spotted a body of water 1,000 feet below them. Thirsty, they decided to descend to this small lake, and as they looked at the five brooks that trickled outward and down the mountainside, McIntyre realized they had found the origin of the great Amazon. This daring expedition would lead to the revelation that the twisting and turning river is longer than the Nile by nearly 100 kilometers, and would stir interest in uncovering the mysteries of this region of the world that had been almost completely hidden to Westerners.[1]

McIntyre was an old-school explorer who relied more on guts, brawn, and instinct than on technology to help him navigate. I remember meeting him near the town of Pucalpa, Peru, the last navigable Amazon port. It was late in the spring of 1979, and I was an eager young man with a fresh Ph.D. looking for an unexplored niche in anthropology. I had already spent nearly six years traveling to the Peruvian Andes and Amazon and had become a regular in the "Last Friday" club, a once-a-month gathering at the last waterhole in the jungle that served cold beer. At that time, many of us Westerners who had come to the edge of the unexplored Amazon were searching for the legendary Mayoruna, a shy and elusive people who foraged and hunted in the deep jungle, so that we could study their ways. What made the Mayoruna so exotic to us was that they believed themselves to be jaguars who inhabited the bodies of men and women, and who tattooed their faces to look like jungle cats, even wearing whiskers during their ceremonies. Moreover, we were enticed by the rumor that they were able to "beam," transmitting their thoughts telepathically to one another.[2] The possibility that we might uncover and understand the secrets of the Mayoruna was exhilarating.

The only way for us budget explorers to launch an expedition to the remote regions where there were reported Mayoruna sightings was to hire one of the Irish pilots who worked at the local Christian mission to fly us on their seaplane on a Saturday, their day off, and pick us up the following week at the same spot. These extraordinary flyers risked their lives, and ours, as they landed their aircraft in turbulent river waters where logs the size of trees floated by. By far the biggest challenge, however, was getting them to remember the following week where they had dropped you off, as this was before GPS technology existed, and every bend in the river looked exactly like the next. We used to carry an emergency flare that we hoped would be dry enough to light the following week when the buzzing of the single-engine plane circling above could be heard again. Needless to say, McIntyre not only found the Mayoruna before any of the rest of us did, he traveled with them for many months as they sought the source of their own river and what they called "the beginning of time itself."

During those years traipsing around the Amazon, inspired by McIntyre's discoveries, I came across the opportunity to study with many shamans and healers. Many of them were masters who worked with the ayahuasca vine, a plant with hallucinogenic qualities that is used ritualistically in their culture, which fascinated me. I remember observing one of these shamans, don Ramon, during his nighttime healing ceremonies, as he would load his pipe with jungle tobacco and turn to one of his patients and "sing his jaguar down from the tree." I asked him what he meant and he explained that like many people, the patient lived in constant fear, and that this fear was the result of a trauma experienced early in life that had not healed. He said, "This man's soul is like a terrified cat who escaped danger and quickly clambered up a tree, where it remains, hissing at anyone who comes near. The cat must come down, relax, and resume walking on the terra firma of the rainforest, or there will be no healing of the illness this fear has engendered in him."

As he worked with his patients, don Ramon would speak to them softly, reassuring them that their family was safe, that they were safe. Sometimes, he would massage a patient's belly, explaining that "here is where the jaguar resides within each of us." I told him that in the West, we call the primitive, fearful response to trauma the "fight-or-flight" response, because it causes a creature to run away from danger or lash out in self-protection. The old shaman nodded, and said, "Yes, but when the danger has gone, an animal no longer holds on to its fear, while people will often remain in this state for many years."

The more I thought about it, the more excited I became about the potential of don Ramon's jaguar medicine. His explanation made total sense. Resetting a fight-or-flight response could free a patient from the devastating physiological effects of stress. While the fight-or-flight response can save our life in an emergency, we know that it is damaging to remain in that state for an extended period. During fight-or-flight the body produces and releases cortisol, adrenaline, and norepinephrine, hormones that shut down noncritical functions in favor of high-energy bursts, enhanced alertness, quickened reflexes, and faster blood clotting, all of which are needed in times of danger.

The danger is that our physiological response to chronic stress is the same as during instances of danger. Our fight-or-flight hormones continue to wash through our system, and we soon have an oversupply of cortisol and adrenaline. Excess levels of cortisol break down tissues in virtually every corner of the body, accelerating the aging process. High cortisol levels weaken ligaments, muscle, blood vessels, and bone and can cause elevated blood sugar levels and high blood pressure, eventually leading to easy bruising and thin, nearly transparent skin that we associate with the elderly. Abnormal function of the fight-or-flight system has also been correlated with inflammatory diseases and deficient immune function. While in this state, the body suppresses the healing hormones we need to recover from stress. And while most animals have systems that allow them to shake off the fight-or-flight response as soon as danger has passed, we humans seem to have lost that ability.

I watched don Ramon and other shamans "bring the jaguar down from the tree" during their healing rituals and saw the immediate difference in their patients, who were visibly more relaxed and energized. Later, the healers would employ certain core processes, including what they called "extraction" and "soul retrieval."

The extraction process draws out the "heavy" or noxious energies that have settled in the patient's body or his "luminous energy field" (LEF): the energetic envelope, or information field, that surrounds the physical body. This is the detoxification stage of healing, and it sometimes also involves ingesting plants that induce vomiting or herbs that cleanse the GI tract. The shamans explained to me that these illness-causing energies were often the result of envy or anger that had been directed at the patient by someone else. When lodged in the LEF or in the outer layers of the skin, these energies had to be sucked out of the patient. The shaman would place his mouth over the affected area of the body, suck audibly, then turn and spit out the invisible poisons. Sometimes, the shaman would even vomit fiercely as his physical body rejected the noxious energies he had removed from his patient. Other times, the shaman would use a stone or crystal to extract and contain them.

Many of the shamans I studied during my tenure in the Amazon, and later in the Andes, explained to me that the LEF contains a blueprint for how we will age, how we will heal, and how we might die. Encoded within this matrix are all the gifts and ailments we inherit from our parents, as well as data from all the traumas we have suffered in our life-times. Stories of betrayal, abandonment, and loss are stored in a holographic fashion in the tides and streams of life force swirling about in the luminous field, creating dark, heavy spots among the whirls of lighter energy. If we have a family history for heart disease or breast cancer, this information is encoded in our LEF until we are healed of this legacy. In the Amazon, they refer to such legacies as "generational curses" handed down from parent to child to grandchild. The shamans explained to me that when a sorcerer wants to inflict harm on a victim, he merely needs to activate the codes in the LEF to manifest a generational disease in that person. Conversely, a healer could also trigger the gifts latent within a client's LEF. In effect, these shamans believe that the LEF provides instructions to our DNA to express certain genes.

For many years, I considered their stories about creating health or disease in others to be implausible, but then I wondered, if diet, exercise, meditation, and stress can inform gene expression, couldn't intention do the same? What about the well-documented power of prayer to heal? Could someone with a malevolent intention send that toxic desire to exploit another's weaknesses, in the same way that a benevolent prayer could heal?

After resetting the fight-or-flight system and detoxifying the patient, the shaman practices what is called "soul retrieval." This process summons the parts of the self that the patient has lost as a result of previous traumas. Don Ramon believed that these events, which the shaman called *susto* or "fright," may have split off parts of the patient's soul when she was an infant, or even in utero. Jealous spouses or competitors could also have stolen these soul parts—the confident self, the trusting self, the self who loves freely and feels worthy of being loved in return—in the patient's adulthood.

To retrieve these talents, possibilities, and potentials that have retreated to the hidden recesses of the patient's psyche, the healer will enter a trance state and allow his consciousness to temporarily depart from his body and journey to the "lower world," or what we might identify as the collective unconscious. There, the healer can discover and bring back those qualities of the personality that have been disowned, and that will allow a patient to embark upon their destiny. At this stage of the healing, the shaman will also prescribe certain herbs and foods that will help the body to rebuild and restore physical health.

Shamans say that the soul has such a longing for wholeness that it will re-create the conditions that caused the soul loss, because it hopes that another opportunity for healing will result in our integrating these fragmented aspects of the self. Unaware of their soul's wounding, the person will change jobs but end up with a similar boss, move to another city and wonder at how she ended up with neighbors who are just like those she left behind, or divorce the abusive spouse and end up in an identical marriage. If the shaman can discover the source of the original wounding, he can heal it, and break the self-destructive patterns. He does this by recovering the quanta of life force that were lost and returning them to their rightful place in the patient's LEF.

Shamanic medicine is not a panacea, and shamans themselves will go to the emergency room when they have an acute condition. Western medicine remains the best trauma medicine that we know. Yet shamanic healing, with its emphasis on treating the body, mind, and soul as inseparable and continually influencing one another, can offer us fresh perspectives on dealing with the chronic conditions that afflict so many.

Recently, I invited a small group of travelers with me on a trip to the Amazon. Among these was a retired neurosurgeon who had suffered a stroke several years earlier and had lost significant motor function on the right side of his body. He was unable to set his right heel down, and had to walk very slowly with the aid of a walking stick. After a session with a renowned jungle shaman, he was able to set down his right heel for the first time in years. The following week, he accompanied me on an expedition to the Andes where he hiked up a mountain at 10,000 feet altitude unassisted. When I asked him what had happened, he simply said, "I have my stride back." The lost self who could walk forward confidently and unimpeded had returned, and his body was reflecting this profound change in the state of his soul.

## NOTES

1. L. McIntyre, "Amazon: The River Sea," *National Geographic,* 1972.
2. Petru Popescu, *Amazon Beaming* (New York: Penguin, 1992).

# MAYAN SHAMANISM AND 2012:
## A PSYCHEDELIC COSMOLOGY

*John Major Jenkins*

*Shamans understand that the human brain "is modeled after the celestial vault and the human mind functions according to the stars, which are the ventricles and sensoria of the cosmic brain . . . there exists a close relationship between astronomical observations, cosmological speculations, and drug-induced trance states."*

—GERARDO REICHEL-DOLMATOFF (1982:176)

### PART I. SHAMANISM AND ASTRONOMY AT IZAPA

Observe Stela 6 from an early Mayan site in southern Mexico called Izapa. This is a classic depiction of the shamanic journey into the underworld, into the raging maw of unknown dimensions of time and space, within the deep psyche yet buoyed on the undulating waves of the celestial seas.

What's going on in this 2,000-year-old carving? Prominently, we see a frog or toad with its neck craned back and mouth open. In Mayan symbology, the mouth of the frog, jaguar, or snake (or cave, even) symbolizes the door to the underworld. Its forked tongue sticks out and appears to jostle a tiny figure in a canoe. Shamans, traditionally, go on a journey into the underworld, and this carving clearly depicts precisely that. But there's more going on here. Notice the little dots or holes on

56

*Diagram 1. Stela 6. The shaman and the DMT toad at Izapa*

the toad's shoulder. These are what scholars call "vision scrolls." This toad has been identified as the *Bufo marinus* species, whose parotid glands, located on its back and shoulders, secrete a powerful hallucinogen: 5-Meo-DMT. This compound is a relative of the better-known DMT, but modern explorers of consciousness have reported unequivocally powerful experiences with the 5-Meo relative. It's sometimes described as being abysmal, shredding all identity back to the unconditioned void, leaving the aspirant gazing into the bottomless maw of emptiness. Psychonauts like Terence McKenna who prefer hypnogogic, image-rich hallucinations, have confessed to not liking the 5-Meo relative. Still, one can suspect that shamans of a certain gonzo bent would appreciate having access to this yawning abyss.

We don't know how the early Mayan shaman may have prepared the gland secretions, to enhance or purify the effects. One assumes that the substance was smoked, since ingestion requires an MAO inhibitor to be orally active. (The South American brew, ayahuasca, is imbibed orally and consists of a DMT-containing plant mixed with an MAO plant.) However, chocolate was, and still is, grown at Izapa. Modern cacao has mild MAO-inhibiting properties. Like tobacco, the ancient species of cacao was much more powerful. Perhaps there was at ancient Izapa a visionary shamanism fueled by toad juice potentiated by chocolate, what we may call cacaohuasca.

At the very least, Stela 6 preserves evidence that the Izapan shamans used a powerful hallucinogen. In addition, ritual mushroom stones have been found in this part of southern Mesoamerica, dated to Izapa's heyday (400 BC–AD 50). Although psilocybin mushrooms are reportedly no longer found in the region, there is documentation that they were once prevalent. A surviving mushroom cult among the Mixe and Mazatec Indians in the state of Oaxaca (further up the Pacific coast from Izapa) may provide clues as to what the ancient Izapan mushroom religion was like.

The monuments of Izapa provide clues about how shamanism leads to profound cosmological models. The little shaman sailing into and out of the maw of the underworld on Stela 6 is amplified on Stela 67:

*Diagram 2. Stela 67. Izapa. The Sun diety reborn at the end of the Age*

The human figure on this carving is identified as a sun god, probably First Father (One Hunahpu), of Mayan Creation mythology. He's in a canoe which represents the Milky Way. This carving is located in the middle of the north wall of Izapa's ballcourt. In Mayan art, ballcourts represent the Milky Way. The little seating declivity in which First Father sits is a feature that is located along the bright band of the Milky Way in the region of Sagittarius—a dark rift caused by interstellar dust. This feature also figures prominently in Mayan mythology, where it is called the Xibalba be—the "road to the underworld." The First Father deity (also known as the first shaman) sits in this portal.

So, as on Stela 6, he is entering or exiting (or "in") the underworld. His arms are outstretched, which is a gesture that means "period ending." In the context of shamanism, this has several meanings. The Maya believed that, at the end of a cycle, time momentarily ends and the laws of the world are suspended. In the shamanic voyage, eternity or the timeless ground of manifestation can be accessed. Touching the root or source of the world, the shaman can divine secrets, foretell future events, and develop magical healing abilities. These ideas are eschatological in nature, involving the ultimate ends of things, and relate to Neoplatonic concepts of the individual soul and the world soul being linked (being, in fact, identical); their unity is revealed to seekers, initiates, and shamans "at the end of time."

On another level, the "period-ending gesture" indicates which sun (or day; kin = day and sun) the Sun deity is. In Mayan time philosophy, each day has its own face, meaning that successive days are different deities. In the calendar there are twenty different cycling days, but the four "pillars" of the year (the two equinoxes and two solstices) also have their special deities. The end of the solar year occurs on the December solstice, when the period of night is greatest and the year is reborn. For this and other reasons, the First Father solar lord represents the December solstice sun. The carving is encoded astronomical information. First Father sits in the dark rift in the Milky Way—a very specific celestial location. This suggests a cosmology with profound implications.

Let's look at this cosmology via another carving at Izapa that is symbolically similar to the one we just examined. Stela 11 faces the December solstice sunrise horizon, confirming that the solar deity portrayed is, like the similar one on Stela 67, the December solstice sun.

*Diagram 3. Stela 11, Izapa. The December solstice sun in the dark rift of the Milky Way. This is the galactic alignment that culminates in the years around 2012.*

Like the solar deity on Stela 67, his arms are outstretched. Yet here, he isn't in a canoe, but in the maw of a frog deity that is very similar to the DMT toad on Stela 6. Remember, the mouth of the frog-toad is the portal to the underworld, the Xibalba be, the dark rift in the Milky Way. So, this is how the shaman journeys through the underworld in these iconographic portrayals. What is astounding about these mythic carvings is the unequivocal astronomical references. Let's review what's going on in the part of the sky referred to in these scenes.

The dark rift in the Milky Way extends north from the ecliptic (the path of the sun, moon, and stars):

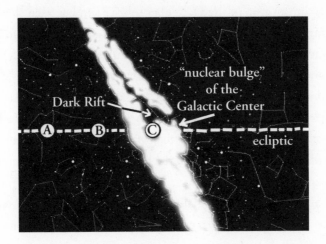

*Diagram 4. The ecliptic, the Milky Way, the dark rift feature, and the precession of the December solstice sun into alignment with the dark rift. A = the position of the December solstice sun 4,000 years ago; B = the position of the December solstice sun 2,000 years ago; C = the position of the December solstice sun today (in era-2012).*

The ecliptic crosses over the Milky Way at a 61-degree angle, forming a celestial cross that the Maya mythologized as their Sacred Tree, or Crossroads. The dark rift begins in the nuclear bulge of the Milky Way, which is the visually large area in which the center of our Milky Way galaxy is located. The sun, every year, moves once around the ecliptic; it thus crosses through the dark rift and the nuclear bulge once every year. The exact date on which this happens has been shifting, due to a slow movement called the precession of the equinoxes. This astronomical phenomenon is caused by the slow wobbling of the earth on its axis, with one wobble completed in approximately 26,000 years.

The shifting is best defined by using one of the solar year's quarter points, such as the equinox; thus, the familiar phrase "the precession of the equinoxes." However, the shifting applies equally to the solstices. As a result, the position of the December solstice sun has been slowly shifting along the ecliptic for thousands of years, converging with, crossing over, and slowly passing background features such as stars, constellations, and, most importantly, the bright band of the Milky Way. The December solstice sun will, in fact, be aligned with the dark rift in the Milky Way in the years around 2012. A striking fact in all of this is that the 13-baktun cycle of the Maya's Long Count calendar—a period of 5,125.36 years—ends on the December solstice of 2012, December 21, 2012.

In this way, what is essentially imagery relating to the shaman's journey into the underworld also encodes, on another level, a profound cosmology of galactic proportions. And that cosmology, what we might call a psychedelic cosmology, implicates another Mayan tradition—the Long Count tradition that gives us the much discussed 2012 cycle ending date. According to the pioneering research I've pursued since the late 1980s, Izapa is the place that formulated the Long Count cosmology and the Mayan Creation mythology that goes along with it. I call this a psychedelic cosmology because powerful entheogenic substances were clearly utilized by the shamans and skywatchers working at Izapa.

The profound integration of celestial, psychological, ritual, and mythopoeic elements at Izapa bespeaks the psychedelic influence, because those tools of vision open the consciousness to higher states of awareness in which multiple dimensions are seen for what they are—mutually interweaving and interpenetrating aspects of a unity that is simply not apparent to the "normal" consciousness that functions on more limited planes of perception.

## PART 2. PSYCHEDELIC COSMOLOGIES

Psychoactive mushrooms and other powerful mind-altering substances were being used in the area of Mesoamerica that gave birth to the Long Count calendar. This is an important factor to consider in explaining the rapid transformation from the Olmec to the Mayan culture, the rapid birth of a new cultural paradigm. A new version of the old mythology sprung up at the same time—the Popol Vuh/Hero Twin myth—and was first recorded on the monuments of Izapa. The Hero Twin myth is an esoteric World Age doctrine designed to describe and explain, in mythic terms, the astronomical process by which the December solstice sun converges with the dark rift in the Milky Way. The Long Count and the Popol Vuh arose within a context in which powerful consciousness-enhancing substances were being used. And the Long Count, we will remember, is designed to end during a unique era of astronomical alignment pointing right at the Galactic Center.

Could the use of hallucinogens explain how the ancient skywatchers became aware of the Galactic Center? Is it just a coincidence that the Galactic Center is near the crossroads believed by the Maya to be the place of World Age creation? Could the use of consciousness-enhancing drugs facilitate such awareness? And, we must ask, what mysteries does the Galactic Center contain? Did the Maya somehow access information or energies resident there? Does their cosmology reflect information obtained shamanically, intimations of a complexly interweaving multi-dimensional cosmos? The sheer profundity and nearly impenetrable insights that are clearly present in Mayan cosmology suggest this is so. Mayan cosmology is based in experiential insights derived from using shamanic tools of vision, and to get an idea of the kind of worldviews that arise in cultures that use these substances as viable sources of information about the nature of reality, we can look to the cosmic models devised by hallucinogen-using Indians in South America: the Desana, Warao, and Kogi Indians.

The Desana, who live on the equator in the Vaupés Territory of the Northwest Amazon, developed a complex geometrical cosmology. The founding myth of the tribe, which explains how their equatorial homeland was chosen, involves a supernatural hero who searched for a place where his staff, when held upright, would not cast a shadow. This is true for the equator on the equinoxes. The shamanic image of this event is that of the staff as a ray of sunlight, a divine sperm, which fertilized the earth. The guiding principle of the Desana thus is, as explained by ethnographer Gerardo Reichel-Dolmatoff, a "search for the center," for the "Center of Day" (1982:167).

The Desana envision space as a great hexagon bounded by six stars centered upon Epsilon Orionis, the middle star in Orion's belt. Desana shamans also perceive this six-sided shape in the structure of rock crystals and honeycombs. The Milky Way is an important celestial dividing line for the Desana, and the entire celestial vault is envisioned as a cosmic brain, divided into two lobes by the great fissure of the Milky Way. According to Reichel-Dolmatoff, "The Desana believe that both brains, the cosmic and the human, pulsate in synchrony with the rhythm of the human heartbeat, linking Man inextricably to the Cosmos" (1982:171). Here we glimpse profound cosmological concepts developed by the ayahuasca-using Desana. Despite living simple lives as hunter-gatherers in the ever-dwindling jungles of the upper Amazon, the Desana utilize shamanic tools of insight and vision to arrive at a profound multidimensional model of the cosmos.

For the Warao Indians of Venezuela, the Earth is a flat disk floating in the cosmic ocean. A "Snake of Being" resides in the outer sea encircling the earth. The horizon thus serves as the outer rim of the Warao cosmos. The sky is conceived of as a canopy, supported at the zenith by the cosmic axis:

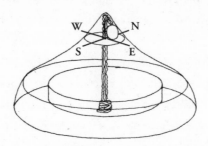

*Diagram 5. The Warao cosmos. After Krupp (1983:320)*

At the base of the cosmic axis lies a knotted snake—the Goddess of the Nadir—that has four heads, each facing one of the cardinal directions. At the highest level of the Warao cosmos, up where the bell-shaped canopy narrows, there is an egg-shaped place of shamanic power. Warao shamans journey to this supernatural zenith by ascending "ropes" of tobacco smoke. Tobacco is the only mind-altering substance Warao shamans use, but the strength and amount they use carry them into the lofty regions of hallucinatory trance. Thus, like the Desana, the Warao shamans' complex multilayered cosmology is informed by drug-induced journeys through the inner planes.

The Kogi, descendants of a spiritual and secretive group in Columbia, also created an astounding and complex cosmology whose religion, philosophy, and cultural traditions are comparable to the high cultures of Mesoamerica. In fact, the Kogi are often compared to the traditional Lacandon Maya of the Chiapan rainforest in Mexico. The Kogi utilize horizon observations of the sun as well as solar zenith-passage dates. Like the Desana, the entire Sierra Nevada in which the Kogi live is imagined to follow a hexagonal plan. The corners of this huge rock crystal correspond to six sacred geographical sites, while their counterparts in the sky correspond to six first-magnitude stars centered on Epsilon Orionis. The Kogi retain complex initiation rites involving multitiered levels of a shamanic priesthood, and place special emphasis on astronomical record-keeping, which sets them apart from nearby tribes. The use of vision-producing substances was certainly a factor in the creation of their cosmovision.

These examples clearly illustrate the kind of complex multidimensional cosmologies that arise as a result of using vision plants to induce shamanic states of mind. The exploration of time and space is an eminently human drive. Mapping space gives rise to highly geometrized mandalic systems, a cosmology incorporating the multidimensional ecology of beings living in our world. Charting time is somewhat trickier, and involves very closely watching and recording the changing position of stars. I feel that this temporal aspect of cosmology-building was also influenced and, indeed, facilitated by the use of powerful vision plants.

### PART 3. SKY CLEFTS, SERPENT ROPES, AND TRANSDIMENSIONAL WORMHOLES

The "hole in the sky" is portrayed in Mesoamerican art as a Creation Place or birthplace. They are also called "sky clefts" and are considered to be portals to the Underworld, or Otherworld. A sky cleft is located in the highest point in the sky, in the center of the cosmic crossroads. (In Mayan cosmovision, the Underworld is the night sky.) In terms of actual astronomy, we are talking here about the dark rift near the Milky Way/ecliptic crossroads. Mayan concepts of birthing involve deities descending along "serpent ropes" from the sky cleft. The Deity Nine Wind, illustrated in the Codex Vindobonensis, descends out of a sky cleft. Sky clefts are extremely abundant in Central Mexican codices, the symbolism of which can be traced back to Teotihuacan (AD 150–AD 750) and, ultimately, to the Olmec cleft-head motif.

Various forms of sky clefts are also found in the Mayan codices, demonstrating the widespread use of this very basic Mesoamerican concept. These sky conduits are portals to other realms through which deities are "birthed" and descend to Earth on serpent ropes, bringing with them otherworldly knowledge.

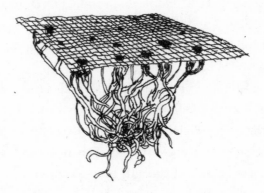

*Diagram 6. Wormhole connections in space-time. After Klein (1982:12)*

In Mesoamerican ideas about world creation, cosmogenesis takes place via a kind of weaving process. Reality is thus undergirded by a system of threadlike links. In other words, space-time itself is woven together in ways that human beings, stuck within the three-dimensional space-time "fabric" of observable reality, cannot readily perceive.

This philosophical model developed by Mesoamerican thinkers is actually extremely progressive, for modern physicists also describe a network of threadlike links between distant places, quantum "wormholes" in space-time that tunnel through a higher dimension. Physicists even joke about making faster-than-lightspeed journeys to distant stars by accessing these holes in space.

Did the Maya access these "wormholes" in their conjuring ceremonies? Did they "birth" into local space-time beings from other realms? Did they travel to distant worlds through these "serpent ropes"? If we may indulge in a little science fiction or, perhaps, metaphysical fact, then we may propose a complex Mayan science of shamanically invoking a "wormhole" in local space-time, an opening to the transdimensional realm that ultimately gets its power from the Black Hole within the Galactic Center, and traveling through it to other worlds. The focus of this shamanic invocation is the Galactic Center, signified by the visible dark rift; serpent cords descend and open, providing local space-time access to the Cosmic Source and its eternal riches. In the deepest sense, Mayan philosophers conceived of this "evocation of creation" or "ritual summoning" as a type of birth (Taube 1994).

But what does it mean for a serpent cord to descend and open? Who was traveling through the hole in space-time? Is such a scenario just a fanciful fairy tale, or could it have involved the actual activities of Mayan kings and shamans? To begin answering such questions, we can consult Mayan iconography, which frequently portrays ancestors who have been conjured through shamanic vision rites peering out from the mouths of serpents. These serpents are often shown descending from a sky cleft, and gods and ancestors also are born (or appear) into this world through these sky clefts. As one scholar wrote, "It is likely that this cleft is a pre-Hispanic form of the Glory Hole—a celestial conduit . . ." (Taube 1994:660). The Glory Hole is the hole at the top of the cosmic house. So, the sky cleft is a hole in the center of the sky, at the center of the crossroads designating the celestial throne. Since the center of the crossroads is the location of the sky hole as well as the celestial throne of Mayan kings, ascending to the cosmic throne must have a lot to do with vision journeys, conjuring, king accessions, and magical birthing.

These processes and concepts are intimately involved in the understanding that the Milky Way is the Great Mother, and the dark rift is her vagina or birthplace. It is the place of transformation that the prospective male king must enter in order to be reborn as the king, a divine being. That these things are templated upon the alignment of the December solstice sun with the dark rift in the Milky Way—on the 13-baktun cycle end date, December 21, 2012—is mind-boggling. We can poetically describe the Maya's end-date cosmology as follows:

King-shaman is born from the Jaguar Mother and, enthroned upon the lap of the Galactic Center, forever dispenses authority while communing with the sacred source—the Great Mother Goddess. The throne of the Jaguar Mother manifests when the First Solar King (the December solstice sun) joins with the Cosmic Mother (the Galactic Center).

*Diagram 7. The Mayan king enthroned in the Galactic Center*

Underlying these activities and interests of Mayan king-shamans is the role played by mushrooms and other psychoactive substances in the formulation of the Long Count and the Hero Twin myth around 300 BC—indeed, in the formulation of Mesoamerican cosmology as a whole. Given that these tools of vision were in use at that time, we should not be too quick to draw limits on what these king-shamans and astronomer-priests could or could not have accomplished. The Long Count calendar as Galactic Cosmology is the unique result of a shamanistic experiment seemingly conducted in secret, over perhaps three hundred years in the dimly understood Pre-Classic era. The tools of cosmic knowledge used by the ancient visionary cosmologists of Mesoamerica to discover and fine-tune their Galaxy-centered cosmovision were the same ones used by seekers of gnosis in other times and places—vision plants.

In his introduction to my 1998 book, *Maya Cosmogenesis 2012*, Terence McKenna wrote:

Can the Maya dream of renewal at the conjunction of winter solstice and Galactic Heart redeem our civilization? I believe that it can play a significant part, and that part of the resacralization of the world that must accompany any valorization of post-historical time involves the recognition of the deep power and sophistication of the aboriginal mind—not only the ancient aboriginal mind, but the contemporary aboriginal mind as well. As we awaken to the power of the moving sky, as we awaken to the powers that inform and illuminate many of the plants that have found their way into aboriginal medicine, as we struggle with the vastness of the universe of space and time and our place in it, as we do these things, we follow in Maya footsteps.

The galactic knowledge encoded on the carved monuments of Izapa, in the Creation Myth and the Long Count calendar, was discovered within the context of the use of mind-expanding plants and preparations, the pharmacopeia of traditional shamans. The integration of movements in the outer sky and movements in the inner collective psyche of humanity is a nondual unification that psychedelics can reveal. What I've termed a *galactic cosmology* is named so not simply because it utilizes the galaxy as an armature of the sky's shifting, but because it perceives human evolution from a heightened, enlarged, galactic level. After being lost for centuries, this galactic cosmovision is now reemerging. With its attendant spiritual teachings, it promises to help us restore our deep connection to nature, the universe, and our true selves.

### REFERENCES

Klein, Cecilia F. 1982. "Woven Heaven, Tangled Earth: A Weaver's Paradigm of the Mesoamerican Cosmos" in *Ethnoastronomy and Archaeoastronomy in the American Tropics,* edited by Anthony Aveni and Gary Urton, pp. 1–36. New York: New York Academy of Sciences. Annals of the New York Academy of Sciences, vol. 385.

Krupp, E. C. 1983. *Echoes of the Ancient Skies: The Astronomy of Lost Civilizations.* New York: Oxford University Press.

Reichel-Dolmatoff, Gerardo. 1982. "Astronomical Models of Social Behavior among Some Indians of Columbia" in *Ethnoastronomy and Archaeoastronomy in the American Tropics,* edited by Anthony Aveni and Gary Urton, pp. 165–181. New York: New York Academy of Sciences. Annals of the New York Academy of Sciences, vol. 385.

Taube, Karl A. 1994. "The Birth Vase: Natal Imagery in Ancient Maya Myth and Ritual" in *The Vase Book: A Corpus of Rollout Photographs of Maya Vases,* vol. 4, pp. 652–685. New York: Kerr and Associates.

*This article incorporates excerpts from my book,* Maya Cosmogenesis 2012 *(Bear & Company, 1998), and from my essay, "Through the Smoking Mirror: Astronomical Alignments and Mayan Shamanism," published in* Conference Proceedings of the American Psychotronics Association, *July 2002.*

# AYAHUASCA AND KABBALAH

## Jay Michaelson

In 1954, Aldous Huxley published "The Doors of Perception," a famous essay observing that the effects of mescaline were remarkably similar to the unitive mysticism of the world's great religions, particularly Vedanta, the philosophical-mystical form of Hinduism which Huxley practiced. It caused an immediate sensation. Many in the public were outraged by its pro-pharmacological spirit, and many in the academy accused Huxley (like William James before him) of flattening different mystical traditions, and of disregarding distinctions between "sacred and profane" mystical practice.

But many more were inspired. Huxley's essay, and other works like it, set the agenda for 1960s spirituality, and what later came to be called the New Age movement. He provided a philosophical explanation of what was important about mescaline—that our perceptive faculties filter out more than they let in, and that mescaline, like meditation, opens those doors wider—and a personal account of what a "trip" was like. He showed how entheogens (as they later came to be called) could be a part of a sincere spiritual practice. And he perhaps unwittingly imported a certain Vedanta agenda of what the "ultimate" mystical experience was like: union. As has been argued by many scholars over the last few decades, this claim of ultimacy—that *unio mystica* is the peak form of mystical experience, with others defined by how close they approach it—is actually a rather partisan one. Why is "union with the All" superior to, or more true than, deity mysticism, visions of Krishna/Christ/spirits, and the text-based mysticism of the Kabbalah? Sure, for Vedanta it is—but that's just Vedanta's view.

Two generations of spiritual seekers have been influenced, for better and for worse, by this hierarchy. From the naive hippie to the sophisticated yogi, Jewish Renewalniks to Ken Wilberites, hundreds of thousands of spiritual practitioners have implicitly or explicitly assumed the prioritization of the unitive over all else: The point is that "All is One."

Most of these constituencies are also, like Huxley, influenced by the psychedelic experience, primarily that of mushrooms and LSD. While most contemporary spiritual teachers have long since given these substances up, in favor of meditation and other mystical practices which afford the same experiences in a more reliable container (and one greatly enriched by self-examination and introspection), if you ask them, as I have, they'll admit that the psychedelic experience formed an important part of their spiritual initiation. Whether it's what got them on the road in the first place, or confirmed their earlier intuitions, psychedelics have set the agenda for a huge percentage of contemporary spiritual teachers, across religious and spiritual denominations, and many of their followers as well.

These two trends—that All is One is the point, and that it accords with the psychedelic experience—have occasionally led to a distortion of religious and spiritual traditions. In the Kabbalah, for example, unitive mysticism is only a small part of a wide panoply of mystical experiences. Yes, there are texts which speak of annihilation of the self (*bittul hayesh*) and a unification with God (*achdut*). But these are, truthfully, in the minority. Many more are visionary texts, describing theophanies of all shapes and sizes; or records of prophecy or angelic communication; or less explicitly unitive accounts of proximity to the Divine. Yet there's a sense, among teachers of contemporary Kabbalah—and I'm not referring here to the Kabbalah Centre (where Madonna goes), which does not teach Kabbalah proper, but rather a unique and sometimes weird synthesis of Kabbalah, the Human Potential movement, and New Religious Movements like Scientology—that unitive mysticism is the *summum bonum,* the ultimate good.

Some Kabbalistic texts agree, but many others do not. For example, Rabbi Arthur Green, today one of progressive Judaism's leading teachers, in 1968 wrote an article (under a pseudonym) called "Psychedelics and Kabbalah," explicitly analogizing the psychedelic experiences to aspects of Kabbalistic teaching—but selecting those aspects of Kabbalah and Hasidism which fit the experience. Naturally, Green was also influenced by the many forms of non-Jewish mysticism popular at the time, most of whom asserted that All is One, but in that essay, he makes clear that the psychedelic experience affected how he understood Kabbalah. Green, like fellow practitioner-academic Daniel Matt, has been enormously influential: Their anthologies of Hasidic and Kabbalistic texts are read far more widely than the texts themselves, and are widely assumed to represent the mainstream of their respective traditions.

I am not taking a position on whether this "distortion" is for good or ill; in my own practice, the nondual/unitive perspective plays a central role, and I am grateful for it, whatever its sources. But I have a hunch that it is about to change.

The reason it is changing is that more and more Jewish spiritual seekers are pursuing nonunitive paths. This includes earth-based ritual, shamanic ritual, and other disciplines which, while they may hold the view that All is One, provide experiences of differentiation (energies, elements, visions, etc.). But perhaps more importantly, it includes drinking ayahuasca, smoking DMT, and visionary shamanic-entheogenic practices which offer different experiences from the unitive one. The ayahuasca trip, unlike the mescaline one, is not especially unitive; indeed, one of its hallmarks is the sense of communication with other life forms or consciousnesses. And while a sense of All is One is sometimes reported in the midst of the ayahuasca experience, it's more common to read reports of visions of phenomena—manifestation, not essence.

Some of these accounts are strikingly similar to texts from the Hechalot and Merkavah schools of Jewish mysticism, which flourished between the second and ninth centuries. In the texts from this period, we read detailed accounts of heavenly palaces, Divine chariots, and angels; of ascents to other realms which seem somehow to be in outer space or an extraterrestrial locale; of a sense of great danger, but also great awe, beauty, and love; and of beings which travel on some kind of cosmic vehicle. The descriptions are visionary and auditory, much like the accounts of ayahuasca visions. They are "shamanic" journeys, both in the sense of being journeys of the soul to other realms and in the sense of a transformation of the self. They yield information, prophecy, revelation, theophany. And they are not really about All is One.

Hechalot and Merkavah mysticism is studied in the academy, but it is little known in the contemporary spiritual world. It's complicated, arcane, and literally otherworldly. But just as the unitive moments of Hasidism appeal to those who have had a unitive experience on mushrooms, so, too, the visionary aspects of Hechalot and Merkavah mysticism appeal to those who have had a visionary experience on ayahuasca. The similarities are striking.

What's more, Hechalot and Merkavah mysticism, related as it is to gnosticism, provides one of world literature's richest libraries of otherworldly mystical experience. It's eerie how similar some of these millennia-old texts are to the records contemporary journeyers provide of the ayahuasca trip: the sense of being in "outer space," the tenuous links to consensual reality, the sense of danger, and above all the colorful descriptions of chambers, angels, songs, palaces, ascents, descents, fire, music, and so much more. It also provides a sense of history, context, and "belonging" to those who affiliate with Judaism, Christianity, or gnosticism; like unitive experiences, nonunitive visionary/ecstatic experiences have a lineage within these traditions. Perhaps, too, it might offer guidance for those seeking to integrate such experiences into their lives.

To reiterate, I am taking no position on whether unitive or non-unitive experiences are "better," and see nondual essence and dualistic manifestation as two sides of the same ineffable unity. My point, simply, is that much of contemporary Western spirituality derives from a particular psychedelic experience and a particular form of mysticism it approximates. With the increasing popularity of ayahuasca and similar medicines, the former element has changed—and I think the latter will too.

In the esoteric world, this kind of change and interchange has always been with us. Hechalot mystics learned from the gnostics, who learned from the Jews, who learned from the Babylonians. Medieval Kabbalists learned from the Sufis, who learned from the Hindus, who learned from the Buddhists, who learned from other Hindus. One need not make the facile, and false, claim that all mysticism is the same thing in order to recognize that mystics across space and time have understood themselves to be gesturing toward the same truths, albeit in very different ways. And those differences advance, not obstruct, the progress of realization. After all, when one can ultimately know nothing, it helps to learn from everything.

# PSYCHING OUT THE COSMOS

## Daniel Pinchbeck

According to contemporary cosmology, our solar system emerged from titanic accidents. Gases swirling together in the void of deep space randomly formed stars and planets; eventually, the whole show will collapse back into nullity. This perspective, developed from the Renaissance to the present, stands as a great achievement of the modern mind. It also deviates radically from the ancients' conception of a universe saturated with meaning and purpose, where human activity reflects the movements of the celestial bodies. The basis of Hermetic philosophy was "As above, so below." Seemingly crushed by the rise of scientific materialism in the West, this worldview has now been rephrased in a new book that proposes a startling reversal of paradigms.

Scrupulously researched and carefully argued, Richard Tarnas's *Cosmos and Psyche* (Penguin, 2006) is the product of thirty years of thought and study. A Harvard-educated professor and a founding director of the California Institute of Integral Studies, Tarnas is already known for *The Passion of the Western Mind*, a surprise 1991 bestseller that surveys Western philosophy from the Greeks until today and is used as a standard text in many college courses. With his new work, Tarnas has staked his success and academic reputation on a radical thesis. The new structuring metanarrative that he explores, in 550 carefully argued pages, is not some postmodern deconstruction of systems and methods, but that cornerstone of antiquity and the often derided New Age: astrology. According to his thesis, the orbits of the planets—especially the so-called outer planets—are synchronized with developments in human consciousness, and their movements can be correlated with cycles of scientific progress, cultural breakthroughs, war, peace, and revolution. Ignoring the zodiac signs explored in tabloid horoscopes, Tarnas focuses instead on planetary transits—geometric relationships between the bodies of the solar system—and the correspondence that these alignments seem to have with the dynamics of civilization.

For those with no sympathy for astrology, *Cosmos and Psyche* will prove an implausible stretch. Tarnas knows that he faces a difficult task in getting this material taken seriously in mainstream circles—let alone the skeptical and intellectual enclaves of academia that embraced *The Passion of the Western Mind*. In conversation, he says that *Passion* was, in a sense, a "Trojan Horse," and that he had always intended that book to be followed by his new work, which seeks to revive astrology as a serious intellectual discipline and provide a cosmological missing link between the human world and the greater universe in which we are embedded. *Cosmos and Psyche* offers us, ultimately, a rejoinder to Copernicus—where the astronomer shifted the Earth from the center to the periphery, Tarnas proposes a reintegration, in which the evolution of consciousness reflects the ordering principles of a larger whole.

Tarnas does not believe that the planets directly influence human behavior, in some straightforward cause-and-effect manner. He concurs with the psychoanalyst Carl Jung, who wrote, "Our psyche is set up in accord with the structure of the universe, and what happens in the macrocosm likewise happens in the infinitesimal and most subjective reaches of the psyche." When we look at a clock, the hands indicate what time it is, but they do not make it be that time. Similarly, Tarnas argues, patterns in human culture are meshed within larger cyclical processes of the solar system. He believes the planets function like Jungian archetypes, complexes with multiple meanings that can influence the individual and collective psyche in myriad ways. By studying astrology, we can learn to read what time it is, in an archetypal sense.

What are astrological transits? As the planets orbit the sun, they form geometric angles in relationship to the Earth and to one another. An individual's natal chart maps the particular pattern of relationships that exists at the moment of birth. Throughout our lives, the planets—said to be "transitting"—weave further geometries that intersect with this original matrix. If the planets represent archetypal complexes, then the expression of these energies—their particular intensity or quality—depends on this constantly shifting set of relationships. How or why such geometric alignments of planets might correspond with large-scale trends in a civilization, or psychological patterns in an individual, is another question. Such a correlation is impossible to account for with modern scientific methods, as it is not based on any transmitted force or direct influence, but on a deeper realization that human consciousness is meshed within the larger universe, a fractal that organically expresses the larger pattern of the whole.

Classical astrologers knew of only seven spheres—Sun, Mercury, Venus, Moon, Mars, Jupiter, and Saturn. In *Cosmos and Psyche,* Tarnas instead focuses on the slower swoops of the outer planets—Saturn, Neptune, Uranus, and Pluto. Because these distant bodies take more time to complete their orbits of the solar system, their conjunctions and oppositions can require many years to complete. It is in this protracted dance that Tarnas believes he has uncovered a convincing system of correspondences, integrating widespread developments in history and culture. Of the outer planets, all but Saturn were discovered within the last two hundred and fifty years. The archetypal astrology that Tarnas promotes is, therefore, an explicitly modern discipline, founded upon our technological capacity to peek into deep space, and aided today by computer programs that can calculate complex orbital patterns in the distant past or far-flung future. "We have, in a sense, been given a powerful archetypal telescope for a vast archetypal cosmos at the same moment that we have developed extraordinarily powerful space telescopes to apprehend the vast physical cosmos," he writes.

Astronomers name new planets when they are found; it then takes decades of observation by astrologers to understand the energies these planets represent, which they discover by studying the effects the spheres exert, first, on individual lives and then on larger periods of cultural development. The oldest-known of the outer planets, Saturn, has long been associated with limitations, discipline, the paternal, melancholy, death, and gravity. During an individual's "Saturn Return," which happens roughly every twenty-eight years, Saturn swings around to the place it occupied at the time of birth, often coinciding with a period of existential reappraisal.

Discovered in 1781, at the peak of the Enlightenment, Uranus (the father of Saturn in classical mythology) is often associated with breakthroughs, liberations, and rebellious upsurges. Tarnas argues that the planet bears close resemblance to the classical figure of Prometheus, who stole fire from the heavens and gave it to mortal humans. Tarnas suggests it was no accident that Uranus/Prometheus showed up in the skies at the beginning of the Industrial Revolution, of the Romantic movement in literature and art, and in the era of the French and American Revolutions. The astronomical event seems correlated with an intense liberating upsurge in the West, as if the physical embodiment of the planet represented the new powers and self-realizations then emerging "into the conscious awareness of the collective psyche."

Neptune was discovered in 1846, and named for the god of the deep seas. The planet represents all things transcendent, formless, subtle, and spiritual. It is also connected with the dissolution of boundaries and structures, illusion, addiction, and "the bedazzlement of consciousness, whether by gods, archetypes, beliefs, dreams, ideals, or ideologies; with enchantment, in both positive and negative senses." Neptune's discovery corresponded with a nineteenth-century fascination with the occult and the mystical. In high culture, this fascination manifested as the "world spirit" of Hegel and the Transcendentalism of Emerson, while the masses, and even some scientists, indulged in explorations of Spiritualism, mesmerism, and phrenology.

Pluto, linked to the Underworld and its ruling deity, made its appearance in 1930, a decade before World War II, at the time of the Great Depression and the rise of the gangster as mass-cultural antihero. "Pluto is associated with the principle of elemental power, depth, and intensity," Tarnas writes. He connects Pluto with the creative/destructive deity, Dionysius, noting that the Greek Hades, who became Pluto under the Romans, was identified with Dionysius by Greek authors such as Heraclitus and Euripides. Pluto/Dionysius represents instinctual upsurge, cathartic, orgiastic, and frequently violent; the archetype empowers "whatever it touches, sometimes to overwhelming and catastrophic extremes."

These four planets take the starring roles in *Cosmos and Psyche*, which can be enjoyed as a vast Shakespearean drama where the action revolves around cosmic principles that influence human lives, social movements, and historical actions. When Saturn and Pluto align in the heavens, for instance, the result is often phases of mass-destruction and planet-wide violence. The spheres were in exact conjunction at the start of World War I; in opposition from 1929 to 1933, during the Great Depression and the rise of Fascism; and in an exact square alignment in August and September of 1939, as Germany invaded Poland, starting World War II. They were within two degrees of exact opposition when the events of September 11, 2001, incited the current phase of global conflict. The Plutonic principle of instinctual intensification appears to catalyze Saturn's downward pull toward "the bottom line, the workings of necessity, the inevitable and inescapable." Acute periods of conservative empowerment, environmental destruction, and social repression are often marked by transits of these two spheres.

When Uranus and Pluto come together, on the other hand, the party starts—and then tends to get out of hand. Dionysius amps up the Promethean urge toward liberation and creative breakthrough, while Prometheus incites Dionysian rampages that often end in violence. The last conjunction of Pluto and Uranus occurred from 1960 to 1972, reaching exact alignment in 1965 to 1966. The 1960s were an Oedipal outburst, marked by volatile movements aimed at political and personal liberation. The entire period, Tarnas notes, "can be recognized as essentially a manifestation of two distinct archetypes—the rebellious Promethean and the erotic Dionysian—acting in close conjunction and mutual activation." Uranus and Pluto were also in opposition from 1787 to 1798, the period of the French Revolution, which had a volatile and emancipatory gestalt similar to the 1960s. Uranus and Pluto formed a square from 1845 to 1856, when a "wave of revolutionary upheavals" passed across Europe.

Tarnas believes that suggestive correlations—such as Uranus/Pluto with radical upsurges and Saturn/Pluto with drastic downturns—indicate that the cosmos "as a living whole appears to be informed by some kind of pervasive intelligence." But where does this leave human will? Tarnas calls, not for fatalism, but for viewing the human condition as one of "creative participation in a living cosmos of unfolding meaning and purpose." While the natal chart appears to give deep psychological insight into the individual, the archetypal forces it depicts are not determinative or predictive, but open to personal expression and conscious mediation. He points out that Charlie Chaplin and Adolf Hitler had similar natal charts, having been born four days apart in April 1889. The similarities indicated by their charts include "harsh life experiences such as sustained poverty and isolation; susceptibility to displays of anger; problematic relationships with authorities combined with dictatorial controlling tendencies." In addition, the men shared "an impulse to experience or create dramatic illusions capable of powerfully moving audiences." But Chaplin and Hitler expressed these archetypal energies in starkly dissimilar ways, exemplifying the creativity and free will of the individual.

With *Cosmos and Psyche,* Tarnas has attempted to do for cosmology what Fritjof Capra's *The Tao of Physics* did for quantum theory, showing how an area of modern rational thought can be integrated with ancient metaphysical principles. Of course, his evidence features psychological and philosophical dimensions that cannot be statistically quantified or materially demonstrated—although hard data such as the quadruple conjunction of Jupiter, Uranus, Pluto, and the Moon at the exact time of the 1969 Apollo lunar landing is quite impressive. However compelling the evidence that Tarnas has garnered, there can be no ironclad proof of a thesis that takes so many intangible and qualitative factors into account. Recognizing this, he notes that part of what he is proposing is that the rational faculty itself must now be contextualized. Skeptical reason must be integrated into a greater understanding that involves intuitive, artistic, and empathic dimensions of the psyche: "It is possible that the deeper truths not only of our spiritual life but of the very cosmos require, and reward, an essentially aesthetic and moral engagement with its being and intelligence, and will forever elude a merely reductive, skeptical, objectifying judgment issued by a single proud but limited faculty, 'reason.'"

The universe, in Tarnas's reading, is closer to a great symphony than a mechanical instrument or mathematical model—and the study of archetypal astrology offers us insight into its deeper harmonics. Since his thesis requires an evaluation of ethical and aesthetic factors as well as material ones, it is up to each reader to decide if Tarnas makes a compelling case. Personally, I have tended to avoid astrology, which seemed reductive and intellectually naive. After studying this work, I will never look at the planets the same way, and I intend to pay close attention to their future alignments in relation to global events and my own inner processes.

Observed through this lens of outer planet transits, what does our own age hold in store? We have recently concluded a long Uranus-Neptune conjunction, spanning 1985 to 2001, when the Promethean spark of creative and technological innovation aided the spiritual and transcendental impulse, coupled with the more problematic dissolution of boundaries and bedazzlements caused by the inciting of Neptunian energies. Tarnas believes that this Uranus/Neptune complex was experienced as "a liminal state . . . unprecedentedly free-floating, uncertain, epistemologically and metaphysically untethered and confused." The development of the Internet and new dizzying networks of communication, as well as the "addictive, druglike, trance-inducing aspect of Internet use," characterized this archetype, as did the rise of raves and electronic music. The forming of the European Union and the fall of the Berlin Wall also exemplified the fast, fluid, boundary-dissolving play of these forces.

Beginning in 2004, we entered into a problematic Saturn/Neptune opposition that lasts, alas, until 2008. During such alignments, Saturnian principles of limitation, death, and repression encounter Neptunian tendencies toward dissolution and the oceanic loss of boundaries. The tsunami in Southeast Asia and the flooding of New Orleans by Hurricane Katrina seem deeply and tragically symbolic of this transit. As Tarnas notes, characteristic Saturn/Neptune themes include "death caused by water, the ocean as source of suffering and loss, contamination of water. . . ." It is a time when "numberless haunting images of death and sorrow . . . [permeate] the collective consciousness." During these alignments, "Social anomie and spiritual malaise are frequent, sometimes intensified to a state of profound alienation." On the upside, the meeting of Saturn and Neptune can also indicate a deepening of spiritual commitment and disciplined response to tragedy. To show what this means, Tarnas points to celebrated individuals with major alignments of these planets in their chart, including the Dalai Lama, Robert F. Kennedy, and Abraham Lincoln; all of them, in different ways, figures "of sorrow and reconciliation" who brought spiritual depth to tragic historical circumstances.

From 2008 to 2020, Uranus and Pluto come into a square alignment, and Tarnas proposes that the Promethean/Dionysian energy of the 1960s will return, perhaps in a new and more tempered form. (According to his model, square alignments often lead to a further development of the possibilities and principles catalyzed by the previous conjunction or opposition of two outer planets.) From 2008 to 2011, Saturn, Uranus, and Pluto will square one another, as they did from 1964 to 1968, "when both revolutionary and reactionary impulses were intensely constellated." Tarnas suggests, gently, that the period we are hurtling toward may be something like the 1930s crossed with the 1960s—think Preston Sturges meets Jim Morrison. At the same time, he is quick to point out that concrete prediction is impossible, as the archetypal energies can take a multitude of forms.

Nonetheless, according to the thesis of *Cosmos and Psyche*, an awareness of which archetypes are currently constellating and approaching can be extremely helpful. The transits of the outer planets indicate ambient mood-shifts in the Zeitgeist that influence all aspects of cultural and social reality, from cultural trends to musical genres, technological developments to historical events. From this perspective, knowing that we have several more years of Saturn/Neptune can help us prepare for the types of challenges, both psychic and physical, we may face.

Awareness of personal and collective transits might also allow us to find, in Tarnas's words, "a more autonomous and creative response to the archetypal forces at work at any given time." The purpose of such knowledge is similar to that of Jungian psychoanalysis, which seeks to reveal the deeper forces pressing on the psyche, so that the individual can mediate them consciously rather than suffer as their unwitting victim. While Tarnas has not given us a crystal ball for divining the future, he may be offering something far more important—a transformative matrix for reconceiving our relationship to the cosmos, as well as some subtle directions for the times ahead.

# SHAMANS AND CHARLATANS:
## ASSESSING CASTANEDA'S LEGACY

*ST Frequency*

When it was published in 1968, Carlos Castaneda's groundbreaking ethnographic diary, *The Teachings of Don Juan: A Yaqui Way of Knowledge,* received enthusiastic reviews from both the academic community and mainstream critics. Castaneda enjoyed immediate success and went on to write a series of sequels chronicling his apprenticeship to Don Juan Matus, a Yaqui Indian and sorcerer from Sonora, Mexico. Combining anthropological observations with engrossing storytelling, *The Teachings of Don Juan* represented to many scholars an exciting new methodology in ethnographic literature, inspiring praise from such figures as Margaret Mead and Yaqui scholar Edward H. Spicer, who called the text a "remarkable achievement."[1] The doctoral committee at UCLA echoed Spicer's esteem for Castaneda, awarding him a Ph.D. in 1972 for his third book, *Journey to Ixtlan.*

With fame came scrutiny, however, and the celebrity anthropologist soon met with controversy that would span his entire career. Questions emerged over the existence of Don Juan, Castaneda's representation of Yaqui culture, and the basic authenticity of *The Teachings* as academics, scientists, and authors identified dubious elements in Castaneda's ethnography. Today, almost four decades after the book appeared and nine years since its author's death, the legacy of *The Teachings of Don Juan* is as much about the consequences of its debated legitimacy as it is about Carlos Castaneda himself.

Richard de Mille, son of Hollywood director Cecil B. de Mille, wrote two books on Castaneda's published works and was one of his earliest and most outspoken detractors. De Mille argued that Don Juan and his teachings are wholly counterfeit. He presented a scathing indictment of academic malpractice, charging that the UCLA faculty and the University of California Press should be held accountable for a spurious work of scholarship.

A major point of contention among Castaneda's critics is the conspicuous absence of evidence to support his claims that he actually did know and study under a Yaqui sorcerer named Don Juan. When a university publishes an account of anthropological fieldwork, it is standard practice to require tangible proofs that the fieldwork actually took place. With *The Teachings of Don Juan,* argues de Mille, this verification was never made. He claims that basic support materials "did not exist either, except in Castaneda's highly developed imagination."[2] De Mille suggests that the book was ultimately printed as a rebellious statement from marginalized sectors of the UCLA intelligentsia against more punctilious rivals. In addition, the university press likely saw in Castaneda's narrative a viable new youth market: wild-eyed denizens of the mushrooming counterculture, hungry for psychedelic yarns of Mexican Indians and peyote trips.

Regardless of the actual details of publication, the book did exceptionally well in both popular and scholarly markets, achieving unlikely success for a work shelved as anthropology. In addition to its scientific classification, *The Teachings of Don Juan* bears the authoritative subheading, "A Yaqui Way of Knowledge." Many critics find fault with this title, noting that the character of Don Juan bears no resemblance to a Yaqui Indian. Spicer, the anthropologist whose positive review lent early and enduring credibility to the text, admits in the same article that it is "wholly gratuitous to emphasize, as the subtitle does, any connection between the subject matter of the book and the cultural traditions of the Yaquis."[3]

Although Don Juan is explicitly named as a Yaqui, Castaneda offers no details throughout the narrative to support this claim, and in fact depicts him engaging in activities associated with markedly dissimilar Indian cultures. Don Juan's use of peyote, datura, and psychotropic mushrooms, for example, is completely divergent from Yaqui tradition and more closely resembles Huichol and Navajo ritual practices. Spicer theorizes that Don Juan, while perhaps of Yaqui descent, is more likely a cultural composite of various Indian and mestizo influences; the subtitle, he assumes, was probably the work of a "publisher [that] went beyond Castaneda's intention."[4]

Spicer is not the only Castaneda critic with relevant scientific experience. Revered ethnomycologist and early psychedelics proponent Gordon Wasson read *The Teachings* soon after its publication and wasted little time composing a letter to Castaneda. Wasson's questions, while politely worded, were directed to clear up what he felt to be anomalies in the mushroom rituals depicted in the book. The notoriously candid Castaneda responded with uncharacteristic eagerness, no doubt excited to correspond with the man whose seminal writings on hallucinogenic fungi were a formative influence for him. Yet his replies, as paraphrased in de Mille's *The Don Juan Papers,* are curiously vague and evasive. Most interesting is his answer to Wasson's inquiries about Don Juan's ethnic origin; in response, Castaneda revises the rough biography offered in *The Teachings,* explaining that the sorcerer is "not a pure Yaqui" and therefore cannot be situated culturally, "except in a guessing manner."[5]

As for the subtitle, Castaneda maintains that it was added per suggestion of the University of California Press who, prior to reading his manuscript, insisted on its inclusion to help categorize the book. To imply that Don Juan is representative of all Yaquis, he says, was never his intention. This admission stands in stark contrast to a comment made by the associate editor of the University of California Press who, in a letter to de Mille, states, "The title of Castaneda's book and the entire text are the work of the author."[6] It seems then that Castaneda himself erroneously labeled his work as an exposition of a "Yaqui way of knowledge," and purposely so—but for what reason? De Mille suggests that, in aligning the book with a relatively obscure Indian tribe, Castaneda not only ascribed a scientific legitimacy to his account, but also sought to fashion a "kind of red man no one had ever met," and in so doing, corner the market on a new pop-cultural archetype.[7]

With the overt nature of the subtitle in effect, whatever Don Juan teaches throughout the text becomes a "Yaqui way of knowledge" by default. It is then unnecessary for Castaneda to prove Don Juan's "Yaquiness" to his readers (unless of course, those readers happen to be Yaqui scholars, in which case he relies on clever obfuscation). In the introduction to *The Teachings,* for example, Don Juan's provenance is described quite briefly, and in rather broad terms:

> All he said was that he had been born in the Southwest in 1891; that he
> had spent nearly all his life in Mexico; that in 1900 his family was exiled
> by the Mexican government to Central Mexico along with thousands of
> other Sonoran Indians.

The "Yaqui Diaspora" is well documented in the historical record, and little is offered in the way of authentication with this short synopsis. Careful to avoid pigeonholing Don Juan into any recognizable ethnicity, Castaneda further muddies the image of his Indian with a caveat acknowledging the sorcerer's murky heritage: "I was not sure," he maintains, "whether to place the context of his knowledge totally in the culture of the Sonoran Indians. But it is not my intention here to determine his precise cultural milieu."

Prefacing the book with this disclaimer, Castaneda effectively shields his ethnography from charges of misrepresentation and fashions his depiction of the "Yaqui" sorcerer in such a manner as to render the Indian cultureless—or as Spicer phrases it, suspended in "cultural limbo." Don Juan's origin is thus couched in ambiguity and skillfully blurred, rendering him both inoffensive to discerning critics and appealingly enigmatic to the lay reader.

However innocuous his presentation might appear, Don Juan nevertheless aroused the suspicions of more skeptical readers who exposed further aberrations in Castaneda's work. As the series progressed, many critics observed glaring discrepancies in the details and chronologies of events, as well as a general drift in tone from scholarly observation toward more whimsical storytelling. Yet even with his first book, Castaneda's literary techniques invited some serious scrutiny. *The Teachings of Don Juan* is allegedly a translation of the anthropologist's field notes from Spanish to English, with occasional bracketed asides imparting the polyglot Indian's original dialogue. Why is it, then, wondered some critics, that Don Juan tutors Carlos solely in their lingua franca—especially when certain concepts would doubtless be more genuinely articulated in his native tongue?

The conspicuous absence of Yaqui terminology in the text raised the eyebrows of more than one scholar in Castaneda's audience, and prominent critics such as Spicer, Wasson, and de Mille sounded the alarm to this anomaly. In his letter to Carlos, Wasson inquires whether he managed to gather any Yaqui translations of the recurring philosophical terms Don Juan uses in his teachings. Castaneda replies that he has, indeed, learned a few Yaqui words but is loath to expound further on the issue. De Mille is far less congenial in his disputation, pointing out that the young anthropologist apparently "learned not one word of Yaqui during his first five years with Don Juan," and then in later writings, makes reference to only two, rather commonplace terms.[8]

Spanish expressions abound, on the other hand, as Castaneda repeatedly employs the words *brujo* and *diablero* to denote those experienced in the knowledge of Yaqui sorcery. Conveniently for Castaneda, *brujo* is sometimes used in Yaqui culture to refer to dabblers in black magic. The nature of sorcery as practiced by Don Juan, however, differs strikingly from that traditionally understood to exist in Yaqui society. Anthropologist Muriel Thayer Painter notes that, according to Yaqui belief, those persons that practice witchcraft (i.e., sorcery) are timorous and feeble—both traits utterly incongruous with Don Juan's depiction as a man who has "vanquished fear" and is remarkably fit, "despite his advanced age." Furthermore, the knowledge of witchcraft is thought by the Yaquis to be "an inborn quality," a power that cannot be taught or inherited. This statement directly contradicts Castaneda's accounts of the art of Yaqui sorcery as a cycle of apprenticeship handed down across generations from a "benefactor" to his "chosen man."

In her book *With Good Heart: Yaqui Beliefs and Ceremonies in Pascua Village*, Painter presents a sampling of Yaqui vocabulary associated with spirituality: *morea*, an equivalent to the Spanish *brujo; saurino*, used to describe persons with the gift of divination; and *seataka*, or spiritual power, a word which is "fundamental to Yaqui thought and life."[9] It is indeed hard to believe that Castaneda's benefactor, a self-professed Yaqui, would fail to employ these native expressions throughout the apprenticeship. In omitting such intrinsically relevant terms from his ethnography, Castaneda critically undermines his portrait of Don Juan as a bona fide Yaqui sorcerer.

Linguistic concerns aside, the Indian depicted in *The Teachings of Don Juan* departs from traditional Yaqui behavior in other significant ways, most notably in his usage of entheogenic plants such as peyote and psilocybe mushrooms. As Spicer and several others have argued, Don Juan's psychedelic forays are "not consistent with our ethnographic knowledge of the Yaquis." His exploits do, however, resemble those of Native American tribes like the Huichols who have a well-documented history of peyote consumption. Anthropologist and outspoken Castaneda critic Jay Courtney Fikes spent several years embedded in a community of Chapalagana Huichols during which time he became intimately acquainted with shamanism and the ritual practices of Mexican Indians. Once a fan of Castaneda's work, Fikes soon grew disillusioned with what he viewed as outright caricatures of Huichol culture.

In his 1993 book *Carlos Castaneda, Academic Opportunism and the Psychedelic Sixties,* Fikes explains how the character of Don Juan was likely modeled on Ramon Medina Silva, the Huichol shaman popularized by the ethnographic studies of Peter Furst and Barbara Myerhoff. These anthropologists were UCLA graduates and peers of Castaneda, and there is convincing evidence that Ramon and Carlos had actually met prior to the publication of *The Teachings.* A dramatic waterfall leap performed by Silva, allegedly with Castaneda as a witness, finds a curious parallel in his second book, *A Separate Reality,* wherein a companion of Don Juan performs similar "supernatural" feats at a waterfall. Further complicating the matter, Fikes also disputes the veracity of Furst and Myerhoff's ethnography, noting that the Huichol shamanic practices they detail are at odds with his own findings. In developing his account of Don Juan, suggests Fikes, Castaneda likely plagiarized from his classmates a distorted portrayal of Huichol culture in the character of Silva, and unscrupulously applied it to his fictional Yaqui sorcerer, thus perpetuating the misrepresentation of Native Americans across cultural boundaries.

The effect of this caricaturing is twofold: First, as de Mille and Fikes bemoan, erroneous ethnographic research is quite difficult to remove from the anthropological record once canonized. By accepting such questionable documents as authenticated knowledge, the truth about indigenous peoples becomes diluted with misinformation and (perhaps more lamentable) the halls of academia are tarnished with the elevation of charlatans to pedestals of high esteem. Indeed, as he remarks in his introduction, Fikes heard "nothing but praise" for Castaneda's first four books in his graduate studies at the University of Michigan in 1975, despite their disputed validity.[10]

Second, the misrepresentation of the Yaqui people as portrayed by Castaneda negatively impacts Native American culture as a whole. In order to assess this detrimental influence of Don Juan and his teachings, one must consider the social context into which he was born. The decade colorfully referred to as the "psychedelic sixties," with its adherence to counterculture ideology and self-exploration through drug use, was an era ripe for an iconic figure such as Don Juan to materialize.

As *The Teachings of Don Juan* introduced thousands of psychedelically inclined readers to its mysterious sage, the deserts of Mexico were subsequently inundated with droves of "Don Juan seekers" determined to find, and be enlightened by, the elusive sorcerer. Anthropologist Jane Holden Kelley reports the harassment of Pascuan Yaquis during the 1970s by "long-haired hippies" in search of Castaneda's muse. Seizing an opportunity, the crafty villagers played along, divesting the deluded youths of money, booze, and cigarettes before they realized they had been duped.[11]

It was not the Yaquis, however, but the Huichols who bore the brunt of the hippie influx throughout the seventies. As Fikes explains, the Yaquis "offer relatively little to guru-seekers" since they do not use psychedelics and are somewhat "more acculturated" than the peyote-ingesting Huichols. He relates accounts of traditional Huichols "harassed, jailed, shot at, and almost murdered by guru-seekers" and offers an anecdote depicting the attempted stabbing of his Huichol "father" by a gringo peyote hunter. These incidents grew more infrequent with time, but the lasting impact of *The Teachings* on Native Americans, asserts Fikes, lies in the marketing of the Don Juan archetype.

New Age "shamans" modeled on Castaneda's sorcerer exist in abundance in today's society. Offering travel packages to psychedelic meccas, these pseudo-shamans profit from the misappropriation of rituals and liturgical objects sacred to Native American religions. While some operations offer legitimate and conscientious experiences of traditional shamanism, others are little more than opportunistic scams. As Fikes contends, such shameless exploitation trivializes "Huichol, Yaqui, or any Native American culture by masking or ignoring its true genius." Furthermore, these profiteers increase the Western fascination with psyche-delic drugs such as peyote, bringing unwanted government attention to authentic Native American practices.

A *New York Times* article from July 23, 1970, describes the plight of Oaxacan Indians suffering from the flood of American "mushroom ad-dicts" and the subsequent crackdown by Mexican authorities; once con-sidered a "great medicine," the fungi are now contraband in Oaxaca. In the United States, similar legislative measures currently threaten Native Americans' religious freedom. The *Smith vs. Oregon* decision of the Su-preme Court, for instance, banned the ritual use of peyote among mem-bers of the Native American Church from 1990 until its repeal in 1993. Within a "War on Drugs" political climate, the mystique engendered by Don Juan and his imitators represents a real and direct threat to the "special rights" Native American cultures have been granted in American society.

Most troubling, the fallout from nearly four decades of Castaneda-inspired drug tourism in Mexico now threatens to wipe out some indig-enous shamanic cultures entirely. According to a recent NPR report, the rampant, unsustainable harvesting of peyote by foreigners and drug traf-fickers from the desert surrounding Real de Catorce has placed the slow-growing cactus in danger of vanishing from the region. The area is held sacred by the Huichol, who regularly pass through the north Mexican desert on shamanic pilgrimages. Once thriving in abundance along their route, the peyote cactus has become increasingly scarce, prompting the Indians to lobby the government for protection of the holy site. If the peyote disappears, so does the unique knowledge system of one of Mexi-co's most vital remaining tribal cultures.

Carlos Castaneda reemerged in the public eye in the early nineties es-pousing the virtues of a meditation technique he named Tensegrity, after a term coined by R. Buckminster Fuller. Consisting of movements called "magical passes" (allegedly the lost knowledge of Mexican shamans in the lineage of Don Juan Matus), this discipline was taught by the author himself to devotees at exorbitantly priced seminar-workshops. Castaneda had, in effect, fulfilled the Don Juan archetype, adopting the role of pseudo-shaman as identified by Fikes. His death in 1998 was followed by the release of his final book, *Magical Passes*, rounding off the Castaneda oeuvre at an even dozen titles. Along with a multimillion-dollar estate, the anthropologist-guru left behind him the legacy of a successful career marred by charges of academic fraud and opportunism.

His seminal achievement, *The Teachings of Don Juan,* has been simultaneously embraced and vilified since its appearance, yet its influence cannot be overstated. Richard de Mille once speculated: "Is Carlos' multistaged confessional narrative the next step in the history of ethnography, or . . . a further development in the novel, an ultimate fiction?" Although the answer remains to be seen, almost forty years later it is evident that Castaneda's work of "ethnography and allegory" has had an indelible effect—for better or worse—on the way the Western world interprets entheogens and Native American culture.

NOTES

1. Edward H. Spicer as quoted in Daniel Noel, *Seeing Castaneda* (New York: G. P. Putnam's Sons, 1976), pp. 31–32.

2. Richard de Mille, *The Don Juan Papers* (Santa Barbara, Calif.: Ross-Erikson Publishers, 1980), p. 19.

3. Spicer as quoted in Noel, *Seeing Castaneda,* p. 32.

4. Noel, p. 32.

5. De Mille, *The Don Juan Papers,* p. 324.

6. Ibid., p. 325.

7. Richard de Mille, *Castaneda's Journey* (Santa Barbara, Calif.: Capra Press, 1976), p. 78.

8. Ibid., p. 52.

9. Muriel Thayer Painter, *With Good Heart: Yaqui Beliefs and Ceremonies in Pascua Village* (Tucson: University of Arizona Press, 1986), pp. 11, 43–44.

10. Jay Courtney Fikes, *Carlos Castaneda, Academic Opportunism, and the Psychedelic Sixties* (Victoria, B.C.: Millenia Press, 1993).

11. Jane Holden Kelley as quoted in de Mille, *The Don Juan Papers,* p. 33.

# BLOOD AND BREATH

*Barbara Alice Mann*

This article comes out of my thinning patience with the plethora of Western works on "Indian thought" that do little more than wrap Christianity in feathers and blankets, preparatory to announcing the discovery of some "universal principle." On the conservative end, missionary-mangled versions of Native traditions pluck one, small episode out of an interactive story cycle, wash its bones clean of any identifying features, and then reinterpret it as anything from a "Sun Myth" to evidence that, upon resurrecting, Jesus visited the Cherokees. On the New Age—or worse, "scientific"—end, stories are mixed and matched with breathtaking disregard for culture of origin, with the aim of supporting whatever agenda is at hand, be it a biblical flood; the fanciful Beringian "land bridge"; or the cultural uplift of us savages by ancient alien [check one]:

- ☐ UFOs
- ☐ Semites
- ☐ Africans
- ☐ Atlanteans

It is hard for traditional peoples to challenge any of this nonsense because Native Americans average only 3 percent of the American population and primarily live below the poverty line, with life expectancies of 47 for men and 50 for women. A major consequence of our complete

dispossession by Europeans is our heavily limited access to church hierarchies, academia, and the popular press, the very factories busily pounding out these tall tales. Moreover, although few mainstream Americans
know as much, it was *against federal law* for Natives to practice their
traditional spiritualities until 1978. Yes, you read that correctly. It was
not until the American Indian Religious Freedom Act was passed in
1978 that we enjoyed any of America's vaunted freedom of religion. Even
so, our religious rights are severely curtained anytime anyone governmental decides we might be Ghost-Dancing too vigorously, again. (The
Wounded Knee genocide of 1890 occurred because the people were practicing a non-U.S.-approved religion.) Our woes did not end with the
nineteenth century.

Between modern killing (90 percent of all U.S. uranium mining is
conducted, very unsafely, on reservations), forced sterilization (42 percent of all living Native women have been sterilized by the government), government kid prisons (called "boarding schools"), out-adoption
of Native infants, and missionary-run, government-backed cultural
genocide—not to mention denial of federal recognition to those hiding
out in the hills and the swamps from all of the above—it has taken
everything we can do just to survive physically, let alone get into the
more delicate matter of correcting stereotypes, lies, and misrepresenta-
tions of ourselves and our cultures. There are so many gaffes, so widely
spread, that the tiny handful of us in any position to start the correction
are, frankly, daunted by the magnitude of the chore.

The task is heightened by the fact that, postmissionary and post-
governmental meddling in our cultures, a large number of modern Natives are left knowing very little about their own histories, cultures, and
spiritualities. Instead of the old stories, they have had colonial versions
forced down their throats, sometimes by their own leaders. Sganyadaiyoh ("Handsome Lake") of my people, the Senecas, is a good example.
In 1799, he fashioned his Gaiwiiyo ("Code"), which severely christianized Iroquoian culture. Today, the fact that he was completely opposed

by the Clan Mothers, lineage chiefs, and holy people of his time is lost in the academic, and worse, reservation, rush to embrace his Code as "tradition," simply because he kept some of the old cultural props, like clans and seasonal festivals. Academia now fawns over his "visions," some of which he acknowledged having made up and others of which he claimed to have forgotten. (As the Clan Mothers asked at the time, what kind of dimwitted prophet forgets his own visions?) Despite these drawbacks, Sganyadaiyoh had the backing of the Quakers, who controlled Iroquoian reservations in his day, and access to Thomas Jefferson, so his Code prospered. Anthropologists wrote it down in English, a surefire method of mainstreaming it. Today, instead of being seen as the caving to colonialization that it was, his Gaiwiiyo is lionized in academia as Real Indian Wisdom. This sort of damage makes it especially hard for real traditional thinking to gleam through the cultural ruins.

In addition, so used to its own ways is it, that Western thought is ill-equipped to grasp Native thought, unprimed. Instead of priming itself, however, Eurosupremacy just assumes that whatever it already knows is pure and sufficient unto the day. This arrogance leads to what I call "Euro-forming the Data," or cramming it into preexisting Western schema, whether or not it fits, by lopping off meaning here and denaturing ideas there, until the result feels comfortable to Europeans. Euro-forming is easy to identify but hard to overcome. I have thought long and hard about the most fruitful entry point into *real* Native perspectives, not only spiritually but culturally, and concluded that our concepts must be grasped through a previous appreciation of our binary math.

As a lynchpin, binary thought is so far from Western linearity, that it is next to impossible for Europeans to crawl into it without a conscious effort. Toward the goal of helping Westerners appreciate something like a Native approach, I have published *Iroquoian Women: The Gantowisas* (third printing, 2006) and *Native Americans, Archaeologists, and the Mounds* (2003), especially chapters 3, "We Can Make a Waukauhoowaa," and 4, "Kokomthena, Singing in the Flames." I will soon have a chapter coming out on our binary gift economics, which I realized only in the summer of 2006 was the basis of matriarchy, generally. Here, I will both review some of my already published material and abstract a bit of my forthcoming materials.

The first thing to understand is something so fundamental to Western thought as to be invisible to Westerners—i.e., the realization that the base number of their culture is ONE, as evinced in such ideas as one god, one life, one way, one soul, one true love, etc. In the West, the only accommodation of Two is the Manichean dichotomy, under which, if there are two of anything, one must be an impostor, a rival, a debasement, an evil to be driven out in favor of the One Right Thing. In any TV movie about twins, we can be certain at the outset that one of them is ≈ EVIL ≈ itself, intent upon destroying The Good Twin. I call this ONE-THINKING.

Native traditions assume a base number of Two. There cannot be ONE unless there have first been Two. The easiest way to explain this is through our (Iroquoian) concepts of The Direction of the Sky and The Split Sky. The Direction of the Sky is the East-West axis, the trail that Brother Sun runs daily. He cannot know where West is, unless he first knows where East is. Similarly, East is meaningless, unless West also exists. Only after we know the Two, may we know the ONE. It is through their cooperation that the single path, The Direction of the Sky, can be descried.

Oops. Now, there is an imbalance: One stands without a sacred Twin, but not to worry. The trail of Brother Sun is crossed by the path of Grandmother Moon, who normally runs The Direction of the Sky, but who, once every generation (18.61 years), favors us by running another trail, that of The Split Sky, showing us how to restore the balance through the North-South axis. Again, we cannot know North unless we also know South, and South is meaningless without North. Together, collaboratively, they create The Split Sky, another, single path. Now, we have a cross, which looks something like a plus sign, a unit of Two constructed by Four. This is what I call TWO-BY-FOUR THINKING, as shown in Figure 1 below.

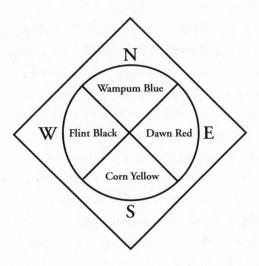

*Figure 1. The Two-by-Four of the Cardinal Directions, shows the traditional, tilted concept of the Twinned Direction of the Sky (E ↔ W) and Split Sky (N ↔ S). Figure created by Barbara Mann. White (E ↔ S) wampum and purple (N ↔ W) wampum are referenced by the background colors.*

In Figure 1, the directions are shown as cocked, not "true" (E ↔ W) or (N ↔ S). This has to do with solstices and equinoxes, important time-keeping devices in agricultural cultures. For our purposes here, it is important to see the interaction of the two sets of sacred twins. Typically, N ↔ W—the Blue Lynx of the north (referencing calving icebergs and glaciers) and the Humpbacked Runner of the Western Rim, Flint—are connected with wrinkled things like death and danger, whereas S ↔ E—the Sweet Woman of the South (referencing corn) and the Sapling, the Strawberry Man—are associated with smooth things like life and safety. E ↔ W is construed as male, and N ↔ S is construed as female. Obviously, they crisscross in the N ↔ W and S ↔ E pairings.

The primary halves are shorthanded in the woodlands cultures as Blood and Breath. West of the Mississippi River, they are more likely to be referenced as Water and Air, respectively. In addition, they are conceptualized as Sky and Earth. These binaries are cosmically observed, with everything that exists tending to belong to one or the other, as shown in Table 1, The Halved Cosmos. Male and Female do show up as interactive halves, but it is important to see that this is as part of a larger concept. M/F is not the concept itself.

Traditionally, people were very careful to know what fit into which category. This included, of course, the two spirits indwelling *everyone*— not just gays and lesbians, as fractured traditions popular in New Age circles maintain. A person born with just one spirit was feared as most probably criminally insane. (That Europeans claimed to have just one spirit explained a lot for us.)

The Sky/Breath spirit, gotten from the father, lived in the brain and dealt with ethical and intellectual issues, whereas the Earth/Blood spirit, gotten from the mother, lived, depending on the culture, in the marrow of the bones or in the gut. It dealt with moral and passionate issues.

### THE HALVED COSMOS

| *Blood/Water/Earth* | *Breath/Air/Sky* |
|---|---|
| Agriculture | Hunting |
| Youth | Age |
| Women | Men |
| Snake | Eagle |
| Square ■ | Circle ● |

Table 1. The Halved Cosmos gives an example of how the complementary binaries work. Table created by Barbara Mann.

Part of spiritual health lay in knowing which spirit was speaking and why. Of course, a life's task was to coordinate the different agendas of each. At death, the two spirits went their separate ways. They did not necessarily reincarnate together. Ghosts are dangerous specifically because they represent just one of these spirits, bereft of the tempering presence of the other.

Of course, widespread across the continent were stylized motifs referring to these concepts. Recently, Western scholars have broken down to admit that Native Americans wrote with two completely independent and mature writing systems in South America predating Cuneiform. There has been a lag in recognizing writing in North America, however, because Western scholars do not comprehend that wampum was a character-writing system and that our mounds were an earth-writing system. Nevertheless, our bedrock binaries are articulated in both. Wampum used white and "blue" (actually, dark blue-purple) beads made from quahog shells to create four possibilities for every character, depending on whether the character (or background, depending on one's vantage point) was white or blue and which half of the double-wampum speech it fit into.

The binary shorthand in mound-writing worked a little differently. There are numerous ways of referencing the cosmic twins, but one of the most popular in the Ohio Valley mound cultures was through the use of the square ■ of Earth and the circle ● of Sky. Figure 2, Square-and-Circle Motifs in Mound-Writing, shows the cosmic connection between Breath/Circle/Sky and Blood/Square/Earth. An interesting alternative to the very common Circle-Square appears in the lower left center, where Earth is entirely encircled by Sky. Figure 3, The Cross Mound, shows an even more interesting twist, with the circle of Sky encompassed by the square, here as a plus sign, of earth. Needless to say, this "cross" gave the early missionaries quite a start, exciting some fairly wild speculation about Jesus' disciples hiking around in North America. (This last is a perfect example of Euro-forming the data.)

Another popular motif included concentric circles and/or semi-circles. Figure 4, Dome and Concentric Mound Motifs, which used the concept

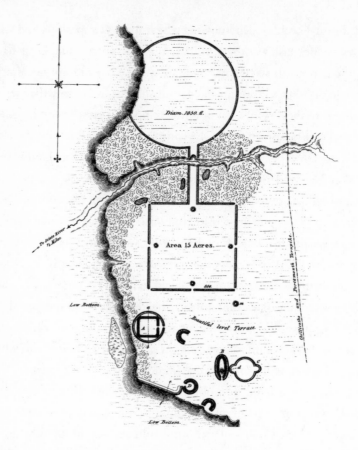

*Figure 2. Square-and-Circle Motifs in Mound-Writing shows how paired earth-writing was deployed. Notice the smaller motif including the Square of Earth within the Circle of Sky. SOURCE: Ephraim George Squier and E. H. Davis,* Ancient Monuments of the Mississippi Valley: Comprising the Results of Extensive Original Surveys and Explorations. Smithsonian Contributions to Knowledge, 2 vols. *(1848, reprint; New York: Johnson Reprint Corporation, 1965), 1: 66, facing.*

of the Great Turtle Island, or North America. Seen in profile, the lower arch represents the turtle's back, or Earth, whereas the upper arch represents the Sky above. The concentric motif is an overhead view of the

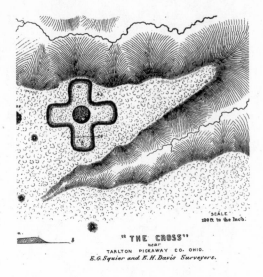

Figure 3. The Cross Mound shows another variation of the Earth-Sky motif, with Sky interestingly inside the four corners of the Earth. SOURCE: Ephraim George Squier and E. H. Davis, Ancient Monuments of the Mississippi Valley: Comprising the Results of Extensive Original Surveys and Explorations. Smithsonian Contributions to Knowledge, 2 vols. (1848, reprint; New York: Johnson Reprint Corporation, 1965), 1: 98, facing.

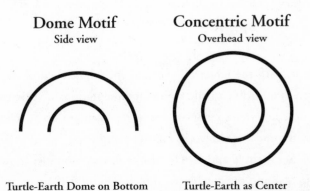

Figure 4. Dome and Concentric Mound Motifs are based on Grandmother Turtle, who carries Turtle Island (North America) on her back. Figure created by Barbara Mann.

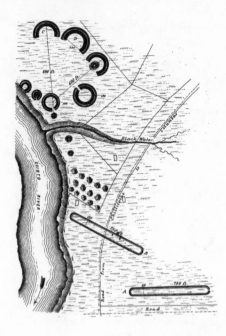

*Figure 5. Semi-circle and Circle Motifs in the Mounds shows both the profile of Earth and Sky as well as the overhead view of the same binaries. SOURCE: Ephraim George Squier and E. H. Davis,* Ancient Monuments of the Mississippi Valley: Comprising the Results of Extensive Original Surveys and Explorations. Smithsonian Contributions to Knowledge, *2 vols. (1848, reprint; New York: Johnson Reprint Corporation, 1965), 1: 61, facing.*

same concept, with the larger Sky around the whole shell of the swimming turtle. In addition to the minor representations of this motif in Figure 2, there are some really stunning representations of it in other Ohio Valley mounds, as shown in Figures 5 and 6.

Figure 5, Semi-circle and Circle Motifs in the Mounds, shows both the semi-circular and the concentric motifs. Figure 6, Concentric Motif in Mound-Writing, shows the overhead perspective, only. It features the interesting Lenape concept of onion-like layers of dimensional reality, peeling inward to the central core of earth.

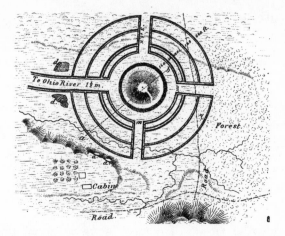

*Figure 6. Concentric Motif in Mound-Writing shows the top-down view of the Sky-Earth binary as complicated in Lenape thought. SOURCE: Ephraim George Squier and E. H. Davis,* Ancient Monuments of the Mississippi Valley: Comprising the Results of Extensive Original Surveys and Explorations. Smithsonian Contributions to Knowledge, 2 vols. *(1848, reprint; New York: Johnson Reprint Corporation, 1965), 1: 76, facing.*

Woodlands social, political, and spiritual life certainly reflected our binary thought, but it is also obvious in our gift economies, which carefully maintained the interaction of Blood and Breath through field and forest, respectively. The Two-by-Four here was Female/Male crosswise from Farming (Female)/Hunting (Male). These root pairs included other associations: Blood-Water-Seed/Female/Field ↔ Breath-Air-Arrow/Male/Forest.

The math of the gift economy was more complicated than this, including three, a concept important to binary math. In woodlands cultures, three is construed as a number of warning, admonition, or special care. For instance, founded in the twelfth century, the Iroquois Constitution featured *three* pillars in its preamble (i.e., as things to be vigilant about in maintaining our democracy). Those pillars are, of course, twinned:

1. *Ne Gashasdenza*
   - The sacred will of the people (Breath)
   - The sacred power of the people (Blood)
2. *Ne Gaiwiiyo*
   - Ethical behavior (Breath)
   - Moral behavior (Blood)
3. *Ne Skennon*
   - Peace (Breath)
   - Well-being (Blood)

Binary economics are gift economies, interweaving the gifts circulating from the Blood half to the Breath half, and back again. The Two-by-Four function here is through the interaction of the Mother (Female/Clan) and Father (Male/Nation) sides of the culture, with all their respective associations of field and forest, as shown in Table 2, Binary Gift Economy, below.

| *Clan Identity* | *National Identity* |
|:---:|:---:|
| Turtle Clan Moiety | Elder Nations |
| *Earth*  ■ | *Sky*  ● |
| Wolf Clan Moiety | Younger Nations |
| *Sky*  ● | *Earth*  ■ |

Table 2. Binary Gift Economy shows the Two-by-Four interchange on the economic level. Table created by Barbara Mann.

Table 2 displays the Two-by-Four interaction between Sky and Earth to sustain life. Although the Clan identity springs from the Mother side, it nevertheless applies equally to the male Wolf clan half. Similarly, although the National identity adheres to the Father side, it includes the younger nations, which are Female. Youth and Age involve none of the Western baggage, but simply indicate that life existed in Sky (which re-

fers to outer space, not the earth's blue atmosphere), before life was initiated on planet Earth.

Hopefully, this whirlwind trip through Native binaries helps to clarify some of the more important paradigms of truly traditional thought.
It should be instantly obvious that there is no room for Manichean polar
opposite, for a solitary God-figure, for singleton souls, or "higher consciousness." Spirituality is not a competition but a collaborative, and no
Single Unifying Theory is desirable or likely.

# INSECTS, YOGA, AND AYAHUASCA

## Padmani

"Fold your wings like this, dear, and tuck them underneath you," said an unfamiliar, though kindly, voice that seemed to emanate from inside my head.

"My wings?" I asked aloud, confused by the instructions. "Do you mean my legs?"

"Yes, yes, bend your legs . . . and your other legs too."

And so began what can only be described as a yoga asana lesson taught to me by a startlingly large praying-mantis-like creature during an ayahuasca ceremony in the Peruvian Amazon.

Paying little heed to a nagging injury that would normally prevent such movement, I did as I was told and suddenly I found myself in a surprisingly deep series of backbends, fit for the pages of a yoga magazine. Before the mind could protest, I moved spontaneously from pose to pose with a sense of ease and playful power. Upon rising, I was amazed to find my body retained all of its newfound strength and suppleness. And with no sign of the old injury, I demonstrated for my duly impressed partner what I'd learned from the praying mantis: a group of backbending poses known in Ashtanga Yoga circles as the "insect series."

As a longtime proponent of the whole yogic lifestyle thing (no meat, alcohol, caffeine, or late nights for me, thank you) I was initially reluctant to participate in the ayahuasca ceremony, despite the Amazonian tea's reputation as a sacred plant medicine of the highest order. Like many, I had heard horror stories about violent ayahuasca-induced purges, and on a practical level, I wondered how I would do my morning yoga practice if the all-night affair left me nauseated, weak, and sore. I also had lingering concerns that the psychoactive brew could somehow undo years of disciplined practice and virtuous living, destabilizing my physical and energetic bodies—not to mention what it might do to my calm mind.

Though curious, I waited almost five years before I agreed to experience ayahuasca for the first time. The change of heart came after a meeting with an internationally renowned yoga teacher who drew a strong parallel between ayahuasca and the mythical ritual drink Soma, which is described in the Rigveda as nothing less than the nectar of immortality: "We have drunk Soma and become immortal; we have attained the light, the Gods discovered" (8.48.3, as translated by R.T.H. Griffith). "Well," I thought, "if it's good enough for the Gods, enlightened beings, and celebrity yoga teachers . . ."

The praying mantis yoga lesson was the first of many yogic teachings that have come to me in ceremony. Sometimes the ayahuasca makes me move around—mostly wild inversions and heart-blossoming backbends—and sometimes it puts me into deep states of meditation where my breath all but disappears into the stillness of my being. Even the dreaded purges feel good and cleansing in a way, not so different from the seemingly strange purification practices prescribed in the ancient yoga manual, the Hatha Yoga Pradipika.

Perhaps most significantly, I was initiated into the practice of Nada Yoga (the yoga of sound) during a ceremony. It happened when I began to perceive what yogis call the inner music, the primal sound signified by Om, which came at first in a dazzling symphony of clanging bells, snare drums, and cosmic sitars. During that same night, the hinge joint of my jaw popped wide open and music and poetry flowed unstoppably from my mouth for several hours. The telepathic message I received (this time from a cheering chorus of insects and amphibians) was that, as a yogi, I have an obligation to literally open my mouth wider and speak out on behalf of those who can't.

Ayahuasca took my yoga off the mat and made my practice practical. At one time, I did poses such as locust, scorpion, cobra, dog, and tree without thinking too much about their correlates in the natural world; they were little more than exercises with fanciful names. Now it seems obvious that before there were yoga studios, designer yoga-wear lines, and sticky mats, the yogis took their teachings from nature. The first yoga teachers were the plants and animals—and yes, the insects, too. They say the practice of yoga is directly informed by nature. Now I finally get on a cellular level why yogis have such a close friendship with the earth: because we're not separate from her.

Much like yoga practice itself, ayahuasca and other plant medicines have the ability to reunite human consciousness with natural and supernatural rhythms. Taken with the correct intention, they can help catalyze a profound shift in our all-too-limited take on things. With the radical deepening and broadening of perspective comes a new brand of happiness—the real stuff that lasts. Experience teaches that when I stop thinking about myself and connect to the other (even when the other is something as alien as a giant praying mantis), I put some space between my mental afflictions and myself. What flows from that space is the taste of freedom.

In the Yoga Sutras, the sage Patanjali explained that spiritual attainments leading to liberation can arise from drugs or chemical means, as well as from yogic practices such as mantra recitation, performance of austerities, and samadhi, which is union of individual consciousness with divine consciousness (Book IV, Sutra 1). Interestingly, practices such as pranayama (breath control) and asana (physical exercise)—the two most important components of modern yoga practice in the West— are considered chemical means, according to Shri Brahmananda Sarasvati, because they work by causing biochemical changes in the body and mind.

One of the primary psychoactive ingredients in ayahuasca is DMT, a powerful hallucinogen that scientists have discovered occurring naturally in the human body. It is reportedly released by the pineal gland (what yogis refer to as the third eye) and stored at the base of the spine, where kundalini shakti is said to lie dormant until activated. Yogis have long known that transcendent experiences are accessible through certain yogic practices. Certainly the "yoga high" is what keeps me and, I'm sure, millions of other yogis coming back to the mat day after day.

While some may scoff at the notion of seeking enlightenment through stretching and psychedelics, the reality is this stuff works. It's not just talk—it's experiential and tangible, and it taps me into something big and juicy. As one of my teachers likes to say, "Plant teachers aren't exclusive to South America, and India doesn't own the rights to yoga." As a modern-day seeker, it feels like I'm just now coming into my spiritual birthright—it just took a giant insect to show me the way.

# GNOSIS: THE NOT-SO-SECRET HISTORY OF JESUS

*Jonathan Phillips*

I always begin "The Electric Jesus" workshops with a simple, yet revealing visualization about our lifelong journey of acquiring knowledge in the West.

Let's start by taking a look back at your first day of school. Perhaps your parents packed you a sack lunch, tied your shoelaces, buttoned up that yellow rain jacket, and then walked you to the bus or drove you to that strange large building with lots of windows. Remember your preschool or kindergarten teachers and how they first taught you the alphabet? You learned the fundamentals of reading, writing, and arithmetic. The stakes escalated as you went through each grade. There was telling time, cursive, the national anthem, fractals, history, even a little earth science. The hormones eventually kicked in at middle school or junior high and you embarked on new adventures involving facts, dates, and important events. Basic algebra turned into quadratic equations, which morphed into trigonometry and possibly calculus. Perhaps you went to college and sat through lectures, labs, novels, tests, papers, even a thesis or two. You might have gone on to do postgrad work acquiring various degrees and doctorates. And after years and years of study, from adolescence all the way into adulthood, did a heroic teacher or professor ever set down the chalk or turn off the overhead projector, look your class square in the eye, and say something like this?

"Look guys, we teach you all these things but none of us really know what's going on. Here we are, six billion humans, living on a bluish green sphere we call Earth. We're a little speck spinning through an unimaginably vast cosmos, and none of us can even answer the most basic questions of our lives: Who are we? Where did we come from? Where we are going? And what is the purpose of this fourteen-billion-year experiment we call the universe?"

In my workshops, I'll occasionally hear tales of a Socratically wise teacher who had the gumption to admit that all we know is that we really know nothing at all. But by and large, there seemed to be gaping blind spots and active denial within our educational systems and institutions toward understanding what might be the true nature of this whole thing we call "reality." With all the cost, time, resources, and energy it takes to put our youth through this extended learning process, our students invariably come out of it full of information but knowing very little.

Fortunately, in our Western culture there are many Christian traditions that believe it is our birthright to learn the answers to these crucial questions about our own existence. According to these seekers of wisdom, we only need the perseverance, guidance, openness, love, and spirit (*pneuma*) to find what we've always (although sometimes unknowingly) been looking for. From the scriptural evidence, it appears that these groups came to understand the most fundamental wisdom we could ever obtain in our lifetime—knowing who we truly are. These wise spiritual seekers and teachers have been labeled "Gnostics" by twentieth-century academics.

The word *gnosis* means "knowledge through direct experience or personal revelation." It's not something a teacher, minister, or politician can tell you, nor can it be learned from a newspaper or book, or even the global mind of the Internet. It's something you must experience firsthand. There's nobody who can do it for you, and there's absolutely no exception. For instance, I can tell you that Paris is the capital of France. It has a population of about ten million people. The city boasts wide,

attractive avenues with some classy old buildings. Its residents like crois-
sants and cafés and they still generally smoke too much for their own
good. I can tell you all these things but the only way to truly know Paris
is to have actually been there and experienced it yourself. The same goes
for higher states of consciousness, or "the kingdom of heaven," as Jesus
would put it. And it's the same for knowing ourselves and our own real
nature.

In the Gospel of Mark, Jesus makes a rather remarkable promise:
"There is nothing hidden that won't be brought to light nor anything
secret that won't be revealed" (4:21). According to him, all the secrets and
mysteries of God, the universe, and our own origins don't have to be
guessed at or alluded to, but will actually be known to us in time. And
just as importantly, these mysteries would, quite literally, I believe, be
brought to "light."

According to many of the ancient Gnostics, most of us have fallen
into a case of cosmic ignorance, which they described as "forgetfulness,"
"drunkenness," or "sleep." Their texts say that we are lost in the world of
illusion and have forgotten our actual origins beyond the material world.
The Buddhists and Hindus called this the veil of maya, Plato called this
the shadows of the cave, and Neo mainstreamed the concept by calling
it "the matrix" on wide-screen theaters around the world.

So who were these Gnostics, and how were they able to break through
this veil to "wake up"? There have been many new scriptural discoveries which reveal the wonderful diversity of early Christianity. It was a
rich tradition full of various sects and circles, many of which claimed
"secret knowledge" of our divine origins. In fact, there is strong evidence that supports the popular idea that Christianity comes from very
deep spiritual lineages known as the Mystery schools. These were ancient mystical initiatory religions where seekers would pass through
various rites of passage as they matured on their spiritual path. At
first, those on the outer circle would be taught that the religious stories they were told were historical fact, but as they progressed into the

esoteric inner knowledge (gnosis), they would learn that these tales served as an allegory for their own spiritual journey and process, and mimicked the rites and rituals they'd encounter along the way. The most common rites of the Mystery schools play out in the drama of Jesus' own story. There's a baptism (spiritual cleansing), a eucharist (communion), an anointing ("Christ" means "the anointed one"), and the death and resurrection ritual, something the mature initiate would eventually go through.

In 1 Corinthians 4:1, Paul says, "This is how one should regard us, as servants of Christ and stewards of the Mysteries of God." The word *Mysteries* appears twenty-two times in the New Testament. Jesus tells us himself about these secret teachings when talking to the disciples: "You have been given the secret to heaven, but to those outside everything is presented in parables so that they may look with eyes wide open but never quite see, and may listen with ears attuned but never quite understand. Otherwise, they might turn around and find forgiveness" (Mark 4:12).

As Jesus constantly reminds us, we aren't witnessing the present moment correctly, because if we did, we would see through the fog of illusion, find forgiveness, and remember who we truly are. Those of us on the "outside" have not been trained by the inner mysteries to see the greater reality around us, so we must learn through enigmatic allegories until we complete the various stages of gnosis. "Jesus said, 'It is to those who are worthy of my Mysteries that I tell my Mysteries'" (the Gospel of Thomas), and it most likely took much effort and spiritual discipline to procure this inner knowledge.

The Mystery schools were strewn across the lands of the Mediterranean and are thought to have originated in Egypt centuries before Jesus made his debut in Nazareth. The correspondences between Jesus and Horus are remarkably similar. Horus and his "once-and-future Father," Osiris, are often interchangeable just as Jesus and His Father are. Horus was called the "KRST," or the "Anointed One," as well as the "Fisher," the "Good Shepherd," the "Lamb of God."[1]

Like Jesus, Horus was born to a virgin, Isis-Meri, on December 25 in a cave or a manger. In the catacombs at Rome today can be found pictures of the baby Horus being held by the Virgin Isis-Meri in what scholars have claimed is the original "Madonna and Child." Like Jesus, Horus' birth was announced by a star in the east and he was allegedly attended by three wise men. As a youth, Horus taught in the temple and was baptised when he was 30 years old. As an adult, Horus performed numerous miracles including, like Jesus and even Buddha, the feat of walking on water. Just as Jesus allegedly raised Lazarus from the dead, Horus was supposed to have raised El-Azar-us from the dead. Before his death, Horus had 12 disciples and at one stage appeared before them, "transfigured on the Mount." After "suffering death" Horus, like Jesus, was buried in a tomb where he was resurrected and ascended into Heaven, or "Amen-ti." And here we have another interesting parallel. Just as Christians end their prayers with amen, the Egyptians ended their prayers with amen-ti—Egyptian for "Heaven" or the "After World." But praying was not the only religious practice Egyptians and Christians had in common. At least 2,500 years before John baptised believers in the Jordan, the ancient Egyptians baptised believers in the Nile. Or in burial chambers. In both cases, the purpose of baptism was to cleanse and revivify individuals—whether alive or dead—into a new state of "eternal blessedness." Furthermore, just as Christians today are assimilated with Jesus through baptism, the ancient Egyptians were assimilated through baptism with their god, Horus.[2]

Just like Horus, the "dying and resurrecting godman" was a prominent feature among many of the Mystery religions. In Greece it was Dionysus; in Syria, Adonis; in Asia Minor, Attis; in Persia (and later Rome), Mithras. The similarities among these mythic figures are uncanny. Much like Horus and Jesus, many of them were born on December 25 (around the winter solstice) to a virgin in humble surroundings (a manger or a cave) with a star in the Eastern sky. They grew up to be spiritual masters with twelve disciples, performing miracles, turning water into wine, giving baptisms and communions, and then dying for three days before making a glorious comeback. Often, they were referred to as "the son of the lamb," "son of God," "king of kings," "the light of the world," and "the alpha and the omega."[3]

Even if you've never been to church, I'm pretty sure you'll recognize the following inscription: "He who will not eat of my body and drink of my blood, so that he will be made one with me and I with him, the same shall not know salvation."[4] But this familiar reference to the communion doesn't appear on a mossy Catholic cathedral but rather on an ancient Mithraic temple. The Mysteries of Mithras were around centuries before Jesus hit the religious circuit in Galilee. Here's a common prayer in Mithraic services: "Be good of cheer, sacred band of Initiates, your God has risen from the dead. His pains and sufferings shall be your salvation." The Mithraic Mysteries were spread across the Roman Empire and you'll find temples in London and even up north at Hadrian's Wall where Roman soldiers were stationed. The Vatican itself sits on top of a destroyed Mithraic temple, where initiates once shared a meal of wine and bread, celebrating their redeemer, born on December 25, who died for three days before coming back to life.[5]

Rather than rejoicing in their commonalities, some of the more "Literalist" Christians were bothered by the similarities of the older Mithras religion and that of their own. "Early 'Church fathers,' such as Justin Martyr, Tertullian, and Irenaeus, were understandably disturbed and resorted to the desperate claim that these similarities were the result of *diabolical mimicry*. Using one of the most absurd arguments ever advanced, they accused the Devil of 'plagiarism by anticipation,' of deviously copying the true story of Jesus before it had actually happened in an attempt to mislead the gullible."[6]

There's quite a bit of evidence out there to suggest that the various Mystery schools had a strong interest in astrology. Horus was not just considered the "Son of God," but also the "Sun of God." In fact, the word *horizon* comes from "Horus-Sun," meaning sunrise. Horus was the Egyptian god of light, the sun, and the daytime, where he would rule until his jackal-headed enemy Set ("Sun-Set") would regain control and bring darkness back into the world. This violent drama of night and day highlighted the dual nature of our universe. Jesus plays a similar role to Horus as "the light of the world" surrounded by twelve disciples who are thought to represent the twelve months of the year, and the twelve signs of the Zodiac. The sun enters each Zodiac sign at thirty degrees (30 × 12 = 360 degrees). Thus, the "Sun of God" begins his ministry at "age" thirty.[7]

In *The Golden Bough*, world myth expert and adventurer James Frazier notes problems caused by the similarities between Attis and Jesus. "In point of fact it appears from the testimony of an anonymous Christian, who wrote in the fourth century of our era, that Christians and pagans alike were struck by the remarkable coincidence between the death and resurrection of their respective deities, and that the coincidence formed a theme of bitter controversy between the adherents of the rival religions, the pagans contending that the resurrection of Christ was a spurious imitation of the resurrection of Attis, and the Christians asserting with equal warmth that the resurrection of Attis was a diabolical counterfeit of Christ."[8] For anyone wishing to pursue the correspondences between Attis, Adonis, Osiris, and Dionysus in greater detail, I highly recommend checking out chapters 29–43 of *The Golden Bough*.

Many of the dying and resurrecting godmen of the Mystery religions are born on December 25, including Horus, Tammuz/Adonis, Mithras, and of course, our Jesus. Why this date? you may be asking. A rather spectacular event regarding the earth's most important energy source takes place at that time. "The sun makes an annual descent southward until December 21 or 22, the winter solstice, when it stops moving southerly for three days and then starts to move northward again. During this time, the ancients declared that 'God's sun' had 'died' for three days and was 'born again' on December 25. So [Christ]mas really is the Birthday of the SUN/SON in every way."[9]

At this time, the constellation Virgo (the virgin) precedes the sun's arrival that day. But, the sun's rebirth and resurrection weren't fully celebrated until it reached fruition during the spring equinox, or what we call Easter today. Given the subtle, yet powerful spiritual/energetic forces the Mystery schools were working with, it might not be surprising that their mythic heroes were symbolized by the continual, powerful nuclear fusion process of our glowing sun. As we'll describe later, our own bodies may also be filled with beautiful celestial energy centers of their own, supporting the old alchemist adage "as above, so below." Perhaps the sun's journey of death and rebirth may reflect our own energetic path to spiritual awakening.

The classic Zodiac cross bisects the twelve signs within a circle and the sun is thought to hang "crucified" in the center as it passes through the equinoxes. Different Mystery school figures may also represent different ages of the Zodiac, each of which lasts about 2,150 years. Mithras kills the bull as we move away from Taurus into the age of Aries (the ram), then Jesus comes along with baskets full of fish to usher in the age of Pisces. When the disciples ask where the next Passover will be, Jesus says, "Behold, when ye are entered into the city, there shall a man meet you bearing a pitcher of water. . . . Follow him into the house where he entereth in." Astrologers may assume the water bearer is Aquarius. When we hear of "the end of the world" in the New Testament, it actually translates as "the end of the age," which isn't that terrifying when you consider the authors might be poetically marking the change in the star calendar, and perhaps new energies coming in and affecting our planet.[10]

Given the astrological significance of the cross, it's not surprising that depictions of crucifixion were popular in the Mystery traditions. A famous second- to third-century talisman depicts a figure that looks suspiciously like Jesus crucified on a cross, but is surprisingly labeled "Orpheus becomes a Bacchoi." Orpheus was a prophet in the Dionysian mysteries and a *Bacchoi* was an enlightened disciple who had completed the stages of initiation. (The first depiction of Jesus on the cross wouldn't show up until at least 200 years later.) Around the same time as the talisman, a Roman graffiti artist drew a bizarre picture on the back of a Roman pillar when the authorities probably weren't looking. This ancient "tag" featured a donkey being crucified on the cross, which just might symbolize the rite of dying to one's lower nature in order to ascend to the higher self. This image is reminiscent of Jesus riding a donkey into Jerusalem, revealing in allegory how we can master our own animalistic nature.

While we're shedding light on some overlooked history, I'd like to take a look at what many Christian scholars consider 2,000 years of inaccurate translations. Let's start off with that all-important Christian word *savior*. It's a Greek term, *soter,* meaning "healer" or "bestower of health," or "one who makes whole."[11] Jesus heals throughout the New Testament but what are his miraculous techniques? Some evidence might be found when he comes across a woman "with a flow of twelve years" who reaches out and touches his garments. "The power drains out of him," for which Jesus turns around, and says, "Your faith has healed you."

But how could the power drain out of Jesus? And what is this power? Could it be that he was using the same power that moves the whole cosmos—energy? Was he vibrating at a higher level and like a supreme Reiki master, did he cure her by passing on these higher healing frequencies? Jesus constantly gives "hands-on healings" throughout the gospels, often telling us "be opened," which is very important in cleaning out the energy channels to heal sickness or disease.

To continue our discussion of mistranslations, I'd like to tackle that extremely loaded word we call *sin*. The term that is usually translated as "sin," *harmatia,* comes from Greek archery, and quite literally means "missing the mark." The word isn't riddled with the shame and guilt that you might expect. It seems to describe those moments when we fall off target and then have to realign ourselves to get back on the path.

So it seems highly unlikely that you would go to hell for "missing the mark," or at least not that place of eternal damnation that we hear about. The translation for hell actually comes from the word *Gehena,* which refers to the "Valley of Hinnom," a place where trash was burned.[12] A spiritual master like Jesus understood the laws of karma and knew that if you do bad things, you might, metaphorically speaking, end up in a trash dump for a while until you figure things out. How many of us have been in Gehena at some point in our lives? And I'm sure for some, it felt like an eternity. Of course, we could "repent" to improve our situation, especially since the Greek word *metanoia* simply means to "change one's mind" or, better yet, "to have a change of consciousness,"[13] which can happen quite easily when you meet a higher vibrational being like Jesus. I've had the fortune of meeting several fairly enlightened people in my lifetime, and can honestly say I left their presence with a changed sense of consciousness.

And what about that fabled goateed guy with the red pointy tail? The term *Satan* comes from the Hebrew word for "adversary." In our minds and mythologies, we've built Old Scratch up to be a wily demon tempting us into horrible corruption, but those on the path will recognize our principal adversary to true knowing as the ego/personality attachment to this world of illusion. Some Gnostics called this the *eidolon,* which we must overcome in order to experience our higher self. Once we've accomplished that through the unfolding process of spiritual alchemy, we can become "redeemed," meaning "released" (*apolytrosis*)[14] from the attachment and suffering of the world. When one "resurrects" (*anastasis*), one literally "rises from sleep,"[15] to become fully awake and an aware being in the cosmic dream.

The Buddha's ears might be heating up, as his name also means "The Awakened One." Could Jesus and Buddha be pointing toward the same direct experience? Might Jesus' "Kingdom of Heaven" be the same as Buddha's "Ultimate Reality"? I have my suspicions.

During "The Electric Jesus" workshops, I always give a little pop quiz. And I admit it's a bit of a trick, but here it goes . . . What is the earliest Christian gospel that we know of? Matthew perhaps? Even though it's placed first in the Bible, it wasn't written until AD 80–90. Then how about Mark, you may ask? Good guess. It's the oldest of the canonical gospels (AD 60–70) but there's another gospel even older than that (fragments predate all the New Testament texts) and it happens to be one of the most poetic and compelling spiritual documents in the world, right on par with *The Tao Te Ching* and *The Bhagavad Gita*. We call it the Gospel of Thomas (AD 40). The text is known as a "secret sayings gospel" and you'll find many of these sayings conveniently inserted into the narrative of the New Testament.

This gospel starts off with a startling promise: "Whoever discovers the interpretation of these sayings will not taste death." You only have to read a few lines further down to find another impossible line: "Heaven is inside and outside you. When you know yourselves, then you will be known, and you will understand that you are children of the living father."

Once again, forgiveness, heaven, and knowledge of our true self does not exist in cloud nine far above; it's right here inside us and around us, just waiting to be explored. Jesus goes on to tell Thomas, "I am not your teacher. Because you have drunk, you have become intoxicated from the bubbling spring that I have tended." Could it be that Thomas obtained a similar spiritual mastery as Jesus? Might the "bubbling spring" refer to waves of energy (and the divine knowledge encoded within them) that were passed from teacher to initiate? These electro-psychic transmissions may have maintained the spiritual lineage of these esoteric traditions. Moving water has often been a symbol of energetic waves or transmission. Just look at the rite of baptism, which Jesus executes with "fire and spirit."

Perhaps the most mystically complex saying in the whole gospel is the following: "When you make the two into one, and when you make the inner like the outer and the outer like the inner, and the upper like the lower, and when you make male and female into a single one . . . then you will enter the kingdom of heaven." In this passage, Jesus becomes a hermetic alchemist, or yogic guru, advising us on how to unite the polarities and duality of the universe in order to discover our divine origins and return home. It's a mastery that seems logically impossible, and only the magic of divine gnosis can bring us to this kind of realization.

Along with Thomas, an enormously diverse number of Gnostic gospels and sacred texts flowed through the numerous Christian circles, some of which can be read today. There's the Gospel of Mary, Philip, Judas, Secret James, Secret John, the Gospel of Truth, Act of Peter, Pistis Sophia, Dialogue of the Savior, Tripartite Tractate, and the list goes on and on. If you're curious about the best way to sink your teeth into these vast tomes, I suggest reading Thomas for the wealth of sayings, then Philip for the sacred rites and rituals of the Christian initiates, then Mary to prove that a girl can do everything Jesus can. If you'd like to bone up on the basic history and beliefs of the Gnostics, I recommend starting off with Elaine Pagels's concise academic study in *The Gnostic Gospels,* then delve into the rich and expansive *The Jesus Mysteries* by Timothy Freke and Peter Gandy.

If early Christianity was extremely diverse with dozens of gospels and various Gnostic traditions spread across the Middle East, you might be asking, "What happened to change all this?" Like most of the problems in history, we may be able to pin this one to the horrors of war. With the Roman Empire smashing Jerusalem and its Second Temple in AD 70, the whole region was in violent tumult. The Romans considered secret or hidden societies dangerous hotbeds of rebellion and Christians, with their radical messianic hero figure, found themselves at the top of this list. Members of the Christian mysteries joined the mass exodus out of the country to avoid persecution while many of the initiation schools fractured into pieces. (A similar tragic situation is happening to the Mandeans, one of the last remaining Gnostic lineages, who are being persecuted due to the war in Iraq.)

Initiates were spread far and wide and those who no longer could experience the deeper mysteries and inner gnosis started up "Literalist Churches," which taught the Jesus story as historical fact rather than allegorical representation. The remaining Gnostic circles called these rigid sects "Imitation Churches," as they did not teach the real meaning of the Mysteries—"the Christ within." Literalist Christianity sprouted up in the Roman Empire, and encountered a good deal of persecution from the state's power structure. But in a sad touch of historical irony, leaders of these new Literalist Churches became heretic hunters, attacking those who still carried the inner teachings of their own religion.

In the second century AD, Irenaeus, the infamous bishop of Lyon, wrote the rather uptight *Against Heresies* to discredit those he saw as his Gnostic opponents. This work almost single-handedly shaped the Orthodox faith and set forth nearly 2,000 years of control by what would become the Catholic hierarchy. Suddenly the word *heresy* (from the Greek *haeresis,* meaning "choosing") was mainlined and used at will to attack and deny any teachings that did not fit in with the growing institutions of power. The drafting of *Against Heresies* was a serious turning point in the history of Christianity, the moment when the once more popular inner traditions lost traction to the growing Literalist Church. Irenaeus immediately began a crusade to narrow the diverse wealth of Christian texts to a paltry four stories.[16]

As the number of Christians multiplied in Roman lands, a power-hungry Emperor Constantine switched the state religion to this mass movement, uniting Rome under "one God, one religion," and yes, one emperor. In 325 he oversaw the Council of Nicaea, where Literalist Church leaders completed Irenaeus' dream of wiping out all Christian written knowledge to a slim few texts. This is what we now call the New Testament.

To me, this act would be the equivalent of free-minded Americans handing over their *Declaration of Independence, The Constitution*, the *Federalist Papers*—the whole basis of our liberty—back to King George in England and saying, "Hey, could you edit these and get back to us?" Of course, many of the most inspiring, liberating, and empowering spiritual texts never saw the light of day in the "old boys club" back in Nicaea. And after completing his long business trip, the now Christian ruler Constantine celebrated his return home by immediately killing both his wife and son. He then remained unbaptized until his deathbed so that he could continue his murderous ways and still secure box seats in heaven.[17]

In 391 Emperor Theodosius passed an edict to close all "pagan" temples and burn their books. Christian hordes set out on murderous rampages smashing all traces of the Mystery traditions from which their own religion had blossomed. The last of the Gnostic circles were annihilated, as were libraries, temples, texts, and the spiritual gnosis that had been passed down throughout the ages. By AD 410 the Roman Empire had nearly torn itself apart and the Visigoths strolled in to finish the job. Only eighty-five years after the Council of Nicaea, the Dark Ages had begun.[18]

But, as the old adage states, "Nothing lasts, but nothing is lost." In December 1945, as the world was ending its darkest and most destructive period to date, an Egyptian peasant named Mohammed Ali of the al-Samman clan came across an earthenware jar near some limestone caves. He feared an evil djin (genie) might be inside, but eventually opened the jar in hopes to discover lost riches. Disappointment set in as twelve raggedy leather-bound codices fell out of the jar. He had no idea of the priceless treasure lying at his feet. In its 1,200 pages, *The Nag Hammadi Library* held dozens of sacred texts that had been hidden away for the last 1,600 years. In it were numerous Gnostic gospels and treatises that had been lost to the brutal dustbin of time. Mohammed brought them home where his mother stayed warm by feeding pages of those ancient texts to her fireplace.[19]

Fortunately, she didn't burn most of the texts and the remaining ones can now be enjoyed by anyone with access to Wikipedia, Amazon.com, or a local bookstore. *The Nag Hammadi Library* contains fifty-two texts in all including: the Gospel of Thomas, Secret James, the Gospel of Philip, the Origin of the World, the Gospel of Truth, the Exegesis on the Soul, Secret John, the Three Steles of Seth, the Gospel of the Egyptians, the Prayer of the Apostle Paul, the Tripartite Tractate, and the Sophia of Jesus. As you can see from these numerous titles, early Christianity was an extremely rich, open, and inclusive tradition when it came to gnosis. The Library even includes texts from the *Corpus Hermeticum* and Plato's *Republic*.

To conclude this chapter of our journey, I'd like to say that I've been absolutely amazed by how many people are awakening to a greater vision of themselves and the cosmos, whether through spontaneous openings or engaging in serious spiritual endeavors. Mass transformation of human consciousness seems to be increasing exponentially all around us as record numbers of seekers practice the techniques of yoga, Reiki, Tai Chi, meditation, and much more. While we embark on this noble journey, it's important to integrate the traditions we grew up with and not just push them away, especially if we want to become whole. As Jesus says in the Gospel of Thomas, "If you bring forth what is within you, what you bring forth will save you. If you do not bring forth what is within you, what you do not bring forth will destroy you."

Regardless of your religious upbringing or current practices, Christianity is within all of us. It's in our language, our laws, our mores, our sexuality, even our calendar, deeply influencing our entire perspective on the world. The gnosis of these newly discovered texts provides a mystical bridge between our own unfolding personal transformation and the cultural forces that ground us and identify us in our shared reality. They offer a place to heal, forgive, and embrace our religious traditions while clearing up some of the mistranslations and misunderstandings of the past. We no longer are limited to looking toward the exotic East for knowledge of the deeper mysteries in life. Like Dorothy, we can click our heels three times, and discover we've actually been there all along.

NOTES

1. "In my Father's house, there are many mansions" (Livingstonemusic.net, 2002), http://www.livingstonemusic.net/godmen.htm top.

2. Ibid.

3. Timothy Freke and Peter Gandy, *The Jesus Mysteries* (New York: Three Rivers Press, 1999), pp. 1–26.

4. Ibid., p. 1.

5. Ibid., pp. 1–3.

6. Ibid., p. 5.

7. Dennis Diehl, "The Original Sun of God," (Ezine Articles, 2008), http://ezinearticles.com/?The-Original-Sun-of-God&id=93709.

8. Sir James George Frazier, *The Golden Bough* (New York: Macmillan, 1992), chapter 37.

9. Diehl, "The Original Sun of God."

10. Peter Joseph, *Zeitgeist: The Movie* (2007), http://zeitgeistmovie.com, part 2.

11. Stephan A. Hoeller, *Gnosticism: New Light on the Ancient Tradition of Knowing* (Wheaton, Ill.: Quest Books, 2002), p. 116.

12. Nancy Detweiler, "Hell=Jerusalem's Garbage Dump," CrossLeft, 4/07/2008, http://www.crossleft.org/node/6051.

13. Richard Smoley, *Hidden Wisdom: A Guide to the Western Inner Traditions* (Wheaton, Ill.: Quest Books, 1999), p. 48.

14. Elaine Pagels, *The Gnostic Gospels* (New York: Vintage Books, 1989), p. 37.

15. Richard Smoley, *Inner Christianity: A Guide to the Esoteric Tradition* (Monterey, Mass.: Bma Studios), Discs 1–2 on audiobook.

16. J. Michael Matkin, *The Complete Idiot's Guide to the Gnostic Gospels* (Indianapolis: Watermill Books, 2005), pp. 23–24.

17. Freke and Gandy, *The Jesus Mysteries*, p. 11.

18. Ibid., pp. 243–251.

19. James M. Robinson, *The Nag Hammadi Library* (New York: HarperCollins, 1990), pp. 22–26.

III

ART

# BURNING MEN

## *Erik Davis*

### PART ONE: CHAOSMOS

And so there you are, in a fireman's coat, hurtling through the wee hours across a parched and dusty lakebed in a 1979 American LaFrance fire truck, a pumper from Danville, Illinois, named Sparky who occasionally spits gobs of fire from a flamethrower mounted on the roof of the cab. This is no ordinary Monday night.

Above you the rare shadow of the earth has morphed the full moon into a dusky half-burnt clementine that hangs there pendulous like some wandering orb on the cover of a 70s SF paperback. In the muted moonlight, you can see for once that the thing really is a sphere, and not a disc—a ping-pong jack-o-lantern arrested midflight. You think upon the old ones and what they must have made of such a vision, so unusual but still predictable to the sharper monkey minds: A call to the gods? An excuse to orgy? Proof that nature is a veil?

"Baby's on Fire" is spewing out of the iPod, and Fripp's incandescent solo mixes with Burning Man's surrounding soundscape of engines, explosions, house beats, and the rising cries of gesticulating passersby who have—wait a sec—just realized that the iconic 40-foot-tall trademark that centers their entire week of organized revelry is prematurely aflame.

– Gnat, am I hallucinating?

– Of course!

– But the Man's on fire!

– Ohshit ohshit. Mhuaahaha! GO GO GO!!!

Later, there will be arguments over motive and ethic, of responsibility and risk and the smoldering coals of living theater. But for now there is only the Event: the disruptive eruption of novelty, of amoral surprise, of the genuinely untimely. The man is burning! Time is out of joint! Later, there will be News and Analysis and Opinion, those grubby hustlers of thought who monopolize the discourse we use to mirror the world. But for now we, or at least those of us on Sparky, laugh with exultation, with ridiculous wayward joy, because our lives happen, really happen, only in the environs of the Event, in that frothy chaos that dances ahead of the march of facts.

The Event is not history: It arises in a different kind of time, metamagical time, nonlinear or at least orthogonal to our quotidian grind. The fire that licked the paraffin-soaked figure that Monday night was also the Ouroboros licking its own tail. In a bar after the festival was over the accused perpetrator of the act spoke to my friend about wormholes and time-slips, and it did seem for a moment that we were once again beholding the old-school burning men of yore, toxic and raw and stripped of firework finery. And dangerously mythic. As we scrambled off the fire truck, a lanky young fellow with a thin but prophetic beard passed us, calling to all with ears in a stentorian Masterpiece Theatre voice: The Man shall burn when the planets align, and not at the hour appointed by man.

Of course, the planets fall from alignment, and man returns with his watch and his appointments, with his News and Analysis and Opinion. At first the news we heard was indistinguishable from fantasy and projection, not unlike the apocalyptic speculations that greeted the rumors of Katrina during the 2005 festival. The rumors of 2007, however, were all about sabotage, about grappling hooks and decoy fireworks and zip lines and Spider-Man-obsessed FX maestros and napalm and ferocious beatings and inside jobs and defense funds and mysterious radio silences.

Gradually, the consensus of facts emerged: At 2:58 a.m., August 28, the Burning Man Festival's most obvious raison d'être was torched. Not long after, one Paul David Addis, thirty-five, was booked into the Pershing County Jail on felony charges of arson and destruction of property, and misdemeanor charges of possession of fireworks and resisting a public officer. He was subsequently released after some pals paid a bondsman to post his $25,632 bail.

Addis's early arrest also arrested the more unsettling reverberations of the Event. Once we have a human agent in our sites, the Event becomes a deed, a human deed, and the questions of responsibility and intention arise. Who is this masked man in the mugshot? Why is he smiling? What were his intentions? How could he justify his actions? How shall we judge him?

I am not interested in these questions right now, except for possibly the one about that fucking smile, the gonzo grin of a lost man sailing beyond regrets. What I am interested in are the presuppositions behind our questions, our interrogations really, and how those hidden assumptions bounce back at us as reality.

With this man Addis to speculate about and to blame, the anonymous ambiguity of the Event narrows into the political psychology of a single guy: a loose cannon, a channeler of Hunter S. Thompson, an old-school if infrequent Burner. But which guy is it? The fellow who gave *Wired* a position paper, or the batshit time traveler who met my pal in that bar after the fact, a guy who described the prank as a "birthday candle" and a wormhole?

When he torched the man, was Addis acting as an ideologue, or a prankster, or an artist? Each of these actors in turn invokes a different set of criteria we might use to judge the act, its ethical dimensions, its efficacy.

I'll get to the more conventional and legalistic frameworks for Addis's dangerous deed in part two. But first I'd like to invoke an esoteric one: Poetic Terrorism. The term comes from Hakim Bey, the same fellow who gave us the "Temporary Autonomous Zone," an underground term that was freely used by participants and observers alike in their quest to tag the events on Black Rock desert back in the day.

In his 1985 pamphlet *Chaos: Broadsheets of Ontological Anarchism,* Bey writes that "Poetic Terrorism is an act in a Theater of Cruelty which has no stage, no rows of seats, no tickets & no walls." Bey provides a brief catalog of possible pranks and wonders, which includes one of particular relevance here: unauthorized pyrotechnic displays. Bey has further recommendations:

> Don't do Poetic Terrorism for other artists, do it for people who will not realize (at least for a few moments) that what you have done is art. Avoid recognizable art-categories, avoid politics, don't stick around to argue, don't be sentimental; be ruthless, take risks, vandalize only what MUST be defaced, do something children will remember all their lives—but don't be spontaneous unless the Poetic Terrorist Muse has possessed you.

I don't know if Addis was possessed by the Poetic Terrorist Muse, or Choronzon, or L'il Abner. For all I know, he was acting from some terrible combination of lust, monomania, and neurochemical turbulence. But from some reports he did act as one possessed, possibly spouting prophetic verse. On his Flickr page, Danger Ranger (board member Michael Michael) has his Addis photo in a set called "chaos technicians," which also includes a shot of a guy who has been ejected from the playa five years running. But as my pal Earth pointed out, since when do we expect our poets to be healthy and balanced? You may not agree that his act was poetry, but it was certainly more than the Great Prank—not just a snarky money shot for the camera, but a shuddering, mythic invocation that briefly summoned another age and sluiced a wormhole into the current festival by invoking the contradictions that compose it, by daring the beast to show itself.

At the same time, Addis's was also, by community as well as legal norms, the destruction of someone else's art, performed recklessly and on a public enough scale that the "terrorism" in Bey's phrase is not entirely out of place. Still, I believe that Addis and all who were moved to hilarity and exultation by his act—even if, like me, they wrestle with the contradictions and paradoxes that hilarity and exultation leave in its wake—must acknowledge that what was vandalized had to be defaced for the poetry, in this most peculiar context, to properly sing. Perhaps you heard the song, or perhaps it sounded like noise, or like some idiot tooting his own horn. Perhaps it stirred something in you you thought had died.

The early burn also reminded me that the best art out there is still the stuff that reveals how the whole show is constructed, not just Black Rock City, or your perception of it, but the whole enchilada—you know, reality. And I'm not just talking about metaphysical, woo-woo, infinite-recursive-loop reality. I'm talking about that more solid fabric of identity, matter, property, image, and consciousness that we navigate daily. And sometimes the only way to show how heavily solidified stuff like that is constructed is to destroy it.

PART TWO: THE ORDER OF THINGS

On Monday night of this year's Burning Man Festival, when Larry Harvey saw the figure he first built over twenty years ago burst into flame before its appointed time, the man's immediate reaction was laughter, a pure and perfect response. Harvey also noted that he laughed only after he knew that the fire was under control and that no one was apt to be hurt. (I'll be honest: I laughed without knowing if anyone had been injured.) Soon afterward, Harvey told a blogger that the early burn would turn the festival into a "narrative of community and redemption," as attendees got to see or assist in the public rebuilding of the statue.

I appreciate where Harvey is coming from, but this sounds like a pretty kumbaya take on what looked to me and many others like an increasingly hidebound institution's inability to react creatively to a disturbing and unexpected marvel left steaming on their doorstep. So many things could have been done at the time—parade the body of the blackened man to Center Camp, or distribute his dismembered planks to the plazas like the chunks of Osiris, or place the corpse in the arms of the new man.

Sadly, the organization did not improvise with the Event. Instead, they acted a bit like a colony of ants and simply cleaned up the mess and replicated the established model. The repetitive nature of the task, performed behind guard and beneath those garish lights without poetry or mirth, spoke less of community and redemption than of the empire of work. The second man was not a phoenix; it was a clone.

Perhaps this helps explain why the official Saturday-night burn of 2007 was probably the most boring on record. Admittedly, I've seen these things into the double digits now. But I am also jaded about being jaded and still enjoy the sparkle, the roar, and especially the first surge of the acolytes toward the pyre. But Saturday night's fireworks had all the whizbang of those little doodads that blink on websites, and the conflagration itself was so drawn out and tepid that many of the revelers around me just walked away or started talking about DJs.

So what made it boring? She that hath an ear, let her hear: because the base structure was too strong. It was too rigid. It didn't give. It didn't surprise. If attendants hadn't manually pulled the scarecrow down, he would have stood there all night, like the living dead.

But I am not really interested in second-guessing the organization. They build a crazy, immensely entertaining, and inspiring city in the middle of nowhere and then tear it down without killing people or getting arrested. They have a lot on their plate.

Here is the question I am interested in: If the Event sparked by Paul Addis did not lead to poetry beyond the gesture itself, did it at least lead to insight? Addis threw up a challenge, legal and political as well as artistic and magical. Were Burners up for it? How did we narrate this unexpected rupture? How did we speak it into history?

I have been frankly amazed at how rapidly so many Burners have deflated the delirious ambiguity of Addis's act by taking it upon themselves to render judgment upon it in legalistic or at least highly conventional terms. It's a curious response. I mean, the Feds are going to have their way with Addis whatever you or me or the "Burning Man community" thinks. So what turned us into op-ed stuffed shirts or magistrates proclaiming opinion in a court of law?

Part of the blame for all this dusty punditry can be laid on the feet of the Zeitgeist. In our era of pervasive blogochatter, everyone feels compelled to have an opinion. My friends, it is a terrible habit, having opinions, the compulsive collection of positions that often only masquerade as actually thinking about something. Moreover, these alignments are often related to deeply established memes which we reproduce without complication by "holding" the opinion. In this way, we unknowingly give over our power—individual and collective—to those larger myths and institutions that organize reality according to convention.

What conventions, you say? There is the militaristic logic of escalation: If Addis is not prosecuted to the fullest extent of the law, copycats will destroy the festival! Then there is the fearful invocation of dark possibilities that didn't actually happen (a rhetorical strategy of control-through-fear we should all be familiar with by now): But something really bad could have happened! Then there was the surprisingly oft heard "customer service" critique, often made in the name of other people and whose basic logic, as far as I can parse it, goes something like this: Hey now, folks paid good money to see the Man burn on Saturday night, and no selfish burst of Dada détournement should keep them from enjoying their spectacle right on schedule!

Far more significant (and insidious) than any of these conventions, though, is the colossal mythology of property: How dare Addis destroy other people's art?! I agree that having your playa artwork destroyed by some yahoo with a jug of propane would totally suck, but the totally understandable complaint here actually conceals two very different views, and it's important to keep them apart.

One view is the sacrosanct status of property that supports the modern nation-state. The other view arises from the collective mores of Black Rock City: an evolving body of informal and contradictory standards that holds certain things about the sanctity (and not) of art. Within the latter framework, it certainly is bad form to destroy someone's art without asking. However, within BRC mores, it would not be entirely out of place (though a minority view I suspect) to suggest that burning someone's art may be considered a form of interacting with it. In a federal court, where only the view based on property holds sway, this argument would never make it past a lawyer's lips.

So let's stay with this second view for a moment. Doesn't the oft-trumpeted gift economy of Burning Man—not to mention the insane degree of consumption that fuels it—indicate that property has a different meaning out there, that it is less important than expression or community or pleasure? In an interview recently conducted by telegraph and semaphore, Danger Ranger made the point that the raison d'être of the real world's police and the military can largely be boiled down to the protection of property.

In contrast, he characterized the Black Rock Rangers—who partly enforce community mores—as an organization founded with the explicit goal of protecting community rather than property.

During our chat, Danger Ranger made an even more important point: The legal status of Black Rock City is fundamentally ambiguous.

"Federal, state and county laws are often enforced selectively by the various agencies that represent those civil entities, because most of the individuals within those agencies realize that this is a unique community with a different system of values. After spending some time in Black Rock City, it quickly becomes apparent that 'The Law' is not a universal standard that can be imposed on the citizens of a community who have collectively agreed to a different set of principles." This legal ambiguity is not just a fantasy of freedom—it actually constitutes the shared reality of that place and time, like, arguably, the micronation of Sealand or an MMORPG or the kinky doings in the basement of a private club.

You can get metaphysical about all this. Consider California's pot clubs or the grow fields that support them—the federal laws simply do not apply in the same way to these spaces, even if the Feds sometimes act like they do. The activities in these territories is, like a quantum particle, an ambiguous behavior that is only resolved according to a political struggle over which perceptions, legal and otherwise, can be used to name and clarify it.

So when Burners invoked specifically legalistic categories like "arson" and "reckless endangerment"—and I did it too at times—they were not just rationally debating Addis's fate. They were actively deflating the productive legal ambiguity of Black Rock City as a self-governing political and territorial space by capitulating, too quickly and without consciousness, to the reality tunnel of the State and, particularly, to its conception of property.

Even in BRC terms the Burning Man is not just another piece of art—and it is certainly not just Larry Harvey's art. Arguably, anyone who pays their ticket and invests that figure with hope and expectation can claim a piece of the thing. The Man is a symbol, an icon, and he is also a logo and a brand whose value Black Rock citizens partly create and sustain through our own creativity and sacrifice. To reclaim or arguably "liberate" this chunk of mindshare by burning it is, while crude and destructive, also to reassert the bootleg value of the figure as a figment of the collective imagination rather than the registered trademark of a for-profit organization.

So here's a question: If we believe that property at Burning Man is in service of community, did Addis's destruction of property serve community?

After Addis burnt the man, the Burning Man board could not come to agreement as to the best course of action. The group that wound up ruling the day was not the Board but the crew who actually built the man—essentially, DPW. In other words, the decision to rebuild the man arose through the ranks, reflecting that particular crew's sense of energetic investment into the figure. In this sense, Larry Harvey's kumbaya was right on, and community asserted itself in the face of destruction.

I wish they had rebuilt the man with more panache, but the act at least reflected the fact that the Man was less someone's property than the fruit of someone else's labor. So while the call to rebuild was a corporate decision, requiring the diversion of funds and the deployment of a labor force (volunteer and not), many of the workers were psyched to do it because their labor was not alienated. And in the complex dynamics of Black Rock City, a bloc of unalienated and skilled laborers have a big claim on the (re)construction of reality.

The strongest criticisms of Addis's act went beyond the call of property. An even deeper meme was drawn from, and that is the supreme call to protect human life—one of the core axioms of our fearful, litigious, paranoid, and death-denying society. Addis should be condemned because he endangered innocent human lives. On the surface, this argument is inarguable, but that is, I would like to suggest, more a sign of its cunning than its logic or essential goodness.

At the moment, there is little to be gained from asking just how dangerous Addis's actions actually were (would we think differently if we knew he had planned it out like a jewel thief?). That his act was in some sense dangerous is clear. But how dangerous do we want Burning Man to be? And even before we address that question, it is crucial to recognize how the axiomatic invocation of safety as a trump card also performs its own violence, its own kind of snuffing out.

Look, for example, at the constricted lives of so many kids today, with their helmets and kneepads and car seats, their time managed, their piss checked, their movements tracked by cell phones and prohibitions against aimless wandering. What has been killed in the process of making them less likely to be killed? Perhaps, in our fearful genuflection before safety, we are deadening our taste for the raw and nervy exultation of cognitive and physical liberty—a liberty which most certainly should include the freedom to attend dangerous and wayward festivals where, if you aren't careful or even lucky, large burning things might fall on your head.

Now don't get me wrong. A bomb-chucking Nietzschean anarchist may sneak into my heart sometimes, but my heart lives in my body, and my body doesn't want burning things falling on its head either. I celebrate all the work people do at Burning Man to prevent needless suffering, and I don't want my friends and compatriots hurt. At the same time I cannot quiet the cosmic imp whispering in my ears:

Does not Burning Man stand alone because, even now, the event still tangos with chaos, with Dionysian fury and explosive devices and actual risk? With, you know, Danger? Sure there were people under the untimely burning man who were pelted with fireworks. Did they read their ticket? Are those words just for show? Do you read them that way? Think of the last time you backpacked: Doesn't knowing that old Griz lurks in the hills give the hike through the high country spice?

I know, I know: My old school is showing. I first showed up at Burning Man in '94, when the event was ugly, deranged, and totally transformative: Cacophony and suicide and discordia rolled into one mobile feast of AK-47s, mescal, and cigars. Larry Harvey may not care for the term, but I believe in the temporary autonomous zone. I felt it; I was there.

Don't get me wrong: I am not pulling an elitist move or claiming the festival was "better" back then. It wasn't. I remain continuously amazed

at its evolution. I am fascinated by the fiery city. But those years catalyzed such bizarre ruptures of reality that they demand a fidelity that I
and some quasi-jaded old-school Burners who still attend the festival
cannot and will not shake.

My sadness these last few weeks is mostly a recognition of how many
of today's Burners do not share that fidelity, which in retrospect makes
Addis's act even more meaningful to me than the poetic prank it seemed
that Monday night.

I believe that 2007 will go down as a watershed year in the evolution
of Burning Man, not unlike the transition from 1996 to 1997, when the
urban model was locked in and the guns were banished. This year, we
witnessed the visible embrace of entrepreneurial capital. We witnessed
the Great Prank that this embrace partly triggered, and that in turn triggered a banal official response. We heard a rhetorical upswing concerning the festival's social relevance, and a corresponding backpedaling
on the spirit of useless expenditure that characterized its past. We witnessed the increasing influence of Burning Man on the culture at large,
from the Adult Swim cartoon to Burners Without Borders to the spread
of Burning Man–style art to festivals and urban landscapes. All of these
mark 2007 as a tipping point, as a crystallization of a different regime.

There is great good and enormous potential in this transformation.
It signals the maturity of Burning Man's urban metaphor, the infectious
strength of its countercultural creativity, and its strong desire to bring
the playa back into the world. The playa has burst; the seeds are scatter-
ing. I say spread 'em! Keep drawing others into the fete. Let's transform
the world with a mobile army of art perverts and postapocalyptic entrepreneurs and hard partiers handy with drills, gray water, and incendiary
devices.

But to boldly go into that brave new burning world, you gotta pass
your ass through the time-slip wormhole of chaos that Paul Addis invoked in flame beneath an ominous moon.

# THE KUBRICK GAZE

## J. F. Martel

*"You don't find reality only in your backyard, you know.*
*In fact, sometimes that's the last place you'll find it."*[1]

—STANLEY KUBRICK, 1969

A lot of ink has flowed over the contradiction that is Stanley Kubrick. He seems to be the kind of artist everyone wants to have pinned, yet slips out of every critical grasp. Interpretations of his work tend toward the extremes: Kubrick has been called a right-wing propagandist and a left-wing militant, a misogynist and a feminist, a fatalistic cynic and a quasi-religious optimist. Few directors have attracted so much vitriol, adulation, controversy, and analysis. Kubrick's own silence about the meaning of his films, combined with his notorious reclusiveness and his disregard for "social responsibility" before critic, church, and state, only added to his mysterious aura.

If it is true that Kubrick's films were rigid and cold, as many like to point out, it is also true that they are mercurial, dreamlike, and deeply personal. Their atmosphere is a necessary outcome of the filmmaker's approach in making them. From *Dr. Strangelove* (1964) onward, that approach can only be called *holographic*. What you see in a Kubrick film is the conscious manifestation of an unconscious play of forces taking place beneath the celluloid surface. Kubrick is more concerned with psychic forces—archetypal, philosophical, and cosmic—than he is with the emotional life of his characters or the diversion of his audience.

The relevance of art in society is a burning question today. In a world on the brink of annihilation or possible transformation, what role does the artist play? Should she forgo the ideals of self-expression in order to create what is essentially propaganda, fuzzy New Agery, or pointed didactic? Should he give up the ghost and occupy his time doing something more productive than playing the fiddle while Rome burns? Can art effect change, or can it really be relegated to mere entertainment, devoid of transformative power?

It is in response to such questions that I bring up Kubrick now. At the risk of seeming idolatrous, I hold him up as a model of how vision and conviction can make art that is relevant, spiritual, and transformative. His genius, combined with his refusal to submit to the dictates of Right or Left, or even to the dark satanic mills of Hollywood, produced some of the most revelatory images of postmodern art. My goal is to show that Kubrick's vision is as relevant today as it was when his films were released—perhaps more so.

### THE GAZE

Kubrick once told Jack Nicholson, "We're not interested in photographing the reality. We're interested in photographing the photograph of the reality."[2] Stanley Kubrick's films are not fictions but psychic documentaries. Suspending our disbelief—à la Hitchcock or Spielberg—was never his priority. Nothing in a Kubrick film is supposed to feel like it's happening in a physical world analogous to our own. Their setting is the mind itself. Kubrick's work belongs to the Gnostic hyperreal; it aspires to direct cognizance of pure thought. As psychedelic tours of history's dream galleries, his films are inherently political, dealing with power and the creation and destruction of values. Most importantly, their core is mystical, even shamanic. Kubrick was one of the few filmmakers to take up André Bazin on his famous ideal of the Holy Moment, which posits that the motion picture camera can extract a slice of space-time and enframe it in Plato's hyperspace, creating a reality that supercedes the historical moment originally captured on film.

Some of the most potent Holy Moments Kubrick filmed feature the Gaze, that uniquely Kubrickian device that appears in all of the films post-*Strangelove*, most famously in the first shot of *A Clockwork Orange* (1971) and in that one-shot scene in *The Shining* (1980) where Jack Torrance begins to slip over the edge. Kubrick valued this posture so much that he often assumed it himself in photographs, giving us the image of a man who is seeing beyond, which is precisely what the Gaze signifies. Whether they are looking into some unfathomable distance or straight at us through the camera lens, the characters who adopt the Gaze are piercing through the illusion of conscious life to spy the deep archetypal forces that shape reality.

In most cases, characters react to the truth that the Gaze reveals by going insane. It's as if the eyes are gateways through which the spirit world can pass into the mind and take control. The challenge is to lift the veil of Maya while retaining our humanity. There is a moment in *Eyes Wide Shut* when Alice, Nicole Kidman's character, adopts the Gaze before the mirror while her husband (both real and fictional) initiates sex with her. In the seconds before the screen fades to black, she turns to us. In that moment we know that she sees everything, and that the experience will either lead her (and, as it turns out, her husband) to enlightenment, or into a deeper dark.

## STRANGELOVE, ODYSSEY, AND CLOCKWORK: THE STAR CHILD TRILOGY

This primacy of the eyes reveals an obsession on Kubrick's part with *clear vision*. The skeptical and often ruthless attitude that he adopted with his cast, crew, and cowriters is symptomatic of this obsession. Nothing can be taken for granted; everything must be broken down, examined from every angle and photographed in its most naked state. For Kubrick, film was a lens through which one can know the world. If he often spoke of the importance of objectivity, he invariably meant *his* personal objectivity. You can see this in the title of the black comedy *Dr. Strangelove or: How I Learned to Stop Worrying and Love the Bomb* (1964), in which one insane general provokes a nuclear war. The first-person title refers to Kubrick's own disillusionment in the face of rational materialism, a doctrine whose inbuilt absurdity the movie exposes with the existential hysterics of a Laughing Buddha.

Kubrick said that his original intention was to make *Strangelove* a serious thriller. It was only when he realized how fundamentally insane the military-industrial complex was that he decided a comedy would better express the gravity of the postwar situation. The final film, however, went beyond the Cold War in its condemnation; it is a critique of the rational materialist doctrine of which the state apparatus of the Cold War was a direct product. How could a truly rational society give birth to such a lose-lose situation, let alone make an atom bomb in the first place? From the credit sequence showing the mating rituals of military aircraft to doomsday, *Strangelove* is a damning send-up not only of the military establishment but also of the governing logic of the modern world, a logic rooted in a deep denial of the irrational depths of the soul.

*Dr. Strangelove* set the stage for two more films, *2001: A Space Odyssey* (1968) and *A Clockwork Orange* (1971), which complete Kubrick's science-fiction trilogy. It also set the stage for the cinema of the mind that dominated his work until his death. As if to make it clear that nothing can be the same after the disillusionment of *Strangelove*, Kubrick ends the film by destroying the world. The mushroom clouds let us know that only a complete collapse of the system—be it in the form of collective awakening or of the destruction of the planet—can make possible a new appraisal of life and humanity. "We'll meet again some sunny day," Vera Lynn croons as the world explodes. Black humor aside, it's as though Kubrick were promising us a solution.

From the first shots of *2001: A Space Odyssey*, the story of humanity's journey from ape to overman, it seems that Kubrick intends to keep that promise. We're back together on a sunny day, but we're not in Kansas anymore. The sun rises over the barren savannah of prehistoric Africa, where a tribe of frightful man-apes, our early ancestors, mingles with the plains animals. Evidently, the demon of *Strangelove* can only be confronted by returning to our origins. In a Joycean time warp, Kubrick's *Strangelove* apocalypse "brings us by a commodius vicus of recirculation" back to the Dawn of Man. Here, the famous Black Monolith will make its first appearance in history, bestowing upon us a new power.

Most critics assume that what the Monolith teaches is tool-making. This isn't wrong but it misses the point: Most importantly, the Monolith bestows imagination. The film makes this clear in the scene where the man-ape smashes the skeletal remains of an animal with a bone. The magic of the moment lies in the primate's sudden ability to *imagine* a connection between the skull and the living creature to which the skull once belonged. Intercut into the scene are shots of tapirs falling dead; these are taken right out of the man-ape's mind. But the film uses the tool to symbolize imagination, and it is in the nature not just of film critics but of human beings in general to mistake the symbol for the thing. In fact, the worship of our creations is what leads the humans of *2001* into an abusive relationship with the supercomputer HAL, whose self-righteous attempt to take control of our destiny is a direct consequence of our blind adoration of technology at the expense of the visionary power that gave it birth.

*2001* is Kubrick's most overtly mystical film, and it has always seemed strange to me that his other films are only rarely assessed in light of it. At the time of its release, many people found the film too ambiguous for words. Kubrick himself thought this frustration stemmed from the literal-mindedness of contemporary filmmakers and audiences. "It's time to abandon the conventional view of the movie as an extension of the three-act play. Too many people over thirty are still word-oriented rather than picture-oriented," he said in a 1969 interview.[3]

To Kubrick, becoming "picture-oriented" represents an evolution in consciousness, the development of an ability to go beyond language, the source of all of those binary deadlocks and either-or's that blind the third eye. The transdimensional "Star Child" who, at the end of the film, turns to us on his way back to Earth is a "picture-oriented" being, capable of seeing through the illusion of Maya. When it turns its Gaze on us, we are reminded of our power to imagine, to envision, and to shape our future. Here the Gaze is an invitation.

In its abandon of all but the rudiments of narrative, its use of trance-inducing imagery and its open-endedness, *2001* is not a movie but an ecstatic vision, and in conveying it Kubrick showed us for the first time the shamanic potential of cinema to induce visionary states. An example of film as entheogen, *2001* sheds the propagandist mantle cinema had worn until then (and all-too-often continues to wear today) to reveal its psychedelic heart.

The Nietzschean journey from ape to man to Star Child that shapes the plot of *2001* is in fact an exploration of man's relationship with technology, which led to global destruction in *Dr. Strangelove.* However, here Kubrick seems concerned with technology's positive potential. Echoing Heidegger, the film suggests that in technology, the process that is transforming nature and humans into "standing reserve," mere resource to be used and then thrown away, there lies a "saving power." Yes, technology and the capitalism that makes it proliferate are the result of a mad quest that threatens all living things, but *2001* proposes that this quest may not be as blind as we think. It may be guided by a higher consciousness. In the film, technology leads us to the discovery that it is within ourselves, not outside of us, that the solution to the problem of technology—a solution Heidegger called *poiesis,* or pure creativity—is hiding.

From the film, it would seem at first that interplanetary travel is the key to that discovery. This is where *2001* becomes allegorical. In reality, technology's saving power has nothing to do with spaceships or space travel but with cinema itself. The Black Monolith that appears at the Dawn of Man, on the moon, in space, and in the astronaut Bowman's psyche at the moment of death, is not simply a throwback to Masonic symbolism or the Philosopher's Stone. The Black Monolith is the movie screen.

This is the big secret of *2001*. I'd never thought of it until it was pointed out by sources on the Net.[4] During the prologue and interlude, where we are made to stare at a black screen for several minutes while Ligeti's alien choirs howl, we are actually looking at the Monolith. We are invited to transform ourselves, to become "picture-oriented," to break out of the prison of language. Kubrick drives this secret thesis home in his subtle cameo appearance. In the scene where the astronauts gather for a photo-op in front of the lunar Monolith, we can see Kubrick holding a camera in the reflective visor of a space helmet. By gazing at us like the Star Child at the end of the film, Kubrick is showing us that the saving power of technology, that new *poiesis* made possible by industrialization, is the cinema. Never before its advent was humanity more capable of transcending language, of thinking in visions.

*A Clockwork Orange* picks up where *2001* left off. Now that the Star Child is born, it is necessary to determine how and if it can be integrated into society. Here, Kubrick's optimism seems to fade. The story of the criminal Alex's encounter with the sinister state apparatus of a kitschy dystopia forms the last chapter of the story that began with *Dr. Strangelove*.

The last shot of *2001*, of the Star Child gazing into the camera, and the first shot of *Clockwork*, of Alex doing the same thing, are a conscious juxtaposition. Alex is the Star Child, the Nietzschean overman come to earth to expose society's entrenched hypocrisy through a rejection of obsolete values. His love of music, his use of dramatic language, his costumes and posturing make him a kind of artist, a mercurial trickster dancing on the ruins of history. His pet snake—a classic shamanic symbol—and his ability to trance out and receive visions of violence make him a shaman. But this is the shaman as sorcerer rather than healer. The complete failure of the tribe to integrate Alex has resulted in his using his power to control, dominate, rape, and destroy. Horrified by his instinctive disregard for the consensual trance of traditional morality, society reacts first by imprisoning him and then by reprogramming his mind. After undergoing the Ludovico treatment, Alex's violent soul is put in a vice, yet in an ironic twist the treatment also stifles his love of music. Kubrick is telling us that in denying our shadow, though we may eliminate that part of us that we do not wish to face, we are also denying the visionary power that makes us human. In the end, only a suicidal leap provoked by his revulsion at Beethoven will enable Alex to transcend the vicious dialectic of his situation.

The common view is that after his suicide attempt, Alex essentially reverts to his old self, becoming a violent sociopath once again. I think this view is incorrect. Though the film understandably skips over his coma, Alex's narration describes it to us as "a long, long black gap of what might have been a million years," a literal dark night of the soul that changes him profoundly. When the psychiatrist comes to his bedside to test him by having him fill in the word-bubbles in a series of suggestive comics, his answers are irreverent but not psychotic. When the minister of the interior plays Beethoven's Ninth for the state's new golden boy, Alex goes into a trance just like he used to, but whereas his earlier visions were of historical violence (a woman being hanged in the Old West, WWII explosions, a tribe of cavemen crushed by an avalanche), his final vision is completely different. He sees himself having sex with a woman, but for the first time the sex is consensual, the woman on top and in control, and a crowd of bourgeois are applauding the act. The film is telling us that revolt against old values isn't enough—the mystic eye and the evil eye are the same organ bent on different ends. Only by recognizing and accepting our shadow will the cancer ravaging civilization go into remission.

The last shot of *A Clockwork Orange* ends the science-fiction trilogy.

From the mechanical sex that opened *Dr. Strangelove* we have come to the dream of a fully cognizant union of male and female. This image of union suggests that in order to evolve, our patriarchal culture must embrace the feminine, a feat we will accomplish only once we have let the shadow of our civilization, where the feminine has been repressed, reveal itself. *Full Metal Jacket* (1987) echoes this theme in the scene where the sniper who guns down three chauvinistic and immature Marines turns out to be an adolescent girl. But it is not until *Eyes Wide Shut* (1999), Kubrick's final film, that the theme of the feminine in the modern world is given its proper treatment.

### FROM ALEX TO ALICE

The Star Child makes at least two more appearances in the three films following *Clockwork*. It appears as Danny in *The Shining* and as Matthew Modine's dualistic Joker in *Full Metal Jacket*. In both those films, the Star Child can only *see* reality; it cannot do anything to help the situation. In order to do so, it must take on a different avatar. It must manifest as a female.

As Tim Kreider argues in his essay "Introducing Sociology," *Eyes Wide Shut* is first and foremost a condemnation of the repressive and decadent patriarchy that continues to govern us:

> The slice of that world [Kubrick] tried to show us in his last—and, he believed, his best—work, the capital of the global American empire at the end of the American Century, is one in which the wealthy, powerful, and privileged use the rest of us like throwaway products, covering up their crimes with pretty pictures, shiny surfaces, and murder, ultimately dooming their own children to lives of servitude and whoredom.[5]

The film tells the story of Bill and Alice, a married couple that embarks upon a dream journey to the dark heart of modern sexuality after Alice

admits to lusting after other men. There they discover that society is en-
meshed in a web of lies in which sexuality is used as currency by the rich
and powerful while common mortals struggle to live up to the tyrannical
ideals of sexual "decency" and pasteurized love.

In the fin de siècle Manhattan of *Eyes Wide Shut,* the clumsy totali-
tarianism of *Clockwork Orange* has grown omnipresent, cunning, and
decadent. In fact no one notices it anymore. The behavioral science of
B. F. Skinner and company, still theoretical in 1971, has now been applied across the board, turning the global microcosm of New York City
into a rat maze of luminous marketing and complacent Christmas trees.
While the husbands and wives of the middle class do their damnedest to
hide their true nature from each other, the reigning elites, portrayed as
members of an international Satanic cult, reap the rewards of absolute
power at masked orgies where women are subjected to ritual hypnosis,
brutal sex, and, in one case at least, murder.

Kubrick showed all of this to his audience but, judging from the reaction of critics and the public, his audience remained unmoved. Programmed to expect sexual fulfillment to come vicariously through the
pornography of sex films and family TV, most viewers sat in the theater
feeling ripped off. The movie seemed to promise some kind of thrill, but
when Dr. Bill, played by Tom Cruise, begins to suspect that all is not
well with the world, the elite Victor Ziegler comes to the rescue with a
cold shower of boring common sense. The orgy, the rites, the murder . . .
it was all a charade, he says, threatening but ultimately harmless. It's almost as if Kubrick appeared at the end to remind us that we are only
watching a movie.

The problem lies in our susceptibility to the hypnotic mechanics of
plot. The typical viewer's acceptance of Ziegler's explanation at the film's
anticlimax signifies that we as a species have yet to evolve out of "word-
orientation," so much so that we are still perfectly ready to dismiss what
we see with our own eyes if it is casually denied by some arbitrary figure
of patriarchal authority.

*Eyes Wide Shut* is Kubrick's most scathing critique of the modern world, but it does offer hope. The hero of the story is not Cruise's Bill but Kidman's Alice, whose name resembles Alex for good reason: She is the Star Child reborn as a woman. For the first time, it is a woman who gets the Gaze into the unconscious, and the consequences are drastically different. Throughout the film, she keeps up the image of the good modern woman. As a wife, she is sexy, intelligent, and serviceable. As a mother, she works hard to pass on to her daughter her submissive qualities. Still, she is unable to shake off the feeling that she is living a lie. Her memories and dreams tell her with increasing urgency that the world she has been brought up in is false. Repressed archetypes of the feminine surge up inside her, seeking entry into the world. The Gaze into the beyond makes it impossible for her to keep pretending that her husband's chauvinistic self-delusions have any substance. When she tells Bill how she was willing to throw away her entire life for a single night with a naval officer she'd never seen before, she opens up the floodgates to the unconscious so wide that it swallows her up along with her husband, who spends the rest of the film swimming through her mind, where she manifests in the form of various Other Women, until ultimately she lets him out again, summing up the wisdom of the ages in a single word.

BILL: What do you think we should do?

ALICE: I think we should be grateful that we've managed to survive through all of our adventures whether they were real or only a dream.

BILL: Are you sure of that?

ALICE: Only as sure as I am that the reality of one night, let alone a whole lifetime, can never be the whole truth.

BILL: And no dream is ever just a dream.

ALICE: The important thing is we're awake now. And hopefully for a long time to come.

BILL: Forever.

ALICE: Forever . . . Let's not use that word. It frightens me. But I do
love you, and you know, there is something very important that
we have to do as soon as possible.

BILL: What's that?

ALICE: Fuck.

Like the closing shot of *A Clockwork Orange,* the final scene of *Eyes Wide Shut* places the woman on top, only now intercourse has been replaced by the formulation of a new social contract. As she walks through the toy store with her daughter and husband, Alice seems completely detached. When her daughter points out a toy baby carriage, she replies that it is "old-fashioned," meaning that the illusion of the nuclear family as the elemental unit of the World Order has expired for her, leaving in its wake the ever-burning energy of human instinct transmutable into creative power. By "fuck" Alice does not mean "making love" or "making babies." She means that it is time we reclaim that power from those who have taken it away from us.

The last scene of the last film represents a historical passage out of the world in which Kubrick's stories were set—the patriarchal world of rational materialism—into a new state where the feminine has been restored to its proper place on the earth.

## ART AND THE EARTH

At the end of *2001,* the Star Child is shown returning to Earth rather than drifting deeper into the cosmos. Indeed, as the overman of Nietzsche's *Zarathustra,* the Star Child is "the meaning of the earth."[6] What Kubrick's films call for is not a return to the abstract spirituality of the heavenly spheres, but the (re)spiritualization of the earth and of earthly life. His mysticism was not transcendent but immanent, his religion not priestly but shamanic. Kubrick's overman is not the eugenics monster of the ex-Nazi Dr. Strangelove and his technocratic disciples, but a human being capable of transmuting unconscious shadows into conscious light. Though human beings have been given the gift of creative vision, fear of and detachment from our own nature have prevented us from assuming our role as the cocreators of reality. It is only natural, then, that control over our fate and our world has landed on the laps of the most deluded and hypocritical among us, the dreamers of the nightmare of history. Kubrick's entire work was a call to awake from that nightmare.

Having said this, I don't think Kubrick went into any project seeking to deliver a specific message. Unlike most of what's out there, his filmmaking never told us what to think about the images on the screen; he knew that to be didactic was to contribute to the cultural and intellectual disenfranchisement of the species. As his classic quote goes, "I have found it always the best policy to allow the film to speak for itself."

The ideas I have drawn from Kubrick's films are also present in the work of artists such as Shakespeare, Michelangelo, Blake, or Nietzsche. Art made with openness to the mystery of being and trust in the imagination produces Heidegger's *poiesis,* sacred art, and the "message" of sacred art is always the same. Joseph Campbell said that the two sides of "true" art are beauty, which lifts the soul, and the sublime, which shatters the ego.[7] This kind of art, the kind Kubrick was making when he was at his best, is by its very nature essential, useful, and transformative, especially in times like these.

The artist's role, then, is to shape the chaosmos into figures that inspire us to create the world. As I write this, the marketing and advertising industry continues its tireless work of populating our minds with the myriad logos, concepts, lies, and clichés of universal capitalism. Only art—independent, democratized, and shared—can save us from this final chapter in the story of world colonization.

## BIBLIOGRAPHICAL SOURCES

Gelmis, Joseph. "An Interview with Stanley Kubrick" from *The Film Director as Superstar*. New York: Doubleday, 1970 (article available at the Kubrick Site: www.kubrick.com).

Heidegger, Martin. *Basic Writings*. New York: HarperCollins, 1993.

Kreider, Tim. "Introducing Sociology: A Review of Eyes Wide Shut." *Film Quarterly* vol. 53, no. 3. University of California Press, 2000 (article available at the Kubrick Site: www.kubrick.com).

Nietzsche, Friedrich. *Thus Spoke Zarathustra*. New York: Viking, 1966.

## NOTES

1. Joseph Gelmis, "An Interview with Stanley Kubrick," at www.kubrick.com.

2. Interview with Jack Nicholson in the Warner Bros. documentary *Stanley Kubrick: A Life in Pictures* (2001), directed by Jan Harlan.

3. Gelmis, "An Interview."

4. Most notably Rob Ager's analysis of the film, available at www.collativelearning.com.

5. Kreider, "Introducing Sociology: A Review of Eyes Wide Shut," at www.kubrick.com.

6. Nietzsche, *Thus Spoke Zarathustra*, p. 13.

7. Campbell, "The Way of Art," at http://www.rawpaint.com/library/jcampbell/jctwoa.html.

# HARRY SMITH:
# AMERICAN MEDIA ARTIST

## *Paul D. Miller aka DJ Spooky that Subliminal Kid*

Harry Smith is probably one of twentieth-century America's greatest hidden treasures. I first got into Harry Smith in the mid-nineties. It was a different time: The U.S. wasn't an occupying power in the Middle East, the price of gas was reasonable, and people all thought vinyl was going to be obsolete. How different things are today!

I tend to think that Harry Smith was a walking remixologist—his memory, as I'm told, was legendary: He'd be able to hear a record that he hadn't heard in decades and would be able to tell you who made it and when, plus what edition the recording came out of. I like stuff like that.

Many people know Harry for his films—I know him for his record collection. If you look at the way he edited film, you can see that he was really into visual rhythm—everything he did was about sequencing and pacing out a series of edits and imagery. I tend to think that he's probably one of the first multimedia artists, and in one way or another, the thread that connects him to the twenty-first century is his fascination with information of every kind. Clips of newspapers, short films made from the shards of his everyday life, pages culled from his favorite esoteric tomes on magic and illusionism—all were grist for his collage-centered vision of how music and film could transform the world. Smith's idea was to apply DJ technique to film—he wanted to show that collage could be edited in a way that would speak about myths and the way people can understand the rapidly changing world around themselves from the information they record.

If you look at other people who were using film in the same way, whether it was Andy Warhol with his "Exploding Plastic Inevitable" or even people like the early cinematographers the Melies brothers—all can be traced as inspirations for the allegorical connections that Smith used to create masterpieces like "Heaven and Earth Magic." Even more so, one can look to Joseph Cornell as a precedent. Cornell is well known for the oneiric quality of his art and films. I like to think that Smith took the "dream logic" of free association to another level. Connect the dots and you realize that his drawings were always meant to be animated to music—you can easily see the linkage between the animations he created and the sounds he used to drive the drawing process.

Many have tried, often in vain, to put into words the strange power of Cornell's boxes—toylike constructions in which playfulness and humor are anchored in profound melancholy. Update the scenario, and you realize that the art form that connects Smith and Cornell is the process of selection—something that Duchamp could have recognized in both of their works. When you see Smith's films, you realize that you've combed through the voluminous diaries that he kept throughout his life in search of his own dreams. What you find are brief flashes of images and short, enigmatic narratives of illumination—the drawn equivalent of Cornell boxes, or the anthology of folk music that was Smith's gift to American civilization.

Antonin Artaud, *The Cabinet of Dr. Caligari,* Picasso's bricolage works, Duchamp's anemic cinema, Oskar Fischinger's musical animations—the connections between Smith's work and art history are voluminous. I'm just presenting them as musical slot machine, something that, like William S. Burrough's chance-process writing, creates a different way of seeing the world. Once you've seen Smith's work, you never look at the world the same way again. Think of his 1952 *Anthology of American Folk*

*Music* as the starting point for his film concepts, and the connection becomes even more clear.

The *Anthology* was a watershed moment in America precisely because it echoed the invisible museum of modern culture through the voices of the people we always think of as at the edge of the American dream. The process of the *Anthology* was parallel to the way Harry edited his films— it was a personal vision filtered through a collection of media. Check the flow: Selections were culled from his amassed personal collection of 78 rpm records, picked for their commercial and artistic appeal within a set period of time, 1927 to 1932. Smith chose those particular years as boundaries since, as he stated himself, "1927, when electronic recording made possible accurate music reproduction, and 1932, when the Depression halted folk music sales."

Smith was an Omni-American: He was an archivist, ethnomusicologist, student of anthropology, record collector, experimental filmmaker, artist, bohemian, and Kabbalist. People who know him as a filmmaker often do not know of his *Anthology of American Folk Music*; folk enthusiasts often do not know he was "the greatest living magician," according to Kenneth Anger.

I just hope that we can remember him from every aspect of his varied and dynamic life, and his films are just as much a portal into the realms of his imagination as his record collection was. I like to think of him as America's original underground DJ. He's been an inspiration for me for many years, and I hope that his work will bring more people into the world that he dreamed about: An America as dynamic and diverse as the records he loved to share with everyone when his films played. With his films, as with his *Anthology*, Smith's spirit of generosity was unrelenting—he wanted people to know about the rare dreams he felt waited at the edge of the American imagination.

# XENOLINGUISTICS I: ASPECTS OF ALIEN ART

## Diana Reed Slattery

*Xenolinguistics: the scientific study of languages of non-human intelligences. Publications in this field tend to be speculative as few people have made the claim to have understood an alien language, at least not reliably.*

—WIKIUNIVERSITY

### HALLUCINATIONS AS ALIEN ART

The key to this discussion is a conceit of the extraordinary vision-producing ability unleashed in consciousness by psychedelics, as alien art: aesthetic productions of an unknown, hence alien, source. Whether the alien is an unknown (normally unconscious) aspect of the Self, an Other, or a blended configuration of Self and Other, can be held in abeyance as part of the high strangeness of the experience. Alien art is construed as an epistemological strategy of the Other in the psychedelic sphere for knowledge acquisition and transmission. This view is in sharp contrast to the notion of hallucinations as mechanically generated "form constants," abstract geometries with no semantic dimension per se.[1] It is closer to the narrative and highly significant (for the experiencing individual) first-person reports in Hebrew University professor Benny Shanon's ayahuasca phenomenology.[2]

These aspects of alien art describe features of the visual field that can simultaneously involve cognitive processes accompanied by vivid feeling states; bodily sensations (or lack thereof); and the synaesthetic involvement of other senses. Alien art begins with conditions of extended perception, an ascending scale of effects from the sensory amplifications of cannabis and hashish through the full-scale wraparound realities of high-dose sessions of DMT, psilocybin mushrooms, and LSD. These visionary states and content are frequently experienced as going beyond the pleasures of "great visuals" or "psychedelic eye candy" to their rhetorical and noetic function, with aesthetics and visual languages employed to deliver a teaching, an insight, a revelation or prophecy, or the sought answer to a problem. It is this signifying and hence, in the most basic sense, linguistic aspect of the psychedelic experience that I am calling Xenolinguistics.

### THE ALIEN DIMENSION IN PSYCHEDELIC EXPERIENCE

The mythologem of the alien encounter—UFOs; abduction scenarios; prophetic channelings; generations of Star Trek; and cult religions such as Heaven's Gate and the Raelian dispensation—have haunted the cultural fringe since the mid-twentieth century brought the first sightings of lights in the sky. These real-time ingressions of alien novelty were preceded by decades of science fiction speculations. Xenolinguistics—the search for, creation, and study of alien languages—has strong connections to science fiction and fantasy, and to the activity of constructing languages, represented by a small but highly communicative subculture of "con-langers."

Xenolinguistics connects to the scientifically framed SETI discourse on interstellar messaging,[3] and appears as a theme in the literature of psychedelic self-exploration, particularly in the work of Terence and Dennis McKenna.[4] John Lilly's work in interspecies communication with dolphins led to his inclusion in the first SETI meeting about interstellar messaging and the search for intelligent life in the cosmos. Lilly went further with his researches by combining his technology of sensory isolation tanks with the technology of psychedelic psychopharmacology. Both his methods and his findings placed him outside the pale of institutionally approved science, especially as he reported extensive communication with extraterrestrial intelligence via the Earth Coincidence Control Office (E.C.C.O.) and described new forms of linguistic activity in the psychedelic sphere.[5] The other major outlaw scientist of the psychedelic sphere, Timothy Leary, received his own extraterrestrial download, The Starseed Transmission, while in solitary confinement in Folsom Prison.

The psychedelic sphere is reported by practicing shamans, mainstream and outlaw scientists, and psychedelic self-explorers to be populated by communicating entities. Horace Beach's 1996 dissertation, "Listening for the Logos: A Study of Reports of Audible Voices at High Doses of Psilocybin,"[6] finds that of a sample of 128 participants (with experience with psilocybin), better than a third experienced communications with a perceived voice. The DMT (dimethyltryptamine) archives at the Vaults of Erowid,[7] a database of psychedelic information, have many reports of encounters with entities while in the tryptamine trance, some of which include reports of alien language.[8] The literature of shamanism contains pantheons of helpful and malign spirits, guides, allies, gods and demons, angels, extraterrestrials, and ancestors.[9, 10] Within these persistent experiences of encounters with entities can be found reports of new forms of language deployed in these contacts with the Other, and a complex of related notions about language, consciousness, and reality.

There is an aspect of each of these perspectives on alien language in my own work: a fictional, constructed language within a story world; the SETI discourse; and contact and communication with the Other in psychedelic self-exploration. I will focus on the role of psychedelic self-exploration which resulted in the creation and explication of an alien language, Glide, through a novel The Maze Game,[11] academic research,[12] and the development of interactive software as writing instruments for this visual language.[13, 14]

Xenolinguistics, in my usage, is the study of language and linguistic phenomena in the psychedelic sphere. Xenolinguistics gives a word to this effort to create a first assemblage of local knowledges, gathered from first-person reports, as from the logbooks of early navigators, about these phenomena. The local knowledges I am interested in are those of the xenolinguists, where the focus, fascination, and subsequent interpretations circle around languagem—different capacities of language from what we call "natural" language. Xenolinguistics reveals forms of language and theories about language itself, and its functioning in the brain/mind, in culture, and in evolutionary processes, both genetic and cultural.

Stanley Krippner reports in 1970 on a variety of distortions of natural language use under the influence of psychedelics, with instances given of both increased and decreased functioning.[15] Roland Fisher studied the effects of psilocybin on handwriting; his experiments had the participants copying passages of writing while under the influence; the writing becomes larger, rounder, more fluid.[16] Henry Munn in his writings on curandera Maria Sabina speaks of heightened eloquence, and of the evolution of writing under the influence of psilocybin:

> Language is an ecstatic activity of signification. Intoxicated by the mushrooms, the fluency, the ease, the aptness of expression one becomes capable of are such that one is astounded by the words that issue forth from the contact of the intention of articulation with the matter of experience. At times it is as if one were being told what to say, for the words leap to mind, one after another, of themselves without having to be searched for: a phenomenon similar to the automatic dictation of the surrealists except that here the flow of consciousness, rather than being

disconnected, tends to be coherent: a rational enunciation of meanings. Message fields of communication with the world, others, and one's self are disclosed by the mushrooms. The spontaneity they liberate is not only perceptual, but linguistic, the spontaneity of speech, of fervent, lucid discourse, of the logos in activity. For the shaman, it is as if existence were uttering itself through him.[17]

This vision of language as a universal ecstatic form of signification, of its source in the Other ("automatic" writing; the mythologies of language origin), and of eloquence that expresses itself visually in a bootstrapping move into new forms of language is a particular feature of the psilocybin trance. Munn describes this process as it is experienced in Mexican cultures:

The ancient Mexicans were the only Indians of all the Americas to invent a highly developed system of writing: a pictographic one. Theirs were the only Amerindian civilizations in which books played an important role. One of the reasons may be because they were a people who used psilocybin, a medicine for the mind given them by their earth with the unique power of activating the configurative activity of human signification. On the mushrooms, one sees walls covered with a fine tracery of lines projected before the eyes. It is as if the night were imprinted with signs like glyphs. In these conditions, if one takes up a brush, dips it into paint, and begins to draw, it is as if the hand were animated by an extraordinary ideoplastic ability.

Instead of saying that God speaks through the wise man, the ancient Mexicans said that life paints through him, in other words writes, since for them to write was to paint: the imagination in an act constitutive of images. 'In you he lives / in you he is painting / invents / the Giver of Life / Chichimeca Prince, Nezahualcoyotl.' Where we would expect them to refer to the voice, they say write. 'On the mat of flowers / you paint your song, your word / Prince Nezahualcoyotl / In painting is your

heart / with flowers of all colors / you paint your song, your word / Prince
Nezahualcoyotl.—Maria Sabina, curandera.[18]

One of the major themes of Terence McKenna's lifework is the explication of the linguistic phenomena released in the tryptamine trance,
and his speculations on the relationship of this phenomenon to the cultural evolution of the human species. For McKenna, language is fundamental to reality and its construction.

> Reality is truly made up of language and of linguistic structures that you
> carry, unbeknownst to yourself, in your mind, and which, under the in-
> fluence of psilocybin, begin to dissolve and allow you to perceive beyond
> the speakable. The contours of the unspeakable begin to emerge into
> your perception and though you can't say much about the unspeakable,
> it has the power to color everything you do. You live with it; it is the in-
> voking of the Other. The Other can become the Self, and many forms of
> estrangement can be healed. This is why the term alien has these many
> connotations.[19]

The specific connection of new language and psilocybin is made:

> What does extraterrestrial communication have to do with this family of
> hallucinogenic compounds I wish to discuss? Simply this: that the unique
> presentational phenomenology of this family of compounds has been
> overlooked. Psilocybin, though rare, is the best known of these neglected
> substances. Psilocybin, in the minds of the uninformed public and in
> the eyes of the law, is lumped together with LSD and mescaline, when
> in fact each of these compounds is a phenomenologically defined uni-
> verse unto itself. Psilocybin and DMT invoke the Logos, although DMT
> is more intense and more brief in its action. This means that they work
> directly on the language centers, so that an important aspect of the ex-
> perience is the interior dialogue. As soon as one discovers this about psi-

locybin and about tryptamines, one must decide whether or not to enter into the dialogue and to try and make sense of the incoming signal.[20]

Observing the varied effects of tryptamines on language, McKenna developed a theory that it was the encounter of early humans with the mushroom that potentiated the development of language. Plant knowledge would be one of our earliest forms of expertise as hunter-gatherers, discovering not only foods from every part of plants (roots, stems, leaves, berries, nuts) but also their medicinal and mind-altering properties. The merit of this speculation is more easily accessed from within the experience itself. From this perspective, the development of computer graphics and animation raise the possibility that new forms of language, particularly visual language, are emerging in our culture.

## A FEW ASPECTS OF ALIEN ART

The perceptual events which I am calling alien art forms occur, by definition, under conditions of extended perception, a sliding scale of alterations from the commonly observed enhancement of music heard or produced under cannabis intoxication[21] to the high-speed, multidimensional visual linguistic constructions morphing at warp speed in the DMT flash, and the unfolding of epic historic tableau under ayahuasca.[22] They are characterized by a sense of high information content in a high-speed "download." Simon Powell describes this high information content as a function of moving to "higher" forms of language, especially symbolic language.

> The symbol embodies a whole set of relations or, to be more specific, it is the point where a huge web of psychological relations converge. To fully understand the symbol is to sense at once all of its relations to other objects of perceptual experience. In other words, visual symbols play a role in a psychological language. (Here, I again invoke the concept of language since language is essentially an information system not re-

stricted to words alone. Language, in the abstract way in which I refer to it, is a system of informational elements bearing definite relations with one another; hence a language of words, of molecules, of symbols, etc.)

Such universally powerful visionary symbols can be thought of as expressions in the dictionary of a "higher" language connected with the human psyche. What I mean by "higher" is that the visual elements in this language are far more rich in meaning and informational content than the words of our spoken language. Moreover, the direct perception of visionary symbols choreographed together in a movie-like fashion— as occurs in the entheogenic state—is to experience meaning in perhaps its purest, most informationally rich way. To partake of a visionary dialogue is to be overwhelmed by the direct apprehension of naked, unmuddled meaning, which arises as a consequence of the highly integrative informational processes liberated by shamanic compounds.[23]

The "unspeakability" or "ineffability" of psychedelic experience appears to be not only an expression of the inadequacy of natural language to express certain experiences, but basic to the nature of the specific linguistic vehicle. Natural language is simply too slow a software to carry the complexity, the simultaneity of multiple meanings, and the speed and quantity of cognitive connections among ideas and images flooding into a psychedelic mind-body state. These perceptions of increased velocity— of thought and of sensory data—seem related to the experience of time dilation in the psychedelic sphere. Time dilation is a function of cognitive and sensory speed and the quantity of information per unit of time: hyperconnectivity, hyperconductivity, and processor speed. When novelty approaches infinity, realities fly apart. Hence: Xenolinguistics.

Powell continues:

Such types of symbol can therefore be considered elements of a high language, a language not of the individual ego-driven mind but of the communicating Other. The symbols are amalgamated concentrations of information coming to life in a mind illuminated by visionary alkaloids. Or, to use Huxley's terminology, the informational forms are transmitted via the psilocybinetic brain. In either case, a Great Spirit, a sacred presence, or Gaian Other reveals itself as being no less than a tremendously vast system of confluential information flowing through the psychedelically enhanced neuronal hardware of the human cortex. As information 'struggles' to integrate, ever more coalescent forms emerge, and these are experienced as the felt presence of the Other actively communicating in a language of potent visual imagery. Information appears as if alive and intent upon self-organization.[24]

This passage points to the experience where psychedelically potentiated language and communicating Other appear to merge into a living language. McKenna's many descriptions of "self-transforming machine elves" and my own perception in altered states of Glide as a living language that teaches about itself as well as many other things seem to belong to similar narratives of experience. This perception of living language in motion and constant transformation takes the self-reflexive activity of using language to describe itself to a meta-level of function, where the language gains the self-reflective quality of consciousness, in communicating about itself—and just about anything else in the universe one may be wondering about.

This alien art of hallucinatory presentation of information is often accompanied by a set of qualities that extend baseline perception. These qualities can include deeper, richer, more varied, more subtle, and in some cases, new colors that make up the visual palette. The complexity and density of the informational field is in part accompanied by an increased amount of very fine cognitive detail and a concomitant shift in the amount of detail from the sensory systems. Attention, a primary function of consciousness, presents a panoply of aesthetic choices, shifting its qualities, in some cases toward an increased slipperiness (a hyperconductivity), sliding frictionlessly from one point of focus to another.

At other times, attention becomes the ability to focus in stillness, to hold an awareness not only of the object(s) of contemplation but of the awareness itself, a kind of "witness consciousness" or mindfulness that allows direct perception of the goings-on in one's mind. One becomes aware that attention can partake of qualities like touch—rough, focused, gentle, smooth, and/or erotic, and applied with various admixtures of emotion.

## LAYERING, TRANSPARENCY, IRIDESCENCE

Another visual/cognitive quality that emerges is the layering of visual imagery. This can appear accompanied by subtle and shifting degrees of transparency and iridescence, of soft flows combined with extremely precise, fine filamental structures and a sense of having X-ray vision and microscopic vision as controllable aspects of the visual field. Macroscopic visions of the structure of the cosmos at astronomical scales can also be presented to consciousness. Transparency becomes a metaphor for all manner of *seeing-through*, revealing in the combined sense of seductive veils and of revelation of a truth, a hide-and-seek God game of gnosis—now you see Me now You don't—of quest and question, a noetic dance in realms wholly outside our natural language's labels and cognitive ordering schemes.

The high-information content aspect of alien art is not a matter merely of quantity of information but can be imbued with qualities such as fecundity, a sense of an abundance of creativity in the flood of images and ideas, and often a prevailing mood, of playfulness, or numinosity, or strange juxtapositions of mood, such as sacred silliness or a combined cathedral and carnivalesque architecture, each mood generating a seemingly endless fount of aesthetic styles.

## PATCHWORKING

Patchworking describes a complex collage-like cognitive-visual process by which different, sometimes drastically diverse, bits of vision-knowledge begin to collect and arrange themselves into larger patterns that incorporate, recombine, and transform the meanings of the individual pieces. Quilt-making is such a process. The illustrated quilt brings together hundreds of diamond and triangular patches from discarded clothing, carefully recycled into a design that incorporates two- and three-dimensional visual aspects. The design shifts depending on whether you view the material within the hexagons as flat six-pointed stars, or as baby blocks (Necker cubes). In the baby-blocks view, one can see two different perspectives. Each perspective in turn recombines the order of the available patches. The surface, playing with these illusions, shifts and moves dynamically among dimensions, as the different views pop in and out of the visual field. A kaleidoscope, containing a handful of irregular bits and pieces of colored glass and other materials, constructs a complex, shifting, symmetrical, nonrepeating stained-glass window of colored light.

In my own session reports, I describe patchworking as making "harmonious compositions out of impossibly disparate items without breaking the narrative dream but rather expanding its inclusiveness."[25] Patchworking in altered states assists in "layering realities," and is "a practice to acclimate you to staying in multiple spaces that are incongruous, noncontiguous, seemingly dissonant." McKenna describes this patchworking aspect in *True Hallucinations,* which is the detailed account of the "experiment at La Chorrera," and the mutual inhabitation by Dennis and Terence McKenna of an interpenetrating altered state of consciousness that lasted several weeks brought on by the ingestion of psilocybin mushrooms.

> Occasionally I would seem to catch the mechanics of what was happening to us in action. Lines from half-forgotten movies and snippets of old science fiction, once consumed like popcorn, reappeared in collages of half-understood associations. Punch lines from old jokes and vaguely remembered dreams spiraled in a slow galaxy of interleaved memories and anticipations. From such experiences I concluded that whatever was

happening, part of it involved all the information that we had ever accumulated, down to the most trivial details. The overwhelming impression was that something possibly from outer space or from another dimension was contacting us. It was doing so through the peculiar means of using every thought in our heads to lead us into telepathically induced scenarios of extravagant imagining, or deep theoretical understandings, or in-depth scanning of strange times, places, and worlds. The source of this unearthly contact was the Stropharia cubensis and our experiment.[26]

Patchworking appears to be an aesthetic strategy whereby the Other, using the stored personal information, emotions, and memories of the individual, constructs new forms and configurations of knowledge about our existing reality, its past and future, and about other worlds and other realities with profoundly alien—different from baseline reality—content. This alien content: Vast machineries, strange energies, different time-space schemata, whole worlds operating on different physical principles, or our own world viewed from a profoundly different consciousness, reveals other rules of organization of worlds, such as underlying structures of reality based on games. Patchworking ecstatically rejoins that which has been dismembered, fragmented, or never connected in the first place in meaningful patterns. As such it shares a functional pattern with the shamanic initiatory experience of dismemberment and rebirth in a new recombinatory body which can travel between worlds and hold consciousness of multiple worlds at once.

## GLIDE AND LIVEGLIDE

My own work, the core of which was developed before the encounter with the McKennas' work, has the shape of an adjacent mythology: A narrative of language origin in psychedelic experience. Glide is an experiment in modeling a visual language whose signs move and morph. It originated in a work of speculative fiction, *The Maze Game* (Deep

Listening Press, 2003), as an evolutionary form of writing from 4,000 years in the future. Its myth of origin speaks of a transmission of the language to the Glides from the hallucinogenic pollen of the giant blue water lilies which they tended. I followed the traditional Glide path for learning the language: study and practice both at baseline mind-body states and cognitively and sensorially enhanced psychedelic states. Part of the learning involved building electronic writing instruments.[27] The colors and patterns applied to the transforming glyphs come from drawings, photos, and video by myself and others. LiveGlide is most at home in live performance in a domed environment, such as a planetarium, but can be shown as recordings on a flat-screen format as well.

*LiveGlide: 2D glyphs moving in three dimensions*

Interacting with this visual language—designing the software, then reading and writing with it, especially in altered states, as a noetic practice, has led to a constellation of ideas about the relationship between language, consciousness, and our perception and conception of reality. One cluster of ideas begins with the notion of the hallucination as alien art. It is in part a rhetorical notion that aesthetics is part of the impact of these novel states of consciousness and their contents. The communication with the Other, the entire noetic enterprise, is baited with beauty as part of its persuasive force. This led to the observation and delineation of techniques deployed by the Other in the communicative process in altered states, often hallucinatory.

As to the shifting faces and perceived identity of the Other, many notions have been forwarded. SF writer Philip K. Dick called the Other V.A.L.I.S.—Vast Active Living Intelligent System. John Lilly called it E.C.C.O.—Earth Coincidence Control Office. Terence McKenna called them self-transforming machine-elves, and has also experienced the alien Other as insect-like. I call them the Glides, and they are shape-shifters as well.

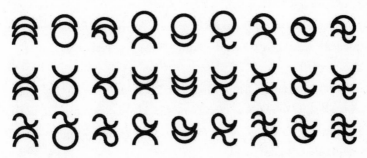

*2D Glide glyph*

But within these experiences, these definitions shift as explanations are sought. Are these others actually another aspect of the Self, buried in the unconscious? This may be more comforting than scenarios of actual alien contact, and is an assumption upon which arguments for mental disorder can be built, but it has little explanatory power, other than to reveal the grab-bag nature of the way the term *unconscious* is used to contain any number of mysteries of human nature. An open mind and a sense of humor may be the best provisional approach to such questions. As the Sundance Kid repeats the plaintive question, "Who are those guys anyway?" and Walt Kelly offers through Pogo, "We have met the enemy and he is us," we can contain the cosmic giggle bubbling up through such speculations at baseline. Yet in the experience itself, it can seem as Simon Powell puts it:

Such chemically inspired neuronal patterning is experienced as being so rich in symbology and meaning that for all intents and purposes it can be considered the result of a living, intelligent, and communicating agency made of information, an agency whose intent can become focused should the chemical conditions of the human cortex be so conducive. Information must indeed be in some sense alive.[28]

## NOTES

1. Heinrich Kluver, *Mescal and Mechanisms of Hallucinations* (Chicago: University of Chicago Press, 1969).

2. Benny Shanon, *The Antipodes of the Mind: Charting the Phenomenology of the Ayahuasca Experience* (Oxford: Oxford University Press, 2002).

3. SETI.

4. Terence McKenna and Dennis McKenna, *The Invisible Landscape: Mind, Hallucinogens, and the I Ching* (San Francisco: HarperSanFrancisco, 1993).

5. John Lilly, *The Center of the Cyclone: An Autobiography of Inner Space* (New York: Bantam Books, 1979).

6. Horace Beach, "Listening for the Logos: A Study of Reports of Audible Voices at High Doses of Psilocybin." Ph.D. dissertation, California School of Professional Psychology, Alameda, California, 1996.

7. Erowid, at http://www.erowid.org.

8. http://www.erowid.org/experiences/exp.php?ID=1859.

9. Shanon, *Antipodes of the Mind*.

10. Alex Polari de Alverga, *Forest of Visions: Ayahuasca, Amazonian Spirituality, and the Santo Daime Tradition* (Rochester, Vt.: Park Street Press, 1999).

11. Diana Reed Slattery, *The Maze Game* (Kingston, N.Y.: Deep Listening Publications, 2003).

12. http://mazerunner.wordpress.com.

13. http://www.academy.rpi.edu/glide.

14. http://web.mac.com/dianaslattery/iWeb/Eye/work-I.html.

15. Stanley Krippner, "The Effects of Psychedelic Experience on Language Functioning," in Bernard Aaronson and Humphry Osmond, eds., *Psychedelics: the Uses and Implication of Hallucinogenic Drugs* (New York: Doubleday & Company, 1970).

16. R. Fischer, T. Kappeler, P. Wisecup, and K. Thatcher, *Diseases of the Nervous System* 31, no. 91 (1970).

17. Henry Munn, "The Mushrooms of Language," in *Hallucinogens and Shamanism*, Michael J. Harner, ed. (Oxford: Oxford University Press, 1973).

18. Henry Munn, "Writing in the Imagination of an Oral Poet."

19. Will Noffke (1989): A conversation over saucers. *ReVision: A Journal of Consciousness and Transformation* 11 (3, Winter, Angels, aliens, and archetypes: Part one), pp. 23–30.

20. Terence McKenna, *The Archaic Revival: Speculations on Psychedelic Mushrooms, the Amazon, Virtual Reality, UFOs, Evolution, Shamanism, the Rebirth of the Goddess, and the End of History* (San Francisco: HarperSanFrancisco, 1992).

21. Charles T. Tart, *On Being Stoned: A Psychological Study of Marijuana Intoxication* (Palo Alto: Science and Behavior Books, 1971).

22. Shanon, *Antipodes of the Mind*.

23. Simon Powell, *The Psilocybin Solution*. Draft of an unpublished manuscript.

24. Ibid.

25. AD_05.03.27. (This is the filenaming convention I established for the research sessions. The AD stands for—playfully of course—Alien Downloads.)

26. Terence McKenna, *True Hallucinations: Being an Account of the Author's Extraordinary Adventures in the Devil's Paradise* (San Francisco: HarperSanFrancisco, 1993).

27. An early description of the Glide project including animations of the Glide glyphs.

28. Powell, *The Psilocybin Solution*.

# PAINT INTO WORDS:
## ALEX GREY INTERVIEW

*Michael Robinson*

*Alex Grey is a visionary artist specializing in spiritual and psychedelic art inspired by entheogens and mystical experiences. His oeuvre spans a variety of forms including performance art, installation art, sculpture, and painting. Grey is a member of the Integral Institute, sits on the board of advisors for the Center for Cognitive Liberty and Ethics, and is the chair of Wisdom University's Sacred Art Department. He and his wife, Allyson, are the co-founders of the Chapel of Sacred Mirrors (CoSM)—a not-for-profit institution supporting Visionary Culture in New York City.*

*MR: What is your personal mantra?*
AG: The great Tibetan teacher Namkhai Norbu introduced me to the Dzogchen Buddhist mantra "Ah," which one visualizes as a white letter in your heart and identifies with as primordial awareness outside of time and boundless in expanse. Also, I like the seed syllables of all the Buddhas, "Om Ah Hung," which you visualize in your head as a white Om, your neck as a red Ah, and your heart as a blue Hung. When synchronized with your breath as "vajra breathing" it helps affirm your own Buddha nature.

*What does the role of Artist mean to you?*
The Artist is a tiny reflection of the One Creative Spirit that generates, and is, all realities. God creates the cosmos with love. God is the creator

of the unfinished masterpiece, "Time-Space Continuum," which each of us helps cocreate. The artist faces the blank canvas and invents new realities, and in a very tiny microcosmic way, this reflects the macrocosm. The highest art aligns us with the "Divine Imagination," as Blake called it, and empowers our soul, catalyzing our path to becoming the greatest person we can be.

*What is the driving force behind your creativity?*
Love.

*What transformative experiences have influenced your life and how has that manifested in your work?*
My artwork is a way to share the transformative experiences I've had, so it would be better to look at my books or website to get a full idea, but I can say the coincidence of meeting my wife, Allyson, thirty-three years ago on the same night as my first LSD trip was the turning point for me. I would never have done the Sacred Mirrors without her to inspire them, and all the paintings celebrate our love and journey together.

*How long does it take you on average to complete a piece of work, and do you ever do several pieces simultaneously?*
I've been working for several years on the painting *Net of Being*; two years on the *World Soul* sculpture; and one year each on *Cosmic Christ* and *Nature of Mind*. Then there are paintings I do in one night, live painting events that last three to six hours. I try not to work on too many pieces at once, but that is part of the reason why *Net of Being* has taken so long.

*Why should people check out your work?*
Because my intention is to plant a seed of liberation in the mindstream of the viewer.

*How does your work affect Consciousness, and what are your views on the evolution of consciousness?*

I've noticed various stages of receptivity to my art. The work points to a mystic core of truth at the heart of all wisdom traditions and affirms an integral universal spirituality. If you have ever had a mystical experience you will understand my work immediately—if not, it may take a while. The human species is evolving and waking up to our self-destructive bender called materialism and the twentieth century. Human evolution will allow access to dormant visionary physiology that allows us to see clearly, to see more easily when people are lying, and to recognize the common heart of love behind all our dualistic thoughts.

# IS THAT A REAL REALITY, OR DID YOU MAKE IT UP YOURSELF?

*Steven Taylor*

*"Any musical innovation is full of danger to the whole State, and ought to be prohibited. So Damon tells me, and I can quite believe him; he says that when modes of music change, the fundamental laws of the State always change with them."*

—PLATO, *The Republic* IV

*"I'm glad to say my dreams came true, that I saw America changed by music."*

—HARRY SMITH[1]

When we were young first-year students in a music college in nowhere zen New Jersey, we were made to take certain classes designed to tune up our basic skills. One such class, "Rhythmics," took fifteen weeks to ensure that we could perform on sight a set of exercises from a snare drum rudiments book. (A teacher's lot is not a happy one.) As luck would have it, our rhythmics teacher was Joel Thome, a composer and conductor of great vision and awe-inspiring dedication. Joel took rhythm, and music in all its aspects, very seriously. He said that if we weren't practicing our instruments for at least five hours a day, we were wasting our time. He lectured spontaneously on the ontology of the now. He covered the blackboards with lists of books that we were to read, and recordings and scores that we were to study. He told me that a Baroque lute duet that I was then practicing was of world-historical importance. But the thing he said that has stuck with me the most was that music was going to save the world.

The idea that music can transform reality predates by many millennia the category "music" as we know it. Before art was understood as a phenomenon in itself apart from its ritual application (a relatively recent and culturally specific development), what we now call music was indistinguishable from magic. There is a wonderful, intoxicating romance that runs from Pythagorean harmonics through Platonic musical ethos to Boethius's codification of Greek tunings, then into the Renaissance cosmologies that prefigured modern astrophysics, on the idea that a change of music is a change of consciousness, culture, and even physical reality. And it's not just an old fantasy, a lot of serious thought and investigation has gone into it. For present purposes, I'd like to sketch a few lines that touch upon music and cultural change.

I began to understand the power of music to work change when, at the age of seven, I stood onstage at the Labour Club talent show in my Lancashire hometown, opened my mouth and sang a song, and the feeling in the room changed. The same thing happened a decade later in my American high school where in the space of three minutes I went from an immigrant misfit to something else entirely, purely on the power of song and the voice that I had inherited from my father, who'd had a reputation in the Manchester pubs as a good turn. Music, it seems, worked a shift in the various social milieus in which I found myself, and this sense of music as a kind of subtle magic expanded to encompass larger and larger contexts as time went on. Many wonderful music teachers contributed to this, and then a particular watershed moment came when another magician from a different field of music came to the college and I was asked to accompany him in performance.

Subsequently, over the course of two decades, I performed internationally with Allen Ginsberg in every imaginable type of venue, and through him I met and worked with other socially conscious artists—

those whom Amiri Baraka calls "culture workers"—whose work had played a part in the twentieth-century cultural shift that we now link back to "the sixties," but whose roots really go back through centuries of social change in which the arts played a role.

All of the artists with whom I worked, from the internationally famous to the virtually unknown, had in some way embraced the ancient idea that music held the power of transformation. Their politics, however, were not those of Plato. He favored oligarchy over democracy, and as can be seen from the above epigraph, advocated that the government ban new forms of music (by which he meant all of the arts) as a threat to the state. As my bandmate in the Fugs Tuli Kupferberg paraphrased it, "when the mode of the music changes, the walls of the city shake." If our culture, as seems to be the case, has in some ways retained Plato's sense of music's power to change society, the mid-twentieth-century push against the oligarchical tendencies in the state could be expected to champion new modes of music toward what Ginsberg called "democratization in the arts."[2]

Do new forms of artistic activity point to deep transformations in society? A lot of serious thought has gone into exploring this question, and much of it occurred in the twentieth century, when social scientists began to look closely at the relationship between particular forms of performance practice and the larger social forms in which they take place.

When computers first became widely available for social science research, anthropologists began compiling databases through which various culturally specific customs and practices could be sorted and compared. It became possible to see broad patterns of relationship, on a global scale, between economic activities, religious practices, social norms, and forms of art.

In the 1960s, musicologist Alan Lomax developed a research program for applying these methods to song (Cantometrics) and dance (Choreometrics). He concluded, perhaps not surprisingly, that the favored song and dance forms of a particular group tend to reflect the major economic activities of the group. For example, in societies where the majority of the food supply is provided by the solo male hunter, the favored dance and music forms tend to feature the solo male, and where much of the food is provided by women working in groups to gather or garden, showbiz tends to favor female choral song and group dance that looks like horticultural labor (bending, dipping, reaching, etc.).

This may seem rather obvious, but Lomax extended his conclusions to a level of detail relating, for example, the sound quality of the singing voice to customs regarding sex. He believed that a tight-throated vocal sound is heard in societies where sex is strictly regulated and largely unavailable outside of marriage, and that an open-throated sound is heard where sex is more readily available. (On this view, the sound of Gregorian chant would seem to support centuries of gossip about the secret life of Christian monastics.) Lomax's work has been criticized as biased, too selective of facts, and too sweeping, but relating art form to social form is not easily dismissed. It has been the case, for example, that U.S. country folk accustomed to manual farm labor in coordinated teams of men and women under the direction of a single male supervisor tended to go in for square dance.

What Lomax observed among what he called "traditional cultures" others have applied to modern societies. Ortiz Walton, for example, pointed out that during the era when the U.S. economy was based on large-scale manufacturing, the most prestigious form of musical ensemble consisted of a large group of musicians organized into departments (sections), each one with a supervisor (first chair), all led by a single manager-in-chief (conductor), and realizing a plan (score) provided by a designer (composer). He also pointed out that the workers in this musical ensemble punched a time clock and belonged to a union.

More recently, jazz historian Ted Gioia has connected the emergence of "free jazz" in the 1960s to the "freedom riders," "freedom schools," and larger freedom movement brought on by the civil rights activism of the same period—a breaking of old boundaries and the empowering of a multitude of voices exemplified on the bandstand by ensembles un-constrained by a composer, a song form, an arrangement or prescribed tonal framework, and the whole taking place without regard to the large recording corporations that have just caught on to the last wave of cool and want you to play by those rules.

So it seems that art forms tell us about how our society is organized, and new emergences in the arts can speak to us about changes in larger social structures, but they can also instruct us about the changing nature of our sense of self. Literary theorist Paul Oppenheimer has written that the invention of the sonnet in the thirteenth century—a form of poem tending to topics of personal reflection and meant to be read silently to oneself when verse had been spoken or sung aloud since ancient times—heralded the "birth of the modern mind." But which came first, the new poem or the new person? Is art merely illustrative of cultural conditions, or does it play a role in motivating cultural shift?

The anthropologist and performance theorist Victor Turner noted that music is universally associated with heightened states of conscious-ness, what he calls "communitas," a feeling of oneness that both affirms and erases everyday boundaries, which is invoked in "liminality" (from limen, threshold). Liminality refers to being between states, or in a tran-sitional phase. In a medical context, it can refer to being between life and death. For anthropologists, it indicates the in-between state an initiate experiences in a rite of passage from one social status or existential level to another. In the context of performance theory, it is a space of indeter-minacy and flux opened up in, for example, mass-participatory music/dance performance, where cultural shift can occur.

In a participatory performance, the personal boundaries of the indi-vidual are blurred and a collective emerges in which the individual is de-centered, becoming something larger or less fixed than her conventional social role. Music/dance suspends, for a time, our usual sense percep-tions, putting us into a state which, says Turner, "is almost everywhere held to be sacred or 'holy,' possibly because it transgresses or dissolves the norms that govern structure and institutionalized relationships and is accompanied by experiences of unprecedented potency."[3]

Turner based his research in settings where a whole village might participate in a music and dance event, but his observations could be applied to many contexts. I experienced this sense of reality shift most potently at various alternative rock venues in Europe and America in the '80s and '90s. It happened at my first ever show with the hardcore band False Prophets at CBGB. Having come from a more formal performance world, I was at first put off by the people sitting on the stage, in what I thought of as "my" space, seemingly unaware that musicians might need some room in which to work. But twenty seconds into the first number, all at once a wave went through the crowd and all of space exploded into what folklorist-alchemist Harry Smith (a regular at our early shows) later called "the most ecstatic dance I ever witnessed." I remember thinking at that first show, "this is what music is for."

Later, when my tours with the band yielded a book-in-progress that led to graduate studies in ethnomusicology, I discovered that Turner had accurately described the feeling I had experienced in the punk clubs, the sense of being in between, neither inside of nor outside of myself, in a place where individual identities are not lost in undifferentiated wholeness, but rather seem to phase in and out. This sense of a flux of personal boundary is not anxiety-producing. It is ecstatic, and as Turner notes, uniquely powerful. It is an electrical charge punctuated by the stunning visual effect of flashing colored lights and wild motion in a dense mass of bodies, rendering what I can only describe as a living, swirling, psychedelic impressionist landscape—Monet's garden at Giverny waving wildly in the real world and constituted in (by, as) incredibly powerful sound.

I also found in my studies that our experience of the anarchist collectives, particularly in Europe, that hosted many of our shows, seemed to reflect the scholarly literature on musical style reflecting social style. Among people who valued and practiced this music and dance, community business tended to be conducted in nonhierarchical group settings, what the organizers at the Flora Squat in Hamburg called "hard-core breakfast." Clearly, here was a style of music whose participants were committed to radical social shift.

Economist Jacques Attali has described one of the more radical theories of music and cultural change. He argues that when social shift is about to occur, it shows up first in the music. The more a particular style of music is prophetic of change, the more it will be regarded not as music but as noise. Upon reading Attali, I reflected how, when the Beatles first broke on the radio in my hometown, thirty miles from Liverpool, my parents (along with many elders and critics of the day) said, "that's not music, that's noise." Then, after the civil rights movement and the '60s counterculture produced advances in civil liberties and new demands for greater democratization of society, rock became the soundtrack of the mainstream, and today, the Beatles' music seems tuneful, benign, and not so far removed from the jazz-inspired songs of the previous generation. If we accept that music enables change by challenging norms, we can also see a connection between music and language that helps to give poetry its prophethood of change.

At a conference in the late 1960s, the linguist Roman Jakobson was asked: What makes a verbal message into a work of art? His answer is instructive. First, Jakobson described what he called six functions that are present in all verbal communications.

Most of our communications feature the denotive function, where the emphasis is on the speaker and a simple message, such as, "I'd like you to be at that meeting on Wednesday." Also common is the conative function, which delivers more or less the same information, but emphasizes the hearer, "Please be there." There will also be an emotive function, which will dominate when the hearer thinks, "Whoa, what was that about? It sure wasn't about that Wednesday meeting." The phatic function dominates when the communication is really about contact rather than content, as when Judy and I talk about the Wednesday meeting just so we can interact, but the denotive content is not at all important. Our talk might as well be about the man in the moon. The metalingual function dominates when the conversation is about the conversation, "What did you mean when you said . . . ?" And somewhere, usually buried under all this complex message mix, there is the sense that one is getting a message. This is the poetic function.

The poetic function doesn't dominate very often. We're usually too busy trying to do the ordinary business of everyday communication to be concerned about "Oh my God, I'm getting a communication." Ordinary speech tends to play down the poetic. But language art, Jakobson says, is distinguished from other types of speech by its emphasis on the poetic.

Jakobson associates this function with musical affects, pointing out that the impact of a simple phrase may be boosted by poetic constituents such as rhyme and rhythm, as in the slogan "I like Ike" or Julius Caesar's "Veni vidi, vici." But the poetic function doesn't just make a message memorable, it also works a split. It gives you a message and at the same time tells you that it is giving you a message. In effect, you're getting two messages. With "I like Ike," you're getting a simple message—"this guy voted for Eisenhower," and you are getting the more troubling message that words, what linguists call "signs," are strange things. The poetic function makes language appear strange.

At a certain level of emphasis on the poetic, the speaker and the hearer seem strange too. Writers such as James Joyce and Gertrude Stein made a point of repeatedly pushing this button. It is simply not possible to read *Finnegan's Wake* or *The Making of Americans* and get lost in the story. The story is hard to track, or may be nonexistent, because the language is more like music than speech. When the means of delivering the message calls attention to itself apart from what it appears to be saying, the listener can experience a sense of instability. When linguistic meaning goes into flux, it can invoke a liminal state.

Julia Kristeva, a linguist and psychoanalyst who has built on Jakobson's work, has written that music pluralizes meaning, and that poetic language is therefore threatening to conventional categories of self and state.

What we commonly call the self, or the "I," or "the subject" is, according to Kristeva, a subject-in-language. "I" she says, "is quite literally the subject of a sentence." We learn to organize our world according to preexisting categories (such as those described by personal pronouns—I, you, he, she, etc.) that are built into language. "I" is not a constant or particularly stable thing, rather it is instantiated at each thought or utterance of "I." It is a product of repetition, a kind of insistence on a certain category of meaning which is given by our culture. Music can invoke a condition prior to speech, before our enculturation into the "I" and its macroscosmic partner, the state. The poetic function troubles the conventional categories of self and state, and so is an agent for change.

> Poetic language . . . is an unsettling process—when not an outright destruction—of the identity of the meaning and speaking subject. . . . On that account, it accompanies crises within social structures and institutions—the moments of their mutation, evolution, revolution, or disarray.[4]

Another theorist linking art with a sense of strangeness and potential for change was Theodor Adorno, for whom art's revolutionary potential lay in its sense of being artificial and incomplete. The totalitarian impulse wants to portray its view of the world as real and complete—indisputable and immutable, all settled and sewed up. Conservatives are "realists"; liberals are "sadly deluded idealists." Systems that favor the rightist mind-set are portrayed as natural and correct, something to be conserved, not changed.

Art destabilizes this sense of certainty and fixity by saying, in effect, "Look at me, I'm an invented reality, I'm arbitrary, artificial, completely made up." By doing this, art hints that maybe the rest of our reality is arbitrary and made up too. And if reality is a made thing, then it can be made differently. Adorno's metaphor for art's incompleteness was Penelope's tapestry, which she wove all day and picked apart all night—the never-completed task she used as an excuse to put off her suitors. Art is never complete. The poem and the painting can be experienced a thousand times, differently each time. In this sense, art instantiates flux. This is why fascists try to control it or kill it.

As an artist, I take apart reality. It's not so much that the artist proposes an alternative reality, but rather that the abstract categories "I" and "reality" continually deconstruct in art. This doesn't mean that I don't take out the garbage, or feed "my" cat, or love "my" wife and child, and what some would call "my country." It means that I believe that the state of humanity is necessarily and always liminal. We are and always have been in transition, and the reality of change is visible and audible in the changing modes in which we have expressed our various concepts of self and society at various places and times.

If the world is to be "saved," it will happen in the realization of the necessity of change on all fronts, a shift from a paradoxical model that claims to be conservative while acting destructive, to one that recognizes that conservation can only occur in change. This is what music has to teach us. This is what Joel meant when he said that music would save the world.

### NOTES

1. In 1991, Harry Smith was given the Chairman's Certificate at the Grammy Awards ceremony. The presenter of the award noted that Smith's 1952 Folkways Records edition, *The Anthology of American Folk Music,* had inspired a generation of musicians, and that Harry had demonstrated a lifelong commitment to the idea that music can be a vehicle for social change.
2. Personal communication, 1993.

3. Victor Turner, *From Ritual to Theatre: The Human Seriousness of Play* (New York: Performing Arts Journal Publications, 1982), p. 128.

4. Julia Kristeva, "From One Identity to an Other" in *Desire in Language: A Semiotic Approach to Literature and Art* (New York: Columbia University Press, 1980), pp. 130; 124–25.

# MOBY CLICK

## David Rothenberg

A scientist I once spoke with said that my idea of learning the music of whales by playing along with them was the worst kind of egotistical folly. But recently I met a scientist with quite a different approach.

Michel Andre is one of the world's great experts on the acoustics of the sperm whale. He had long been vexed by the problem of how to tell one whale from another when recording a cacophony of clicking noises made by groups of these Moby Dick–type whales foraging underwater.

Andre heard layers of overlapping rhythms that made no sense to him. He remembered that European musicologists, when first visiting Africa, could not understand how the large groups of drummers in countries like Senegal could keep their own part going in the midst of so many other contradictory beats. In fact, these drummers have maintained their own signature rhythms in the din of the crowd since childhood. From these years of practice, each drummer knows how his pattern sings out in the spaces between all the other patterns. You must be an expert in the discernment of rhythms to successfully play this music.

With this in mind, Andre invited a Senegalese drummer, Arona N'Diaye Rose, to listen to his recording of a four-member unit of vocalizing sperm whales. The sabar master was immediately able to distinguish the beat of each of the four clicking whales from the others. He also believed that what the scientists heard as cacophony was actually an organized rhythm, based on a dominant beat coming from one of the whales, which Rose felt was analogous to the signature rhythms marking the social structure of an African tribe.

"I couldn't believe it," said Andre to me at a café in Barcelona last week, close to his laboratory. "We knew there were four whales because we took notes during the recording, but all we heard was a confusion of clicks. I asked Arona how he could tell there were four different animals. He said, 'I don't know how—but I know.'"

Since that listening session ten years ago, Andre has been seeking funding to continue his research. But his story is the same as I've heard from many scientists: It is invariably difficult to get support for descriptive work. Applied science, especially work toward managing whale "stocks" or populations, is always easier to fund. An approach that combines biology with music—for all its intercultural promise—is the hardest to support. Should the funders be research agencies or cultural exchange groups? Neither wants to touch anything so firmly on the charged border between one approach and the next.

Andre has been developing more mathematically rigorous, or "objective," ways of categorizing whale clicks. Building this system is a prelude to being able to study the relationship between clicks that come from different whales with greater accuracy. It would also be a method that takes account of the precise rhythm that goes on between the clicks, how they fit into a larger patterned context. This complexity is what Rose heard in the recordings, and Andre feels we should not ignore it.

"We need to study the whales' perception, not our own perception," he said. "Scientists are more used to counting, so we count. We have to learn from the insights of polyrhythmic drumming to perceive the value of rhythm at work in the clicks themselves." So at the same time as trying out wild ideas, like collaborating with drummers, Andre is also applying more sophisticated mathematics, for more rigorous results.

Andre believes it is the relationship between the clicks that is most important. He also thinks that "reading" the clicks as music might help figure out what's really happening. But it's going to take musicians, scientists, and whales spending a whole lot of time together to get meaningful results.

"Sure, it's subjective if a drummer just listens once," said Andre. "But if I ever get to work with Rose for several months at a time, learning his perception and his approach toward analyzing the combinations, then I hope to learn something of his rhythmic intelligence that has been passed down through many generations. Yet we still don't have the funding to bring a drum master onto our team. Rose was certainly onto something. He immediately sensed an organization to these whale sounds that none of us in my lab could hear."

Perhaps one day the powers that grant funds to make science possible might see fit to support musicians and scientists working together more deeply. But at the moment, only about ten people in the world have even the slightest understanding of the codelike tappings produced by these legendary, mammoth beasts. How will we figure them out? The problem with whale science is the same as the problem Brian Eno pointed out years ago regarding digital communication: "It's got to have more Africa in it."

# REALITY 2.0

## *Antonio Lopez*

Speaking to the Associated Press, John Fahey, president of the National Geographic Society, lamented, "Someone once said that war is God's way of teaching geography, but today, apparently war or even the threat of war cannot adequately teach geography. . . . More American young people can tell you where an island that the *Survivor* TV series came from is located than can identify Afghanistan or Iraq. Ironically, a TV show seems more real or at least more meaningful, interesting, or relevant than reality."

What Fahey failed to realize is that the real war is not far away, but in a contested realm where the border between unmediated and mediated space is increasingly less defined: our minds. It turns out that CBS's *Survivor* really is the territory when it comes to locating ourselves in an increasingly mediated world where surveillance and life on camera is more tangible than the media-sanitized war in Iraq. *Survivor* is literally a battleground where people are navigating identity that waivers between authentic and compartmentalized media personas.

The most pervasive change caused by technology for the individual is the sense that communication machines increasingly mediate our experiences. For example, studies show that teenagers are spending upwards of eight hours a day in media spaces, such as the Internet, text messaging, and watching television. Often these activities are happening simultaneously. To what extent does this change the individual, and how are these changes reflected in popular culture?

Forty years ago, in his lecture "Different Spaces," Michel Foucault predicted that people in advanced technological societies would increasingly migrate into an indeterminate space he called "heterotopia," which literally means "other place." This kind of realm is simultaneously real and imagined, such as the space where a phone call takes place, or within the informational sphere known as hyperspace or cyberspace. Foucault argued that before industrialization Western society was characterized by time; that is, we organized ourselves based on how we situated ourselves in relationship to time. Inventions like the telegraph have separated communication from transportation, thereby making information "timeless." Before the telegraph, mediated communications was based on how long they took to be delivered. Afterward, they became instantaneous, thus changing our "communication bias," as Harold Innis would call it, to one of space.

How are we coping with navigating this new borderless realm, which is not bound by geography but rather negotiated by our engagement with hybridized technology? Often the best way to understand societal shifts such as these is to look at popular culture. It's undeniable that so-called reality television has become the most popular kind of entertainment on television networks. This phenomenon is prevalent because it is the one arena that is actually grappling with how we define ourselves in mediated space. For instance, *Survivor,* the huge CBS hit, exemplifies how reality TV is coping with our identities as technologically mediated people. The show situates its contestants in a media constructed space with specific rules and parameters. The premise is that prescreened contestants are "shipwrecked," but as cultural interpreters, we must ask, from what? Let's suppose that the show's participants are refugees from the mediated world, and their job is to sort out the proper roles and behaviors necessary in order to "survive" a life in media space.

Our anxieties concerning this new technological space are justified. Post-9/11, our society has become increasingly one of surveillance, and the boundaries between our public and private selves are blurring. Likewise, people increasingly sport personal capturing devices, such a cell phones, PDAs, and digital cameras that make anyone vulnerable to having their image seized. As commerce moves more into the Internet, our identities are increasingly tied to our data patterns. The alarm of identity theft exemplifies perfectly this fear that the technological persona is subject to mobility and capture by unknown parties. Add to this mix the glamour our society attaches to the mediated persona: Everyone will be a star, as Andy Warhol predicted. People now get their three minutes of MySpace or YouTube fame, especially as the proliferation of reality TV, webcams, Internet gossip, and blogs make it easier to distribute our virtual personae across the globe. Given the contradictory attitudes concerning mediated space—i.e., we fear identity theft and surveillance, yet we want to be famous and hence publicly adored—it's no wonder we are confused.

The immense popularity of *Survivor* is due to its ability to situate average Americans in a fishbowl of mediated space in order to gauge and measure their reactions. After all, as Thomas De Zengotita argues in his book *Mediated*, negotiating technologically arbitrated space requires that we become performers, or "method actors." What we see in these shows is that people are constantly straddling the line between playing (hence performing) in a game, and believing they are in a real place. There is a continual question of whether or not fellow contestants are really friends, or are mere allies. In "reality" we have friendships, in a game (or mediated "fake" space) we have associations. Blurring the lines of game space, reality management euphemisms now creep further into our lives, with places like Wal-Mart, the ultimate of mediated retail environments, calling its workers "associates."

Reality TV programs and anxiety over the invasive presence of technology also raises the much larger question: What is the real geography of our times, if any? This was grappled with by the *Matrix* film series; its vast popularity has to be at least partially attributed to its discussion of the increasing inability to distinguish between real versus simulated reality, the assumption being that there is a distinction, i.e., there is such a thing as "real." Popular entertainment clearly reflects our society's ambivalence and anxiety about whether we are living in an authentic world, or one merely mediated by technology. Either way, undeniably we have entered into a new technological sphere that alters our sense of place. For this reason it is good to keep an open mind about popular culture because in many ways it maps our deeper anxieties.

For example, the Sci-Fi Network's contemporary version of *Battlestar Galactica* presents a particularly interesting story that reflects our new quandary. The show's premise is that human-created technology, a race of robots called Cylons, goes to war against their creators by nuking their parent race and destroying their home worlds. As a consequence, the few human survivors drift in a centerless outer space in search of Earth, a future home that will give them a sense of place. They "jump" from sector to sector as if they are typing in galactic hypertext codes, traveling in clunky old aircraft-carrier-like reality bubbles through boundless space, much like us with our alphabetic literacy and industrial-age education zipping around the net in search of meaning and community. Meanwhile the newest Cylon models are indistinguishable from humans and are attempting to mate with them in order to create hybrids that will fulfill their desire to connect with God, who exists as an intellectual concept inside their computerized minds. Ironically, Cylon-engineered blood is a potent medicinal that can cure human cancer. The humanoid Cylons have many copies, like the multiple identities we now use in cyberspace; several have infiltrated the human space colonies, many of whom are unaware of their robotic origins. How the humans and Cylons learn to harmonize is not unlike *Survivor* participants attempting to balance their humanity with a life of mediation.

As TV programs cross migrate into convergence media, we see the traditional mass-media model breaking down. Not only are programs mobile between different formats and players, there is also fan interaction via the Web, video games, and other immersive features that have made new media more complex and interesting. For media activists, new media challenge our core assumptions about how media function, from the breakdown of the one-to-many communications model to the many-to-many form it is taking, to the disintegration of the world as viewed from print.

What we once took for granted—that a book is the basis of truth and perception—is challenged all around us. What many don't understand is how books are bound to Enlightenment thinking, that is, the concepts of nationalism, individualism, and privacy are specifically related to the rise of printing-press culture. Books took power away from kings and priests, but they also made us silent, isolated readers who abstract the world according print's form. A great visualization of this occurs in the last scene of Truffaut's *Fahrenheit 451*. In order to evade the wrath of the totalitarian thought police, the print-loving rebels choose to memorize one book each in order to save humanity's literary heritage. In the end we see a group of disconnected people wandering through the forest reciting books to themselves without interacting with each other. The "book people" look decidedly unhappy (though I think this was the opposite of Truffaut's intent; I think he just translated a morose worldview into his film). Print also biases our perception to see the world as concrete and divisible into discreet pieces (consider how the page is laid out with its neat columns and letters breaking every sound into bits of information). If print is solid and concrete, new media is liquid. Like it or not, Aquarius, with knowledge flowing like water out of his jar, is an apt figure for our times.

Further pop-culture evidence of the changing reality landscape was demonstrated by a recent iPhone print ad featured in *National Geographic,* which shows a strobed finger navigating a Google map on the phone's touch-sensitive interface. As an unmistakable allusion to Michelangelo's "Creation of Man" that famously depicts Adam's finger reaching for God, this could mean three things: Either God is the networked universe to which the iPhone is a portal (hence all is God), the iPhone is God, or the iPhone is the engineered bridge between the known space of the Cartesian domain to the emergent one of the networked economy. This would complete the circuit started by the Renaissance in which God's love is delivered through the fingertip to humans—but now humans can distribute it equally, and return it. The other explanations are probably simultaneously true as well, a conundrum for a traditional media literacy reading that solicits one truth. Because the Renaissance began the psychological descent into humanism, which replaced the medieval world emplaced by God with one shaped by human perception, now humanism is being replaced by "cyborgism." I take cyborg to be a neutral term here, simply meaning that we are hybrids with the technology into which our minds and bodies are networked. In this ad, fingers touch a screen, drawing us into the in-between-not-here-nor-there acoustic realm of heterotopia. This ad can be a useful ecological metaphor because it visually demonstrates Gregory Bateson's formula that we are human-plus-environment. What he means is that because the environment sustains our bodies, it therefore cannot be excluded from our definition of ourselves. The cyborg is human-plus-electronic environment.

The iPhone ad further alters traditional notions of reality by adding one more factor into the equation: The multiple-exposure finger that dances on the interface like a Cubist painting. Recall that Cubism was the first Western art movement to incorporate a sense of simultaneity into painting, a reflection of the emerging art form of film and the new theory of relativity. This image instructs us to dip our finger into data liquid so we can connect with our world's vast rhizomatic network graphically represented by a Google map, thus putting the world at our command in the way that maps allow us to master geography. Because this is from *National Geographic,* the ad appeals to the explorer within us all but assures us that wherever we go we will be in control, despite the treachery of nonlinear space. Additionally, iPhone has eliminated the limitations of a hardwired interface, it changes depending on the context of our input choices, revealing an emerging bias of contemporary culture: The tactile is replacing sight as the central sensory experience of our age. This is not to say that sight isn't a kind of "touching," but more and more our bodies are getting involved with new media, whether it is with multimedia rock concerts, joysticks, Wii controllers, or cell phones as they increasingly become body appendages. If you watch people talk on cell phones you never see them stand still. Often they pace in small circles, demonstrating how much our bodies are in fact engaged with communication. With the iPhone, "I think therefore I am" becomes "I touch therefore I am."

Ironically, the final kicker is that this ad is also a photograph, which represents the most codified product of linear perspective technology: the lens. So in one media sample we see multiple media techniques recycled by the inclusion of linear perspective, chiaroscuro lighting technique, Renaissance humanist philosophy, Cubism, Cartesian space (in the form of the map), hyperspace, tactile media, and networked communications. The iPhone forces us to grapple with our changing conceptions of space that go beyond maps and media objects. To contract a Sun Ra song, "Space Is the Place," we could say that much of our new media experience is a hybridized "splace."

Too bad Descartes didn't deploy more of his senses. Maybe our scientific revolutions would have had Earth as a partner rather than as a specimen reduced to a field of visual objects that can be condensed and cataloged into conquerable parts. For this reason, Reality 2.0 may be more than the death of the real, as Baudrillard would have us believe. With these changes to our spatiotemporal orientation we shouldn't abandon critical engagement, but perhaps view the new gods in our media mirror from a more agnostic approach. It may turn out that these new creatures, like the Cylons in *Battlestar Galactica*, are more biological than we suspected. After all, these doppelgängers are our electronic extensions. We just haven't figured out how to situate them on a cognitive map yet.

IV

SEX

# THE TESTICULAR AGE

## Charles Eisenstein

Thinking in a Taoist yin-yang framework, typically we would clas-
sify male as yang and female as yin. But in her 1993 book *Reuniting
Sex, Self, and Spirit,* Genia Haddon claims that this association is a product of our cultural gender biases, and not intrinsic masculine or feminine physiology. She describes a masculine Yin and feminine Yang that
our culture typically represses, ignores, or fails to cultivate. The result is
to make it difficult to be a complete man or woman in our society.

All beings desire to fulfill themselves and to move toward wholeness.
When the masculine Yin is underdeveloped, men in their search for
wholeness might seek it outside themselves, in a female partner, or they
may take on effeminate qualities themselves, or the repressed Yin might
occasionally burst out in an exaggerated form. The same goes for women
and their neglected or repressed Yang. But what, exactly, are these neglected masculine Yin and feminine Yang qualities?

Let's start with the masculine (I am a guy, after all). The masculine
Yang we are all familiar with. It is the phallic dimension, and its qualities
are what define masculinity in our culture: active, taking the initiative,
goal-oriented, linear, exploring, forging into new territory, impatient,
aggressive, rising above, taking charge, dominating, setting the pace,
strong, firm, erect, getting to the heart of the issue, adventuring, courageous. These are certainly male qualities, but they are not the qualities of
the complete man, because they do not reflect the other defining feature
of male anatomy: the testicles.

The testicles, lying quiet underneath the penis, represent the masculine Yin. The testicles are the generative reservoirs of the seed, the life-essence. Unlike the penis, which is given to occasional action, the testicles' function of producing, storing, and conserving harks to male Yin qualities like patience, steadfastness, supportiveness, solidity, stability, reliability, and resourcefulness.

The feminine Yin we are again familiar with. It is embodied in the qualities of the receptive vagina and the nurturing womb: passive, accommodating, receptive, inclusive, welcoming, submissive, nourishing, and trusting. Our culture has equated these qualities with femininity, but there is much more to femininity than that. The feminine Yang has been left out.

The feminine Yang is embodied in that other important function of the womb: to give birth. Birth (and menstruation) show us feminine qualities that our culture denigrates or ignores, which Haddon groups under the descriptor "exertive"—literally, "pushing out." These include pushing forward, transformation, bringing forth the new, urging forward, propelling, dissolving the old (as in menstruation), forceful, bearing down, demanding, assertive, active in emergency, acting in concert with natural forces, harnessing the energies of the moment. Haddon explains the difference between the feminine and masculine Yang as follows: Both are assertive, but while the phallic Yang is goal-oriented, the feminine Yang acts from a field of reference. One is forging *toward*, the other is birthing *from*.

Male or female, all of us embody all four of these qualities to some extent. For several thousand years though, it has been the masculine Yang and feminine Yin that have dominated our understanding of what it is to be a man or a woman. They have also created the civilization we know today. I have explained in my book, *The Ascent of Humanity*, how we are on the cusp of a civilizational transition greater than the fall of one civilization and the rise of the next, but to a whole different *kind* of civilization. One way of understanding this shift is that we are moving toward an age in which the masculine Yin and the feminine Yang will be in ascendancy.

Notice how deeply our programming of male-Yang dominance reaches. Even by speaking we tend to reinforce it. I just said that the masculine Yin and feminine Yang will be in *ascendancy*. Think about that word and what it implies.

My book's cover artwork, Pieter Breugel's *Tower of Babel*, hints at the inevitability of this transition. The Tower, obviously a phallic image, embodies the ambitions and limitations of the phallic program to attain heaven. Its upward thrust cannot go on indefinitely. Part of the painter's genius was to portray the hubris and absurdity of the builders' ambitions. Their project is obviously doomed, no more plausible than the aroused male desire to have sex forever. He can only reach a certain height, and then a period of regeneration is needed—you might call it a testicular age.

So it is with our civilization's millennia-long thrust to reach ever higher, ever deeper, to forge into new realms, to conquer every frontier. We have reached unimaginable heights indeed, but all around us we see the base of the Tower crumbling, as one crisis after another besets us. The upward thrusting is nearly exhausted. We are seeing in these few decades its highest climax.

The vast womb of mother nature and mother culture has long nourished our growth, but now we are growing up against its limits. Whether in a body or on a planet, this is what triggers birth. We are rapidly entering a state of emergency. It is here that the feminine Yang takes over, bearing down and pushing us forward according to a spontaneous and irresistible rhythm into a new world. We can no more imagine what this world will be like than a fetus can imagine the world outside the womb.

Just as the feminine Yin has complemented the male Yang for the last few millennia, when the female Yang qualities come to the fore in coming centuries, it will be the masculine Yin that supports and sustains them. Already we begin to perceive the necessity of these testicular quali-

ties of conservation, regeneration, patience, forbearance, and steadfastness. As the collective Female of humanity and the planet bear down in
this emergency to birth us into the future, the collective Male will be at
hand, calm, steadfast, solid, and reassuring. These will be the traits that
come to define masculinity, while the phallic traits will retreat for a while
to a lesser role.

During this birthing, humanity will experience a life-and-death journey just to survive. When we are born into that new world, we will realize that our species is just in its infancy. This process is beginning in
earnest in our lifetimes, and it may take centuries to complete. I do not
know the specifics, but in my heart I sense the coming of a more beautiful world. I hope in my lifetime to see its outlines coming into focus.
Sometimes I think I even see its light beckoning. Do you?

# TRANSFORMING REPRESSION OF THE DIVINE FEMININE

*Wahkeena Sitka Tidepool Ripple*

A gentleman came to see me some time ago. He was carrying many wounds around his sexuality, related to his adolescent use of pornography. Because he held so much anger toward his father, due to the emotional charge of that relationship, he expressed it while masturbating to pornography. As he grew into an adult, his entire relationship to sexuality was expressed as an act of aggression, the releasing of his pent-up negative energy; he was never able to merge his heart with his sexual energy. He acted out his aggression with women he held in low esteem, women who he found easy to judge, always magnetizing himself to women who had self-esteem and unresolved abuse issues. At the same time, he was never able to be present with them. He often disassociated from them in a porn fantasy.

He never sensually embraced women. He was unable to be present with them in the body, loving them or worshipping their juicy feminine shakti. With the women he loved and held in a strong heart connection, he was unable to cultivate sexual energy or desire. It was this split, this huge emotional wound, that he desperately longed to release, to transform. So he came to see me.

I'm a tantric bodyworker. He left a mind-blown man. He'd never been so fully present in his body during a sexual experience in his entire life. Indeed, he had his very first full-body orgasm. He asked for help, he stated his intention for transformation, and received what he asked for because he was clear about what he wanted.

Our society is finally pulling its head out of the sand, letting go of its denial. Many of us are looking for transformation, rejecting the global catastrophe that threatens us in favor of the vision of a harmonized global village. But we've denied so many pervasive problems for so long, now many of us feel hopeless about the global situation, certain that we will see Armageddon, World War III, complete economic collapse, or the end of time as touted by (mis)interpretations of the Mayan calendar system.

Those of us awakening to the global situation are calling for transformation. But at the same time we fear the exciting potential this desired transformation will release in us. The change that must take place needs to occur within each individual. The barometer of this transformation's success will be how each of us responds personally to events that transform our lives from the comfortable and known to the ineffable and unknown.

The publication of the essay "Can Sex Work Be Shamanic?" in *Alternatives* last year changed my life profoundly and dramatically, in ways I never imagined. It began as an innocent endeavor. I never considered my own transformation that might ensue as a result of publishing it. I simply felt driven to express something, and was glad to be offered the opportunity to present ideas and experiences I felt could contribute to the evolution of consciousness, which is ultimately all I care about. I had finished a two-hour Thai massage with Peter, the editor of *Alternatives*, on the last day of my Thai training at Breitenbush Hot Springs, and he asked about my background. Peter felt I had a special energy. In the conversation that followed I opened up about the Tantric work I do. He offered me an opportunity to publish an essay, and so was born "Can Sex Work Be Shamanic?"

Truth be told, I'd been asking that question for years. The essence of the essay belies the deeper unspoken question: "Can Sex Be Shamanic?"

There is latent potential within each of us that is held in the field of our sexuality, and this potential often lays dormant and unawakened. Each of us has the ability to experience sex as union, an ecstatic full-body vibration of love. You can connect deeply, psychically with your partner, meditating simultaneously on profound physical ecstasy as well as the energy, always staying present, staying connected in the heart space, staying clear and in the flow of juicy yummy bliss. Down this path lies the potential for sexuality to awaken the kundalini and shift consciousness, awakening the visionary potential of multidimensional third-eye activation. Ultimately, this path leads to the opportunity to experience the deep feeling of transpersonal sex, where we're not making love with the personality of our partner, but with the divine source—"God" or "Goddess"—as we begin to channel our divine energies while in the heightened sexual state.

I believe sex can be a transcendental, holy union. Indeed, this has been in my experience. Those who know firsthand the massive floods of energy moving through the body, and the subsequent transformation of consciousness from "mundane" to "awakened ecstatic," need not question the opportunity that exists, even though most people are unaware of and unavailable for this level of freedom and bliss.

But to return to the massive shifts that happened to me after the publication of that article, first came a lot of attention, more attention than I knew how to deal with. I received more e-mails and requests for meetings than I knew how to handle. So I caved in, dropped off, and focused on my personal life. Then a documentary filmmaker asked to work with me about the topics I discussed.

But the ultimate bomb hit two months after the essay was published: My landlord gave me an eviction notice. He'd discovered my work, my websites, my essay. He handed me an envelope filled with my writings and said I was "flying above the radar," not being discreet enough. I was given three weeks to move out of my cozy nest, the home I worked so hard to create, the massage temple space I worked so hard to cultivate. It was heartbreaking. I'd lived there for only eight months, following nine months of living out of a backpack and traveling around Guatemala, Mexico, and California—all I wanted was "home" that entire time. An intense sadness crushed me completely and I grieved for days. But before the grief set in, my response to the eviction notice was total calm, knowing that this was divine guidance and that the spirits of the universe were communicating with me through this experience. They were instigating more transformation for me. It made perfect sense.

The timing of the eviction was also ironic. The two previous months were among the happiest periods of my life. This had nothing to do with the essay. Rather, it was due to the deepening of my ability to embody my spirit in my body that brought me the greatest happiness. For the first time in my life I felt like I was coming home. Not home as in a place. Not the kind of home that is created through materialistic acquisition. I was coming home into my self. I felt more present, more awake, clearer, more relaxed, more authentic, more fully plugged into my body. I did not feel disassociated from my body or my sexuality. In fact, I felt like my entire life had led to this time of finally gathering the various parts of my being and bringing them fully into the temple of my body. I felt whole.

Some amazing puzzle pieces aligned to make this happen. On Christmas day I received a phone call from a man who I'd been in love with for the previous year—the call helped me let go of his energy, which I'd held on to. I also began a daily smoothie regimen that included maca, cacao, acai, and vitamineral green. It transformed my digestive system, cleared me of all stagnancy and bloating. Once my digestive system cleared out, I released the energetic blockages I held in my lower belly (my second chakra), and released a lot of sexual energy. I returned to a largely vegetarian diet and made the most of my food. I received bodywork from a bodywork genius who tore me apart and helped me realize that I have hips. And most importantly I was cultivating a relationship with a gifted computer wizard, a genius for making phat psychedelic electronic dance beats. First we began cocreating music together, and then we began co-creating sexual energy together.

Becoming sexually activated with my musical compadre reawakened me to the power of sexual energy. In the heightened sexual energy state, when I am ramped up in ecstatic states of physical bliss, when the outer walls of my labia are hard, when my yoni is an enormous orb of hot heat glowing from my root sending pulsations of bliss through my whole body, when I am that present and that free to be insanely joyful—that is when I become my full self. All parts of my being are collected and brought into my body. I can feel an enormous shift within my subtle energy body, and it feels like I become a goddess. The Goddess steps fully into my body. I feel activated, alive, liberated, blissed out, and powerful.

One of the most amazing things about sexual energy and states of union is the experience of releasing every last bit of tension held in the body. When every single cell in the body is infused with high states of pleasure and the body is deeply relaxed, the body does not hold on to any more tension—and neither does the mind. When the body is open, the spirit walks in.

What I am referring to is at the center of Tantric practice. After much meditation upon Tantric wisdom, I realized that the intention or goal of Tantra is to create the merging of dualities. It evokes the union of heaven and earth, the union of masculine and feminine, the union of body and spirit. Through Tantra we can bridge dualities and emerge into a state of wholeness. The Tantric path is about the interweaving of our energies with the fabric of the whole, the available chi of the universe. This is a deep path that requires intense dedication so you can master an awareness of energy, and become energetically aware of the movement of energy in the body.

Many spiritual philosophies speak of the "higher self" as if we are by nature lower selves, disconnected from our higher enlightened selves. I think our psyches are deeply split: Split between our inner masculine and feminine, split between our conscious surface-level awareness and our ignored unconscious denial dream self, split between our divine selves and our "shadow" ego selves. To merge and marry these aspects of our selves is to create wholeness within ourselves. That is the goal, because this is how we can finally experience complete peace and clarity and joy and freedom.

For the past year I have been praying, sending my intention out to the universe, to fully embody my spirit in my body. I long to fully anchor my divine self and see my divine self as my true self, to not identify with the unconscious confusion and chaos self, but to identify with my conscious, fully aware authentic self. Because I want to see Heaven emerge on Earth, I feel I must anchor my heaven in my earth body. Clearly in no time in my life did this occur more profoundly than when I stepped fully into my sexual energy and meditated in deeply blissed-out energy.

Imagine what the world would look like if there were millions of women who were anchors of ecstatic bliss energy. Imagine if there were millions of women who were eschewing convention and walking their path toward their authentic nature, who let go of the norms of social conformity in favor of following their heart bliss. Imagine if the world was filled with juicy mamas who love to be loved, and love to get loved on. Imagine if millions of women were fully in their bodies, fully activated in their sensuality, fully released into their creative liberation. What kind of world would we be living in? We would live in a world where people would rather make love than cut down trees or enslave other people. We would live in a world where we wouldn't need prostitutes. We would live in a world where everybody was met and loved, cared for and nurtured, such that the only thing we would want is to make sure others are getting enough too. We would live in a world where the top priority is to take care of one another, because taking care of each other is taking care of the whole. We as individuals are a part of that whole.

But we don't live in that kind of world. And I don't need to remind you what kind of world we live in instead. I could list the environmental degradation, the wars in other people's homelands, the widespread deaths of bees, the corruption in the highest levels of our society. . . . We live in a world that has suppressed the feminine for thousands of years. Our culture killed all the witches, all the holders of esoteric magic and wise women who knew the plant secrets. Our culture put corsets and bustles on women and disfigured their spines so they couldn't relax into their bodies. And a woman needs to have a good, flowing, healthy, undulating spine in order to have sexual power.

Our culture told people to have sex within the confines of marriage. Our culture put high heels and makeup on all the women in order to disfigure their hips and hide them behind masks of inauthenticity. Our culture has not told women that they are beautiful for their authentic beauty. Instead we have a culture of women who get rhinoplasty and Botox. At the same time, other cultures have maimed and bound the feet of women to look like lotuses, and have dismembered the erogenous jewel of a woman's sexual body—the clitoris. Christianity and Islam, as well as other religions, have suppressed women and our sexuality. Many in our culture have been told to only be sexual with one person for procreation within the confines of marriage and to have sex with a sheet between bodies, with a hole in the sheet for the penis to go through, so no pleasure is possible.

How many clients have come to see me over the years that haven't made love with their wives for fifteen years? The numbers of men who haven't been lovingly met and haven't received intimate nurturing are astronomical, enormous. I once met a sad man who only a year before had separated from his wife of sixteen years, whom he hadn't had sex with since the day their first and only son was conceived within the first year of their marriage. His wife refused to display any signs of affection throughout their marriage. She wouldn't hold hands, hug, or cuddle. This is an extreme example, but it paints the picture of imbalance between genders that is sadly rampant. I feel that a culture of men who haven't been loved, met, or nurtured is a culture doomed to act out that extreme emotional wounding by cutting down trees, degrading the environment, creating wars, and enslaving others. I believe the root cause of all planetary and social imbalances is a result of sexual repression and gender imbalance.

Men have been just as suppressed from their authentic sexuality as women have. But we live in a culture where, generally speaking, women's power has been repressed by dominant masculinity.

There can be no more denying that the suppression of women has kept them from achieving their authentic nature and their sexual power. The tools of physical disfiguration—corsets, foot-binding, and clitoral modification—as well as the guilt-trip tools that dissuade the psyche from pursuing physical pleasure, have kept women from knowing their true power, from standing in their bodies as radiant, ecstatic, blissful beings of joy. I am not a feminist who is angry and vindictive about four thousand years of patriarchy; I do feel, however, that in today's society we don't need to do that anymore.

Many women are waking up to their authenticity, to their creative potential and divine, liberated selves. I know countless artists and witchy wise women who are creatrixes within this matrix. These are beautiful women who delve deep into their creativity, journeying with their art forms—painting, poetry, song, handmade clothing. These women journey and dance, and honor their bodies. These women nurture themselves, educate themselves about how to best take care of their health with healthy food and plant-based medicines. These women love one another and support their sisters, encouraging one another to grow and become more expansive and creative. This new wave of women is the embodied resurgence of the Divine Feminine on Planet Earth.

But the suppression of women is buried deep into our collective subconscious. Even though our culture has seen waves of women's liberation since the seventies, many women still don cloaks of disfiguration and sublimation. In my neck of reality—where my women friends are brilliant artists, juicy mamas making homemade bread and doing plant and sweat ceremonies, dancing ecstatically and going on healing retreats—I am in a bubble of empowered, powerful women. But I recently went to a Mormon church on Easter, and walked into a room of women giving their "testimony" about their "faith." The room was filled with women who didn't seem present or in their bodies. They didn't speak with conviction about their faith. They didn't share stories that expressed their hearts. Instead, they gave testimony to a belief system that they had been indoctrinated into, but which none of them seemed to deeply believe in. Their shoulders were rolled forward, they wore high heels and makeup and looked so uncomfortable in their bodies.

Over the centuries and throughout cultures, most suppression of women has been perpetuated by women themselves. It is the elder African women who dismember the clitoris of the young girls. It is the elder Chinese women who break the feet of young girls and wrap them in cloths. But we must not give in to bitterness or feel victimized about these injustices. Instead, we should realize that we can take our power back. If we want to live in a world that is whole and healthy, we must decide to become whole ourselves, because we are each facets of the whole. When you are a weak link in the circle of the whole, then you aren't doing your part to hold together the integrity of the whole. If we want to live in a world of balance, we need to reembody the Divine Feminine.

When divine, powerful, goddess women reach critical mass on Planet Earth, you know that big shift will happen. It will make more women want to step into their juicy, ecstatic, erotic, powerful, creative selves. The attraction becomes magnetic.

To all you women who don't know how to get from point A to point Z, but think the journey looks appealing and the end result even more appealing, all I can say is this: Be receptive to change. Become an agent of transformation. Do not hold on to what is not serving you.

Getting back to my own story of being evicted, this huge change that forced me out of my comfortable cozy nest in fact offered me six weeks of travel and spiritual pilgrimage. After my journey I moved into a home more beautiful and divinely magical than my old one. Often the doors of transformation take the form of something that seems horrible and heartbreaking at first. But when we surrender to the magic of what is, we make ourselves available for potent potentials of miraculous meetings.

One of my major realizations after the eviction and then hanging out with the Mormons is that we live in a culture that is absolutely afraid of sexual liberation. The suppression of sexuality is deeply ingrained in our collective consciousness. It is the repression of it that causes sexuality to be expressed in the forms of prostitution, strip clubs, and online porn. This happens because the men are hungry and need to be fed. We live in a culture that criminalizes whores, denies them recognition and visibility, and secretly tolerates hordes of them because society would go haywire if whores weren't available. At the same time, they are banished as shameful lepers by society.

But if women weren't suppressed in their bodies or their psyches and we were free to be powerful pleasure beings, if sexuality wasn't so deeply repressed and the life force love energy within each one of us so deeply malnourished, we wouldn't have any of this collective shame about owning our right to freely enjoy joy. We would step into ourselves, and we would step into one another, with gratitude for the gifts that each of us is to one another. We would step into our bodies with gratitude for our pleasure receptors. We would honor one another when we each nurture ourselves. Ultimately, by doing so, we would cocreate peace on Planet Earth—because the priorities would shift from war, corruption, media lies, and economic disparity to nurturing, feeding, and loving one another, supporting the achievement of our highest potentials, so we can contribute to the whole by nurturing ourselves.

# FINDING PEACE
## BETWEEN OUR SHEETS:
## TALKING WITH MARNIA ROBINSON

*Adam Elenbaas*

What if one of the largest problems facing human beings is something so simple and so subtle that it's looking us right in the face, sometimes two or three times a night?

*Peace Between the Sheets* author Marnia Robinson suggests that orgasm addiction might be the single-largest problem plaguing intimate, romantic relationships.

When I first read *Peace Between the Sheets* I felt angry. Certainly orgasms are beautiful, natural, and important to forging intimacy. How could they be the bane of my love life? I thought: *This writer must be religious.*

But as I read Marnia's book I was surprised to find that the science and the vast collection of mystical and ancient wisdom teachings surrounding the book's argument were very convincing. I also look around and see scary population rates, numbers that are rising exponentially each year, and a growing desire within my heart to have a healthy, long-lasting, and monogamous relationship.

Marnia admits that she and her husband are not religious, both enjoy orgasms, and feel no sexual guilt. They simply have strong convictions about this one idea: Orgasm addiction is an undercover problem, creating chaos between our sheets!

*AE: In your book, you talk a lot about why so many relationships struggle, and you are very specific. You think that orgasms are responsible, in large part, for our inability to truly, not just physically, "come together." Explain this. Aren't orgasms the best part of a sexual or romantic relationship? How could they be damaging?*

Marnia: It's not the climax that causes friction. An orgasm feels great, and if it were the end of the story, lovers would be able to do what comes naturally in the bedroom *and* live happily ever after. The problem is that orgasm—especially orgasm leading to sexual satiation (a feeling of "I'm definitely done!")—isn't an isolated event. It's the peak of a much longer *cycle*.

Sex happens in the brain. It's a complex sequence of neurochemical events even more than it is a genital event. (Masters and Johnson were just looking at genitals when they came up with the "arousal-plateau-climax-resolution" model.) I say "brain" because you can stick an electrode in someone's brain, or spinal cord, and produce the sensation of orgasm without ever touching his or her genitals.

Instead of an electrode, your body uses a surge of a neurochemical called dopamine to trigger the sensation of orgasm in the reward circuitry of your brain. Unfortunately it takes as long as two weeks for this deep part of the brain to return to homeostasis after such intense stimulation. While the precise mechanisms are not yet understood, the central player in this natural programmed "hangover" appears to be dopamine.

It's clear that dopamine levels drop after orgasm, and that another neurochemical, prolactin, surges (a sexual satiation signal) to keep dopamine in check. Receptors for testosterone rapidly decline in the reward circuitry, further inhibiting dopamine release.

One can view the orgasm cycle as similar to a drug or alcohol cycle because *it emanates from the same mechanism in the brain,* using the same neurochemical, dopamine. When anything—whether a substance (cocaine, too much sugar) or an activity (gambling, orgasm)—overstimulates your reward circuitry, it produces a high, followed by a period of recovery.

That recovery is, in a sense, a withdrawal. The difference between sex and drugs is that the orgasm "hangover" is so much a part of us, so natural and programmed, that it is hard to recognize—unless, of course, you escape the cycle entirely. It can make you feel uncharacteristically needy, irritable, anxious, depleted, or desperate for another orgasm.

To you it will seem that these traits are just part of your, or your partner's, normal personality. There is often a subconscious urge to do *something* to make yourself feel better. For example, you may reach for a drink, look at porn, curl up in front of a romantic movie with a tub of ice cream, or have an urge to feel your partner up. Your perception is subtly distorted, and it's natural for you to perceive each other as the source of your discomfort. "If only he would be more affectionate or supportive." "If only she would stop processing her feelings and just have sex."

Obviously, we don't all hit upon the same solution. Some people feel this withdrawal as a "needy hole" calling for comfort or attention. Some just feel it as a demanding urge for relief or temporary oblivion. Others are sure that they simply "need space." For some, the craving for another orgasm is stronger than ever—but it doesn't represent true libido. As the ancient Chinese Taoists observed, orgasm, and particularly "Ejaculation, although depleting physical reserves, has the opposite effect on sexual desire. After an immediate postcoital letdown, there is a rapid psychological rebound and an intensification of erotic interest" (*Art of the Bedchamber*, by Douglas Wile, State University of New York Press [1992]: p. 6).

In short, the way we currently manage our sexual energy could prove to be the common biological mechanism behind such diverse phenomena as the one-night stand, the sexless marriage, infidelity, and porn addiction. It contributes to the nearly universal experience that "the honeymoon never lasts longer than a year." It is why close friendships that bloom into love affairs so often turn sour. The culprit is the natural perception shifts that follow sexual satiation, and cause us to find each other less rewarding than before.

I believe this is a natural program, which affects all mammals in some form. Not one mammal or bird is completely *sexually* monogamous. Subconscious, neurochemical mating programs are the way Mother Nature pushes mammals apart. She wants you to fertilize in a passionate frenzy, bond temporarily, and then grow disillusioned and move on to your next partner.

To fool Mother Nature, you obviously have to do something different in the bedroom. This is why the Taoists, and others, recommended learning to make love in a way that doesn't trigger our subconscious mating program—or rather, triggers only the *attachment* part of it, not the *move on* part of it. We can make use of this natural attachment program, which bonds us to our children and parents, in our romances, too, by emphasizing generous affection, playfulness, gentle intercourse, and, of course, by avoiding orgasm. Results include greater harmony and well-being, and, remarkably, less sexual frustration.

*Would you consider your view to be purely scientific, then, or spiritual, or both?*
I believe that all great spiritual traditions call for seeing beyond our own projections of neediness or cravings, for overcoming unloving feelings, and for healing dual perception by perceiving our oneness with others. Therefore, this practice is ultimately a spiritual practice.

However, both my husband and I are not religious. We were fortunate to be raised by parents who believed sex was natural and guilt free, and we loved orgasm. It wasn't until we had both experienced significant health and relationship benefits that my husband, who teaches anatomy and physiology, began digging up the science that helps to explain how managing sex differently can do just what the ancient Taoists and others discovered it can do: reduce cravings, heal, and promote harmony.

*In what way is your research about orgasms different from tantric studies?*
"Tantra" encompasses many different practices, some of which emphasize orgasm, others of which call for transcending it, so it's not possible

to make this kind of comparison. What I'm proposing is definitely different from using each other to fire up sexual intensity to the point of altered awareness.

Here's a description from a friend describing the benefits from this gentler practice, which I think of as karezza (a name given to it by Alice Bunker Stockham, M.D., a century ago), or controlled intercourse:

> Arousal is very much present, and we are both highly motivated to ride these wonderful waves of energy and to ride them as long as we can. We are finding that these are not the waves that either of us have experienced before. Very full heart, and big belly feelings. It is as if we have moved over some threshold. Cuddling and non-goal-oriented touch raise me to a height where I have a dramatically new point of view. I feel like I have entered the flow.

*When you talk about orgasms, are you talking about the release of semen? And if so, then isn't it ok for women to climax but not men?*

Many esoteric sex texts speak in terms of "semen loss" as the problem with orgasm, but the real problem is overstimulation of the reward circuitry of the brain. This is why orgasm can set off subsequent mood swings in women, too. The *loss* idea is right on target, however. After dopamine soars into the red zone in the brain, the body reacts by lowering it below baseline levels. Too little dopamine (or too few receptors for dopamine) *feels* like "something is missing," as if an essential ingredient for happiness is gone. You can easily feel depleted or needy, whether you're male or female. The chief difference between the sexes is that, often, women feel more intense effects during the second week after orgasm, while men feel more intense effects during the days immediately following orgasm.

Interestingly, the ancient Taoists recorded that orgasm, menstruation, and childbirth are all depleting to women. It is primarily the tantric lore that focuses on semen loss, because the Brahmins equated semen with "spiritual light."

*If the best way to experience relational union is to withhold from orgasm, then why does it feel like our bodies are hardwired to go against what is in our best interest?*

There's a commonsense belief that if you do what your body evolved to do, it will lead to well-being and happiness. For example, most people would be healthier if they returned to a Paleolithic diet of whole foods and protein, without refined starches and sugars. By the same logic, if you're designed to pursue orgasm and multiple partners, shouldn't you be happiest if you manage your intimate life accordingly? Perhaps the man-made ideal of *committed relationships* is the problem.

This logic assumes that you're designed for your own benefit. In fact, evolution has hardwired you not for your individual welfare, but for your genes' success. What serves your genes? Lots of fertilization attempts and lots of different parents for your (more diverse) offspring. What serves *you* best? Close trusted companionship (an authentic bond) and lots of affectionate, generous touch. For example, HIV-positive patients survive longer when in relationships. Wounds heal twice as fast with companionship, as compared with isolation. In primates, the caregiving parent, male or female, lives longer. I could go on and on.

The bottom line is that our innate sexual appetite is not a reliable guide to greater well-being because sexual impulsiveness *naturally* leads in the direction of satiation—and even excess—followed by emotional alienation, and the erosion of emotional bonds. As my husband says, our subconscious mating program is working brilliantly; it just doesn't have our individual well-being at heart.

*Do you think that polyamory is in any way a misguided response to the difficulties of orgasm addiction?*

I think polyamory is a very logical solution to the fact that mammals are not monogamous. Hunter-gatherer societies are polyamorous. I also admire the efforts of many polyamorists to master compassionate communication and similar techniques to cope, as lovingly as possible, with the emotional fallout from sexual satiation. In addition, I am attracted to the "group hug," brother-sister feeling of all heart-based communities.

Personally, I still think close trusted companionship has more to offer. One reason is that it is easier to find a comfortable equilibrium for this other approach to sex within a stable partnership. New partners have to contend with a lot of thrilling, but unstable, honeymoon neurochemicals designed to lure those sperm to their fertile targets.

As for orgasm addiction, no, polyamory certainly doesn't offer a cure. Multiple partners and lots of orgasm can make sexual urges more demanding than ever because greater sexual satiation causes more intense cravings during the withdrawal period that follows. Unwittingly, someone with a sexual compulsion is using orgasm to self-medicate during the lows of the cycle—and setting off another cycle at the same time. The image of a hamster in a hamster wheel comes to mind.

A close friend who was very active in polyamory circles said he once thought polyamory offered a solution because he was too needy for any one partner. He figured the solution was to spread himself among many in hopes of meeting his needs. It didn't work, in part because it didn't address the compulsion that was fueling his neediness.

Compulsions aren't "bad," but they decrease your freedom and cloud your judgment, so as a spiritual matter they slow your evolution. Unfortunately, anyone who decides to move beyond a sexual compulsion has to go through an uncomfortable withdrawal period. The people with porn addiction who visit my website find that it takes a good six weeks of abstinence from orgasm to do this. Those with partners willing to engage in lots of affectionate, selfless contact during that time have a much easier time of it. At the end of that transition, people discover their true libido. They realize that their compulsive pattern was not their natural rhythm for orgasm.

*You say that we should refrain from orgasm, but you also say that things like "schedules" are a good idea. Give us an example of a sex schedule. Why is the*

*"sex schedule" a good idea, and doesn't this take the spontaneity away from a
healthy sex life? Isn't it good once in a while to be hot and heavy?*

My husband and I found that making love every night, even without orgasm, caused an uncomfortable buildup of sexual tension. As he said, he
felt like a car engine revving its motor all the time. By the same token, if
we didn't know for sure if we would be having intercourse or not on a
given night, he also tended to rev his engine . . . just in case.

The solution turned out to be surprisingly simple: Spend a night or
two between intercourse nights engaging in non-goal-oriented lovemaking, and schedule when we would have intercourse. On no-intercourse
nights we wallow in lots of eye-gazing and selfless, comforting nurturing
of each other.

By engaging in non-goal-oriented affection, you signal your subconscious that you want to deepen your mutual bond, by tapping into your
attachment, or bonding, programming. Such encounters have the added
benefit of making intercourse itself more fulfilling and less goal-oriented.
You can just *be* with each other. You don't have to *perform*. This makes
sex a very caring, yet carefree experience. Erections come and go, and
you can continue for as long as you like.

As for "hot and heavy," you should have orgasmic sex as often as you
want to feel a sense of alienation from your lover during the two weeks
following. Remember that the greater the buildup, the more intense the
feeling of satiation afterward . . . and the more powerful the subconscious signal you deliver to yourself that it is time to move on to a new
lover. Once you are back in balance, intercourse alone can meet your
true needs for connection; orgasm is actually superfluous. This is a key
tenet of the mystery of sacred sexuality; one that Mother Nature doesn't
want you to know.

That being said, anyone who practices karezza discovers that orgasm
occasionally happens, either while you're making love or sleeping. We
trust that our bodies have their reasons. What still intrigues us is the
power of these inadvertent orgasms to kick off the separation program,

albeit in somewhat milder forms. Having observed ourselves for seven years, we're really clear that we aren't interested in "going for" orgasm. We like the harmony, the easy, relaxed communication, and the profound sense of trust between us.

Each couple has to find their own way. Our one suggestion is to try a solid three weeks of non-goal-oriented affection, with some gentle, karezza in the third week, and *then* return to conventional orgasm—all with the same partner. Only in this way can you really make a sound choice about whether or not karezza has rewards. If you aren't consistent for a couple of weeks, the hangover from prior orgasms is still muddying your perception of your partner, so you won't see all the benefits.

*Do you see any correlations or analogies between addictive sexuality and other habits or behaviors in Western cultures?*

Dutch scientist Gert Holstege, who said that his brain scans of men ejaculating look like brain scans of people shooting heroin, once remarked that we are all addicted to sex. Orgasm is the most powerful (legal) buzz available to us. I believe that when we consciously move from compulsion to equilibrium in our sex lives, we strengthen our sense of inner wholeness. This decreases our vulnerability to *all* addictive activities and substances. Without the feelings of lack, uneasiness, and neediness that mysteriously show up after sexual satiation, we simply aren't as susceptible to manipulation of any kind, whether by advertisers, governments, or porn producers.

Within four months after my husband and I began this practice, his twelve-year addiction to alcohol was under his control. Within a year he was off Prozac and his chronic depression had lifted. I think our sexual cravings have a very powerful effect on our inner compass, our reward circuitry. With a working compass, we can steer in our true best interests. This may be why sexual mastery was considered a powerful spiritual path by the Taoists, the earliest Christians, and others throughout human history.

# GENDER EVOLUTION

### *Kal Cobalt*

"This is Kal," my friends introduced me when I was a kid. "She doesn't wear dresses." At the time, I assumed I was a tomboy. The majority of my friends were boys, and I enjoyed camping and playing outdoors for hours on end. At fifteen, I cut my hair short and continued my trend of boyish clothing. Sometimes, in the winter when a bulky coat obscured my curves, I was mistaken for a boy—something I found oddly thrilling.

Gender reassignment surgery didn't appeal to me because of the poor success rates, but if I could have snapped my fingers and become male, I would have. But I liked being female, too. After puberty, I reversed the gender quotient among my friends, and I found I preferred to deal with women in business transactions (a bit of gender bias that troubled me, then and now). I enjoyed dressing up from time to time, as long as I didn't aim for some sort of feminine extreme. In makeup too thick or heels too high, I did feel as if I were in drag (and not very convincing drag at that), but still, being in a female body appealed to me on several levels.

All of this left me even more confused: Was I, or was I not, male on the inside? I enjoyed writing gay male erotica and found myself incapable of writing erotica with female characters; there were no good literary words for the female anatomy, and my attempts seemed doomed to either read like *Hustler* or Harlequin, with nothing in between. I didn't hate my body, but sometimes wished I were a little more androgynous so I could better pass as male when I felt like doing so.

Then I entered the world of sexual partners, and my confusion was compounded. My first relationship was with a woman, and we often pretended we were both male. This did not bother us, and switching back and forth seemed natural. When that relationship ended, I found myself searching for a new partner but clueless as to how to attract the kind of people I was looking for. Binary orientations have established patterns of behavior and presentation that simplify identifying others: A lesbian with short hair who wears pants is likely to be recognized as lesbian by potential partners. What's the social behavior that signifies: "I don't care what gender you are, as long as you'll pretend I'm a boy every now and then?"

Along with my first lover, I had discovered the world of "slash"—stories written about established fictional male characters having relationships with one another. (Star Trek was the first series in which slash took hold; "slashers" imagined what a relationship between Kirk and Spock would look like.) Around 98 percent of those who write or read slash are women, and come from all points on the orientation spectrum. I have read beautiful tales of hot man-on-man action written by lesbians and been warmed by stories of romantic love between men penned by happily married heterosexual women with kids. As I came to realize just how big this community is, I understood that a surprisingly large segment of the population subverted gender roles one way or another. (Female authors of gay erotic fiction have been abundant and successful for decades, although gender roles have only recently become relaxed enough for some to publish under names that are not male pseudonyms.)

As I gathered more information about those on the cutting edge of gender-smashing, I began to question the term *bisexual* and its implicit nod to a binary gender system. "Bisexual" self-limits to two genders, and in its very construction seems to imply "attracted to men and also to women," rather than "attracted to people regardless of gender." I questioned terms like *monogamous* and *polyamorous* as well—if I did not prefer having one partner at a time, nor having multiple partners at the same time, but instead wished to enjoy relationships in whatever form and number made sense in that particular situation, what was the word for that?

The term *omnisexual* is gaining popularity thanks to an unexpected source: the *Dr. Who* spinoff *Torchwood,* whose main character is an immortal, highly sexed time traveler. "We like to call him omnisexual," says actor John Barrowman. "In our day and age we know 'bisexual' as one or the other," he notes, but as the series addresses multiple sentient species, the limitation of the terminology is evident: "In the fifty-first century, where [he] is from, you can do it with anybody and you can have that intimacy and personal [connection] whether it's male or female or alien, it doesn't really matter."

The show's subversive streak isn't only on-screen; the current *Dr. Who* revival is helmed by openly gay television producer/writer Russell T. Davies, best known for the series *Queer As Folk.* Davies's desire to make the *Torchwood* spinoff more adult in nature was championed by the BBC, as was his choice of John Barrowman, an openly gay actor, for the lead role. It seems unlikely that such liberal staffing would be conferred in the U.S. for such high-level projects, and yet the first episode shown on BBC America was the highest-rated program in the network's history. Perhaps this indicates that the U.S. is moving toward less rigid reinforcement of gender and orientation roles.

As we explore the linguistic straitjackets surrounding orientation and unpack the meanings we have forced upon ourselves as a culture, we open up new ways of understanding ourselves independent of the baggage that language carries for us individually. After several months of describing myself as having "gender issues," a friend of mine told me she thought "gender playful" was more accurate: "You don't have issues. You're perfectly happy with where you are." After some thought, I decided she was right. My own attachment to labels that had identified me in the past blinded me to the fact that I had moved beyond them.

V

# ENGAGEMENT

# IMPOSSIBLE DREAMS

## Stephen Duncombe

To say that the mainstream Left has forgotten how to dream is merely stating the obvious. The political tradition that once dreamed of democracy, socialism, anarchism, and feminism, that holds the Reverend Martin Luther King's "I Have a Dream" speech as one of its finest moments, is now exemplified by the imagination-challenged Democratic Party and monochrome visions of a "sustainable future." There is, however, a new type of dreaming happening on the outskirts of progressive politics.

It's a cold night outside, but inside the St. Mark's Church in New York City it's stifling. An overflow crowd has come to hear Reverend Billy preach. Punctuated by emphatic "amens" from the crowd, the good Reverend energetically exhorts his flock to resist temptation. His choir, dressed in bright yellow and purple robes, launches into a spirited hymn and the audience joins in. Not an unusual scene for a church, except for a few things: Reverend Billy is a performance artist named Bill Talen, behind the pulpit is a ten-foot-high crucifix with a large stuffed Mickey Mouse nailed squarely upon it, and the sermon is on the evils of shopping. With the cadences, mannerisms, and impressive pompadour of a televangelist the Reverend launches into his sermon:

> This is the moment. We stop shopping. The revolution of no shopping. We can start trying to remember what we imagined. We can begin to recall what desire was when it was not supervised.

At first read this is just another arch-ironic send-up of organized religion. But it's also something much more: The service is a genuine experience of communion and shared faith . . . built around an absurd demand: "the revolution of no shopping." His congregation is not some ancient agrarian population where self-sufficiency is a possibility; Bill's sermon is directed to an urban American audience for whom buying stuff is a necessity. Stop Shopping is an impossible dream. And the Reverend is not the only one dreaming such dreams.

It's New Year's Day 1994, the day the North American Free Trade Agreement goes into effect, and out of the mountains of southern Mexico walk three thousand indigenous peasants wearing black ski masks, some carrying rifles, others merely machetes or long sticks, declaring war on the Mexican oligarchy. This Zapatista Army of National Liberation brazenly declares their plan "to advance to the capital of the country, overcoming the Mexican Federal Army, protecting in our advance the civilian population, and permitting the people liberated to elect, freely and democratically, their own administrative authorities."

It's a tall order. The Mexican army is 130,000 soldiers strong and Mexico City is 663 very indirect miles away. Guerrilla declarations are often full of bravado, but there's a hint of something else going on here. The rebel's declaration goes on to state: "We ask for the unconditional surrender of the enemy's headquarters, before we begin combat, in order to avoid any loss of life." Did I forget to mention the size and armament of the Zapatista "army"?

After capturing and briefly controlling the old colonial town of San Cristobel de las Casas, the Zapatistas retreated back into the jungle, but over the next decade their resident poet-in-arms, Subcomandante Marcos, continued to issue communiqués. Sometimes his missives were straightforward commentary on the state of the struggle or responses to Mexican politics, but other communiqués were allegorical tales, narratives in which politics were intertwined with dialogues between Marcos and a little beetle dubbed Durito, or made into surreal metaphor with commentary provided by a fictional character named Old Don Antonio. These are dreamscapes, not rational political communication.

There is much that separates the Church of Stop Shopping and the Zapatistas. The former is a political performance piece playing to an urbane audience, the latter an armed guerrilla struggle of indigenous peasants in southern Mexico. But they do share something: the reach of their imagination. The dreams of Reverend Billy and Subcomandante Marcos move past the real: They are absurd, irrational, and seemingly impossible. In brief, they remain dreams.

Eduardo Galeano, the Uruguayan poet, writes of utopia:

She's on the horizon. . . . I go two steps, she moves two steps away. I walk ten steps and the horizon runs ten steps ahead. No matter how much I walk, I'll never reach her. What good is utopia? That's what: It's good for walking.

This is the goal of these impossible dreams as well. The error is to see them as a blueprint for a new world. Instead they are dreams that we can imagine, think about, try on for size, yet necessarily never realize. They are a means to imagine new ends. Like a poem, these new political dreams are not meant to be read literally. A poem suggests what its language will never allow it to communicate. It evokes rather than describes. Furthermore, a poem encourages the reader to move past the words on the page into a space not yet defined; it builds an edifice to see what's not there. In refusing to be reduced to rational plans, political dreams—like poems—ask us to imagine something truly new.

As such, the impossible dream has the possibility of creating a new world—as an illusion. This is not the delusion of believing that you already have created a new world (Stalin's "actually existing Socialism") but an illusion that gives direction and motivation that might just get you there. As the Parisian forebears of El Sup and the Rev wrote on the walls of their city in 1968: *Soyons réalistes, demandons l'impossible!* Be realistic, demand the impossible!

# YOGA AS SPIRITUAL ACTIVISM

*Sharon Gannon*

I s Activism a natural outgrowth of yoga? Isn't yoga all about focusing inward? When journalists ask me what my message is or what I am teaching, I reply: "Vegetarianism, environmentalism, and the need to take political action." This response is generally met with bewilderment and another question like, "What are the physical benefits of yoga?" I like to answer, "What could be more physical than what you eat, where you live, and what kind of world you share with others?"

I believe that the growing popularity of yoga at this time of global transformation and overall shift in consciousness is not a coincidence. A yogi, by definition, is someone who strives to live harmoniously with the earth. Through that relationship the yogi seeks to purify his or her karmas so that enlightenment arises. Enlightenment is a state in which "Oneness of being" is realized, the interconnection of all beings and things in our world—yoga teaches that we are inseparably woven into the great web of life, matter, and cosmic space.

We are responsible for the health and well-being of our world. But even though it seems that the world needs us more than ever before, it is actually we who need the world for our own salvation—not only as physical beings who require air and water and nutrition, but also in a metaphysical sense. Mother Nature does not require us for her existence, but we need her: This earth provides us with life, and, according to yoga teachings, life gives us the opportunity for enlightenment by giving us the means to work out our past karmas.

Karma means action, not just outer-directed action but thoughts and speech as well. Our lives are made up of actions. We never act alone; all of our actions affect others. At the end of the day, or at the end of our life, the only thing any of us really "has" is our effect upon others. How we treat others determines how others treat us; how others treat us influences how we see ourselves; how we see ourselves determines who we are.

Yoga teaches us that there is no "out there" versus an "in here." Everything we see comes from inside of us, and we create the world in which we live. Our current reality is a projection of our inner reality, which comes from our past actions, derived from how we treat others. If we want our world to change and heal, we must start seeing things differently, and act in a manner that will bring about global health and harmony.

We are in the midst of a planetary crisis that is different from all past crises: Unconscious human activity now threatens the integrity of the biosphere itself. Most human beings do not realize this, nor do they understand that we are the ones causing this crisis. Even those who are aware struggle with the sense of not knowing what to do to help undo the damage.

Luckily, the practices of yoga provide us with very practical skills to enable us to dismantle our present culture, a culture of dis-ease, based upon the exploitation of the earth. If our culture had a mission statement it would seem to be: "The earth belongs to us." It is easier to harm or exploit another being or entity if you see them as disconnected from you, as your possession rather than an extension of your being. This self-centered way of perceiving and treating the earth has led to a global crisis that threatens the very possibility of future life on this planet for all beings.

A yogi seeks self-realization through the perfection of action: A perfect act is a selfless one. By living in an other-centered way rather than a self-centered way, the yogi lives harmoniously with the earth, with all beings and things, and ultimately with her self. To the yogi, the earth is the great mother or the Goddess, who is also the God in us. Yogis don't seek to escape the world, but rather to go deeper into the world, dissolving illusions of separateness and perceiving the physical earth as one's greater heart.

In yoga, this radical way of thinking and seeing is embodied in the practices of asana (steady seat) and ahimsa (nonharming). Both of these practices lead us to political activism. They change our approach to life from asking "How can the earth benefit us?" to "How can we benefit the earth?"

In the second chapter of his renowned *Yoga Sutras*, a two-thousand-year-old text, the sage Patanjali writes on the practical application of yoga techniques, offering the following sutra, or thread: Sthira sukham asanam (YS II.46):

> The connection to the earth should be steady and joyful. Our relationships with all beings and things should be mutually beneficial if we ourselves desire happiness and liberation from sufferings. Our bodies are made up of all of our karmas from countless lifetimes; all of the actions from our past relationships with others. Through the practice of asana one can purify their past karmas.

In Sanskrit *Sthira* means "steady; stable"; *Sukham* means "easy; joyful; comfortable"; and *Asana* means "seat." Your seat refers to your connection to the earth, to all beings and things on this planet. Patanjali is saying here that to attain yoga, your connection or your relationship to the earth, and all of the beings that comprise it, should be steady and joyful. For a relationship to be steady and joyful it must be mutually beneficial. A one-sided relationship based on the selfish needs of an individual will not move one toward yoga or the realization of the oneness of being. As we are now realizing on a global scale, a one-sided relationship based on fulfilling the selfish desires of an individual cannot sustain the whole body politic.

Our bodies are made up of all of our karmas from countless lifetimes, including all of the actions from our past relationships with others. Through the practice of asana we can purify our past karmas and create a harmonious relationship to Mother Earth. By connecting to the earth and creating a steady relationship, we not only create happiness in the world, we create happiness in ourselves.

The easiest way to uplift our own life is to uplift the lives of others. One more way that Patanjali gives us to uplift the lives of others is through the practice of *ahimsa*, which means nonharming. If we want to be happy, then we must not cause unhappiness to others, or to the planet. How we treat others will determine how others treat us. Patanjali says, *"ahimsa pratisthayam tat sannidhau vaira tyagah"* (YS II.35), which translates as: "When we do not hurt others, others will not hurt us." Kindness toward others is the most powerful political act that we can perform on a daily basis.

These two yogic principles of *ahimsa* and *asana* lead us toward perfection of action, which is said to be enlightenment itself. A perfect act is a selfless one. Yoga practices help us to transcend selfish needs in order to be of service to the whole. Yoga teaches us how to get free of fears that contribute to violence, greed, and selfish tendencies.

Some people may argue that spirituality and politics don't mix; if you are a spiritual person, you should disassociate yourself from politics. But the fact is we can't help but be political. Each of our actions, whether of physical deeds, words, or even thoughts, affects everyone all the time. To take one example, our daily eating habits either support local organic farms and socially conscious enterprises or they create profit for horrific industries of slaughterhouses and genetically engineered produce. The work that we choose to do can contribute to other peoples' liberation or their suffering. If we continually act in a way that takes into consideration the well-being of the whole—the people and animals that share our neighborhood, community, town, city, country, and planet—we will have become yogic activists.

If we look at the current world situation from a karmic perspective, we can see that the planetary crisis offers us a great opportunity to purify our karma through right action in the world. Unfortunately, many people have given into cynicism or despair. They look at the global situation and lament the absence of good leaders, hoping to find someone they can follow—a Martin Luther King, Gandhi, or Mother Teresa. Why do they look outside themselves for direction? Yoga practice should teach us inner strength, self-knowledge, and self-mastery. When we have attained these qualities, we don't need to wait for anyone to lead us. We can find the courage to take responsibility for the planetary situation on our own. When we take this on as yogic activists, we step into a great destiny.

# CLEANING UP SOAP:
## WHY THE BRONNER FAMILY IS
## WASHING OUT A FEW MOUTHS

*Jill Ettinger*

What we eat, drink, and breathe is certainly important, but so is what we absorb through our skin. The skin is an organ—our largest in fact. Our internal control centers are all wrapped up inside this giant organ, yet we seem to forget (or ignore) this truth. Perhaps it's because our personalities and identities appear to be forged through our skin's shapes and colors. We deem it as a reflection of our deeper "organless" self, when it is simply just one part of the whole.

Contrary to red carpet commentary and style magazine recommendations, the skin does much more than make us sexy or otherwise. It does more than keep our bones and guts from falling all over the place. It soaks up nutrients; it's both a delivery system and a barrier. The skin is our most corporeal relationship. It's sensual and mysterious. And of course, it must be kept clean.

If cleanliness is indeed right up there next to the holiest of all things, then the Bronner family appear to be a bunch of angels working overtime, ensuring that people are truly getting soaps that are safe and effective, not laced with harsh chemicals.

Dr. Emanuel Bronner was a third-generation German soap maker (and not technically a doctor). He was a quirky pacifist, committed to finding crafty ways of delivering a monumental message of truth and universality. "All one," he called it. "We're all one family." His recipe was a simple blend of quality biodegradable, vegetable-based ingredients (from the label for liquid peppermint): Water, Saponified Organic Coconut and Olive oils (with retained Glycerin), Organic Hemp Oil, Organic Jojoba Oil, Organic Peppermint Oil, Organic Mentha Arvensis, Citric Acid, Vitamin E.

With a small following in the early years, sales experienced tremendous growth as the counterculture movement of the sixties exploded. Dr. Bronner's magic soap fit right in. The symbolic bottle loaded with a unique collection of thoughts and inspiration scrawled every which way delivered a message of "transcendent unity." Like many natural ideals that took hold in the sixties, Dr. Bronner's became an institution. It is a universally loved product found in virtually every health food store in the U.S. (making them the number-one-selling natural brand of soaps in North America), with die-hard loyal fans espousing its effectiveness.

The fourth and fifth generation of the Bronner family has taken Emanuel's commitment to heart by developing fair-trade sources and using only certified organic oils. They've donated millions of dollars to their local community (San Diego county) and converted their signature plastic soap bottles to 100 percent postconsumer recycled (PCR) cylinder bottles and paper labels.

Like the mainstream conventional food industry, personal care manufacturing includes a lot of by-products. There are preservatives, thickeners, and foaming agents born out of other industries, often petroleum. They are sold cheaply to skin care companies, some of whom sell garish products that retail for hundreds of dollars in boutiques and department stores. The only cosmetics one needs, according to Dr. Bronner, is "enough sleep & Dr. Bronner's Magic Soap to cleanse body-mind-soul-spirit."

Caring for the skin is not a modern invention. For thousands of years, natural plant oils, butters, herbs, and flowers have been valued for their rejuvenating, moisturizing, and hydrating properties. Now, industrial convention implies the same experience can be had in a squirt bottle of watered down lotion mixed in a factory, loaded with chemicals.

Browsing through any women's magazine, you're bound to stumble onto countless brands all promising baby-soft, supple skin. Cruise through the aisles of any Whole Foods Market or natural food store and you'll find a similar situation: Bottle after bottle of miracle soaps, crèmes, lotions, and shampoos, but these also exclaim that they are free from the harsh chemicals and parabens of mainstream products, plus they're organic.

Though the natural and organic industry tends to stand for more than just single bottom-line profits, make no mistake, that is priority. And even more so now as Green is the new Vaseline; like they used to say back in the sixties: The times they are a-changin'. Wal-Mart is now the largest distributor of organic produce in America (and just announced that their milk suppliers will no longer be allowed to use growth hormones). Whole Foods Market, who initially thought there were roughly only one hundred spots in the U.S. where their markets would work, are now pushing 300 locations with dozens more in development.

In 2003, Whole Foods became the first certified organic retailer. They worked with third-party certifiers Quality Assurance International (QAI) to ensure stringent protocol is adhered to on their handling of organic products. This they claim is "further proof of Whole Foods Market's unwavering commitment to organics." There is unquestionably an ambient vibrancy in a Whole Foods Market that is more appealing, more resonant than what it feels like when prowling through an overly bright, dirty-but-sterile ShopRite or Safeway. Every product in a Whole Foods seems to glow and ring with an "I'm-reeeeaally-really-good-for-you-so-buy-me" echo.

This is probably why the word *organic* has come to be synonymous with "healthy." While organic foods are free from chemical residues from pesticides and fertilizers, free from genetically modified organisms (GMO), and free from growth hormones—all of which are indeed health factors—an organic claim is not an automatic indicator of the food also being genuinely good for you as in its being a low-sugar, no hydrogenated fats, no artificial colors or sweeteners, high-fiber, vitamin-rich, super miracle health food. Organic or not, a potato chip is still a potato chip. While this should be evident to consumers (who eat them anyway), the harder discrimination comes in those personal care aisles. Skin care, hair care, sun care, after-sun care, lip balms, soaps, lotions, makeup, and on and on. It seems the bigger question may not be which is organic, but why do we need so many products in the first place? If Cleopatra could survive on olive oil and honey for her skin, why do we need so many jars and bottles full of ingredients we can't pronounce? And, how are those organic?

The Bronner family was celebrating their 60-year anniversary (and 150 years all the way back to Germany) at Natural Products Expo West in Anaheim, California, earlier this month. Expo West is the largest natural/organic trade show in the U.S. with attendance near 50,000. Some 2,000 vendors set up their wares, sampling the latest and greatest in innovative categories along with the old tried-and-true standards, like Dr. Bronner's.

As I approached the Bronner's booth this year, I noticed something odd: None of the folks staffed behind it were looking up. They all had their heads down, eyes buried deep into something, reading rhythmically left to right. David Bronner, president and grandson of Emanuel, finally noticed me and handed me a copy of the press release he had been reading. "We're sending all these out here at the show," he said. I was curious, but not surprised to find that "these" were cease-and-desist letters going to some of the leading "organic" personal care brands in the industry including Jason, Nature's Gate, Avalon, Kiss My Face, and Aveda.

The organic personal care industry is rapidly growing. Sales in 2006 were over $300 million (roughly 15 percent of the total personal care market). But the Bronner's have not been taking the growth lightly. They've become incensed at the watered-down chemicals pawning themselves off as organic. The reason for this happening is that the organic regulations for body care are not the same as for food. There currently are none. "We've grown increasingly frustrated with the companies in our industry who seem to feed off each others' misleading practices and show no inclination to clean up their formulations and live up to their organic branding claims," says David Bronner.

From the press release: "The major cleansing ingredient in Jason 'Pure, Natural & Organic' liquid soaps, bodywashes and shampoos is Sodium Myreth Sulfate, which involves ethoxylating a conventional non-organic fatty chain with the carcinogenic petrochemical Ethylene Oxide, which produces carcinogenic 1,4-Dioxane as a contaminant. The major cleansing ingredient in Avalon 'Organics' soaps, bodywashes and shampoos, Cocamidopropyl Betaine, contains conventional non-organic agricultural material combined with the petrochemical Amdio-propyl Betaine. Nature's Gate 'Organics' main cleansers are Disodium Laureth Sulfosuccinate (ethoxylated) and Cocamidopropyl Betaine. Kiss My Face 'Obsessively Organic' cleansers are Olefin Sulfonate (a pure petrochemical) and Cocamidopropyl Betaine. Juice 'Organics,' Giovanni 'Organic Cosmetics,' Head 'Organics,' Desert Essence 'Organics,' Ikove 'Organic' Amazonian Avocado Bath & Shower Gel all use Cocamdio-propyl Betaine and no cleansers made from certified organic material."

Ronnie Cummins, executive director of the Organic Consumers Association, a watchdog group partnering with the Bronners says, "The labeling and formulation practices of these companies are so unsupportable, we wonder sometimes if the garbage manager is in charge of product development and R and D."

"Personal care products are not regulated like food in this country so there are currently no consistent standards for them laid forth by any governing body," says Jeremiah McElwee, senior global Whole Body coordinator for Whole Foods. Not only are organic claims not being regulated in the personal care industry, but neither is overall efficacy. If a product claims to affect a structure or function of the body—as in "reduces fine lines and wrinkles," then according to the FDA, it is classified as a drug and forced to adhere to controlled regulations. But if a product claims to "reduce *the appearance* of fine lines and wrinkles," it is classified as a cosmetic, regardless of whether or not the outcome is identical. That basically means I can bottle tap water out of my Jersey City apartment and sell it to you as a "super-wrinkle-defense-ointment" for one hundred dollars a bottle and not have to prove that it does what I claim. (This stuff really does work by the way—please e-mail me to place your orders.)

The key to the cosmetic industry's success has been in cleverly making product claims to avoid clinical designation but appear to sound as if they are just as effective. They use statements like: reduce or increase appearances, enhance the look and feel of, or eliminate signs of, and so on, creating huge profits for manufacturers and cycles of desperation for those consumers conditioned to fear aging. With unregulated organic standards for body care we not only have products whose efficacy is questionable, but the truth about the ingredients' origins is stretched so thin that even the best miracle-lotion-créme-ointment-oil can't restore them back to something honest.

Whole Foods has taken steps to single out body care products that meet their "clean" regulations. Effective this year they've implemented a "premium body care standard" that forbids ingredients such as parabens, polypropylene and polyethylene glycols, sodium lauryl and laureth sulfates. But the Bronners' expectations of the industry are even higher than those. Along with the Organic Consumers Association, they are raising the organic bar of soap and "plan to pursue legal remedies on Earth Day April 20, if they do not receive responses indicating these companies . . . will cease organic branding by September 1, 2008."

# IF YOU SEE SOMETHING, SAY SOMETHING

*Michael Brownstein*

NYC, 2006

We need your help as an extra set of eyes and ears.
Unattended bags? Suspicious behavior?
Take notice of people in bulky or inappropriate clothing.
Report anyone tampering with video cameras or entering
  unauthorized areas.
If you see something, say something.

I see something.
I see a criminally insane person roaming the halls of the White
  House.
He believes he's the president of the United States.
And I see a rotund bastard with a heart problem hovering in the
  background, pulling the strings.
His crooked smile lights the way to perdition.

In the early-morning chill I see the streets of New York filled
  with people on their way to work.
We think we're home free because John Ashcroft retired.
No more red alerts, no more terrorists disguised as tourists
  worming their way into town.

No more dirty bombs left in suitcases in Grand Central.
Little do we know. Little dare we surmise.

As the rotund bastard with the heart problem said the other day,
   "You know, it's not an accident that we haven't been hit in
   four years."
What's that supposed to mean? That sooner or later he'll feel
   threatened enough to push the hot button again?
And when he does will he be in his secret, climate-controlled
   tunnel halfway between D.C. and Wyoming?
Far from the narrow, dark canyons of Manhattan?

If you see something, say something.
I see something.
I see the forgotten anthrax killers whose bioweapons source was
   not al-Qaeda but our own American arsenals.
I see no global war declared on Fort Detrick or the Dugway
   Proving Grounds, no troops deployed, no actions
   taken.
Our attention always focused somewhere out there (Iraq, North
   Korea, Iran), never in here.

If you see something, say something.
I see a billion dollars a week spent on this war rather than the
   two billion a year needed to lock down leaking Russian
   nuclear facilities.
I see the U.S. military buying anthrax in violation of treaties
   limiting the spread of bioweapons.
I see nanotech embraced for mirage medical cures while its use
   for surveillance and control is ignored.
I see all of us inoculated into a state of permanent low-level
   paranoia.

If you see something, say something.
I see something.
I see our Supreme Leader in the Oval Office fondling "the
    football," the top-secret suitcase with instructions to blow up
    the planet.
Sixteen years after the Berlin wall fell I see thousands of
    hydrogen bombs still on hair-trigger alert in Russia and the
    U.S.A.
I see forty of those bombs aimed at New York City.

If you see something, say something.
I see our protective coating of ironic distance shielding us from
    the truth.
Over the phone I hear "Have a nice day," and "Please speak to
    the system."
And in the stores, behind the Christmas carols, I hear the whine
    of black helicopters making the world safe for democracy.
"Freedom!" I bark, and a miniature poodle on a leash barks back
    at me.

I see something.
I see the U.S. holding the world for ransom.
Again and again the same words keep surfacing: "the national
    interest, the national interest, the national interest."
Reptilian brains having a toxic reaction to testosterone.
Plunging us all into the icy waters of selfish calculation.

If you see something, say something.
I see this trashed-out culture of ours approaching the wall.
Plant and animal species disappearing at warp speed.
Soil turned to dust, aquifers drained dry.
And I see it's too painful to go there.

It's too painful to go there, I'm headed outside for a smoke.

It's too painful to go there, I'm busy learning Italian.

It's too painful to go there, my therapist told me to stay positive.

She said that whatever I experience is up to me, that I create my
own world.

My guru said the same thing.


But it's funny, no matter what they say I keep seeing this
weirdness out of the corner of my eye.

I see undercover agents on every transport platform, watching
over my fellow Americans strapped into bucket seats.

I see my fellow Americans weighed down by schedules and cell
phones and computers and wristwatches.

I see their children swallowing pharmaceuticals to get through
the day.

While in nearby fields the birds and animals look on with
infinite patience, waiting outside of clock time for us to burn
out and disappear.


(The yellow-throated warbler singing, "Is that the best you
can do?

Best you can do?"

"Is that the best you can do?")


I see something.

I see arbitrary national borders separating us from our
humanity.

I hear the siren song of nationalism driving us onto the rocks.

9/11 and the war in Iraq no more than red herrings distracting
us from this fact.

'Cause Iraqis are people just like us. How can their deaths be
worth less than ours?

I see it's time for us to take a look in the mirror.

Notice the frightened children in there, wondering how they got
into this mess.

Realize there's no one in the whole wide world to blame.

Decide to risk everything and open our hearts.

That's the one thing against which the rotund bastard has no
defense.


If you see something, say something.

I see that even though my therapist charges a hundred and
seventy-five an hour and my guru has a lifetime free pass,
maybe they're right.

I'm responsible for what's happening to me.

My beliefs create my experience.

Otherwise why am I swallowed up in rituals of mutual self-
destruction while outside a sweet wind blows through the
trees?


'Cause I see two wolves fighting in my heart, one vengeful and
the other compassionate.

Which one will I feed today?

Will I behave as if the god in all of life matters?

Or will I come after you, blaming and accusing?

Which one will I feed today?

# "I KNOW WE WON"—ABBIE HOFFMAN SPEAKS

## Ken Jordan

The first street theater tricksters—the forefathers of today's culture jammers such as The Yes Men and Billionaires For Bush—appeared on the political stage in the 1960s. At the time, the possibility that activists could spread subversive messages through the mainstream media was a counterintuitive, even revolutionary notion. But with the right mix of TV-savvy images and provocative sound bites, delivered with humor and no small dose of irony, the antiwar, flower power message of the political vanguard was able to reach the living rooms of unsuspecting, disaffected youth across the country, helping to ignite the radical activism that transformed America during that tumultuous decade.

No one was better at genius pranks than Abbie Hoffman. He's appreciated for stunts like bringing the New York Stock Exchange to a halt when he led a band of hippies onto the balcony there, where they rained dollar bills down upon the floor of amazed Wall Street suits, who famously knocked one another to the ground as they dived rapaciously for the free cash. Others may remember Abbie for the levitation of the Pentagon during a 1967 march against the Vietnam War (witnesses insist that it really did happen). But the event that made Hoffman a household name was the Chicago 8 trial, the subject of the recent documentary *Chicago 10*. For months the news was filled with his brilliant, often hilarious, defense maneuvers against government charges that he and his codefendants conspired to disrupt the 1968 Democratic national convention. Abbie transformed the trial into a true theatrical event, a platform for broadcasting the alternative values and politics of the counterculture onto every TV screen in America. In the process, while never wavering from his radical beliefs, Hoffman became one of the country's most famous celebrities.

As this interview shows, he was also a sober, serious strategist who grounded his antics in theory. Few appreciated the subtle ties between cultural gesture and political action as deeply as Hoffman. This converstion took place in New York City a few months before his untimely death in 1989.

*The first big event that put you on the map, so to speak, was when you and a handful of hippies showered dollar bills onto the floor of the New York Stock Exchange. Can you tell me a little about what happened?*
It was the summer of '67. That was when Jerry Rubin and I kind of met, and then we did the levitation of the Pentagon that October. Well, that whole summer, as the year before, it was nothing to wake up at St. Mark's Place on the Lower East Side and say we were going to do some stunt.

*Like what?*
For instance, we would go into a bank, get two rolls of quarters, and start throwing them on the floor. We planted a tree in the middle of St. Mark's Place to get rid of all the cars. Rock bands played in the streets, played in Tompkins Square Park. Every thirty minutes you'd have a new poem, you'd rush out and hand them away on St. Mark's Place. And all the antiwar demonstrations, regularly.

*Who was writing these poems?*
Me, Jim Fouratt, Ed Sanders, Allen Ginsberg, Anne Waldman. It was called the Communications Company. Jim Fouratt had a duplicating machine. We didn't have Xerox then, and we reeled off these poems on multicolored paper. I got married in Central Park, and we did the invita-

tion on a leaflet. Anybody who has a full collection of these leaflets, it would be worth a half-million dollars today! They were great! And it was garbage art really. You just read the poem, threw it away, had a good time. The influences came from people like Allan Kaprow. They were doing Happenings, but they didn't have any political content, see? They were strictly apolitical, so, of course, the rich loved it.

*Did you go to any of the Happenings?*
No, but I read about them, I was aware of them, in the papers and the media. I went to Pop Art exhibits. I went to a big Pop Art show in the Armory, I guess the year before, which had some indoor Happenings. And then there was the Living Theatre, and there was another theater, Richard Schechner's Performing Garage. All this stuff was going on. . . . I think at one point Richard said we were influencing each other. You know, life and art were imitating each other. I mean, walk down St. Mark's Place between Third and Second Avenue, and it was like walking through a circus. You'd see every kind of costume in the world, every sight possible. People barefoot, it was nothing to walk around barefoot. We thought of this stuff very fast. People were handing out flags at the Statue of Liberty saying "End the war." There were a lot of demonstrations down at Whitehall, the draft induction center.

*Everything you did seems to have been inspired by a spirit of fun and a sense of humor.*
And a sense of communicating ideas through the mass media by manipulating famous symbols. We were doing it, actually, before this theory had come around. It was instinctive. I'll tell you one of the more famous ones. On Valentine's Day in '67, we mailed 3,000 joints of marijuana to people all over New York, picked out of the phone book, with a letter explaining, you've read a lot about it, now if you want to try it, here it is. But, P.S., by the way, just holding this can get you five years in prison. We sent it to some in the media. Bill Jorgensen, the local news anchor-

man, almost got arrested on the air for showing it on TV. The cops came right on the set and it was quite hysterical. Half the people on the Lower East Side knew who did it!

*And you had no problems with the cops, they never traced it to you?*
No, no. To come up with the list we'd get stoned, yellow pages and stoned, that's it. There were different rolling teams and all that. Jimi Hendrix gave me the money for it. Ultimately it changed the laws in this state, got the penalties reduced. We used to have a lot of campaigns against pay toilets. We'd go up there, photograph people sneaking in underneath, and put pictures in the underground newspapers with captions: How to get into a pay toilet. So we'd show people who would sneak in under, or taping the lock shut. All these were in *Fuck the System,* later in *Steal This Book,* etc. in that spirit. But the Stock Exchange probably was one of the best of these kinds of acts.

*Tell me something about the Wall Street event. How did it come about?*
Well, I called up the New York Stock Exchange and booked a tour. I said we're bringing a tour group, about eighteen of us. I gave them the name George Metesky, who was the mad bomber of New York, about fifteen years previous to this.

*The mad bomber of New York?*
Yeah, he was just a cultural hero. He was a media freak. When they arrested him he had a big headline in the *Daily News*: "Mad Bomber of New York Captured!" He was living with his mother and his aunt, you know, a meek sort of mild-mannered guy. He just had a thing about Con Ed because Con Ed fired him. So he left little pipe bombs all over the place, like Grand Central Station, and he had the city terrorized! Of course the guy who answered the phone wouldn't remember the name, but I would, as would other people who know the history of New York. I had about three hundred dollars, and I changed it all into singles. It

was either my money or money I raised. Three hundred dollars—that's not much money. You got a bang for your movement buck, let's face it! I could run the country cheap!

*Where did the idea come from?*
Well, I don't want to get arrogant, but the theme of Christ chasing the money changers from the Temple, obviously that idea was there. But maybe I thought about that later, writing about it in *Revolution for the Hell of It,* or something. But it seemed like a good idea at the time, and we had the resources and the capabilities—and we could go to central casting right at Gem Spa, the newsstand at Second Avenue and St. Mark's Place, and get as many people as we wanted right away. People were ready to volunteer for anything, and they were doing their own things. When we got to the Stock Exchange, we got in line with all the other tourists. Pretty soon as we waited in the line to go visit the Stock Exchange, just on the regular tour, somebody must've noticed something freaky, because we were dressed like hippies. We were not dressed like tourists from Iowa, you know, or Indiana. Hippies were still a little bizarre-looking to the general public, there were two cultures. So within a matter of minutes the press was swarming all over us.

*You didn't call the press in advance?*
No, but this is New York City. They get tips. The police, the guards at the Stock Exchange will tell them, there's eighteen hippies down here, they're going to do something. People were giggling, smoking grass probably, you know. You wander above Fourteenth Street looking the way we did, already people are staring at you. You stand in an airport, they stare at you because you look like a runaway from the local circus.

*So you thought of your appearance down on Wall Street as a kind of confrontation?*
Sure. Your very dress, your being was a confrontation. A deliberate con-

frontation. And an affirmation of a spirit, of an art, of a more humane kind of existence. Cooperation versus competition. We didn't have to spell out our ideology because it was pretty clear if you followed our acts, and if you tried to make all the intellectual connections, you'd find plenty of theory. We had utopian visions, like "abolish money" was big. And "abolish work." We were antiwork, antimoney. So the throwing out of money at Wall Street would fit into that. You could say that we were anticapitalists, which we were, but we didn't have an "ism." We had the idea of "free." We kept putting across the idea that it all should be free, since our society's so rich. We had free stores, and you could just go in and take all the clothes you wanted. Free food in the park. Free poems and free rock concerts. The idea was that we were living in "post-scarcity." We had great affluence in that period, as a society. So we should be working toward full unemployment, we should be working toward a society with more quality time. Why work for full-employment? It's boring. Well, of course, because people need money. Well, we're so rich we're just going to divide up the wealth. People have a right to medical care, free medical care, which we all provided on the Lower East Side. We had various institutions that acted as models for a while, as long as we could sustain them. When you'd see a store that says "free store," you could come on in and have anything you want with your good looks. No shoplifting allowed. And people would come in and dump all their junk, and we'd have other people sorting it out. We were building a community of maybe forty or fifty thousand, in New York, on the Lower East Side.

*So when you go to the Stock Exchange dressed like that . . .*

. . . they know something's up. It doesn't take long for a guard, say, for fifty dollars, to call the *Daily News* or Associated Press. And they swarm. You can have a big fire in New York, and you'll have the press there before the fire department arrives.

*Did you stage the whole thing for the press?*

No, I never did anything for the press. Well, we didn't know if we would be arrested. I knew there would be some kind of confrontation, because at some point, the guard's going to come up and say, "No." If we were arrested then the press is there and everything. I mean the story is going to get out one way or another. We didn't know it would be big. The guards tried to keep us out almost simultaneously when the press came, it was all one big commotion. There were a lot of guards, these were guards, not cops, guards from the Stock Exchange. And they said we weren't allowed in and had no right to do this, blah blah blah. And we said, hey you know, what do you mean? We're Americans! Free tour. What the hell, we want to see what it looks like. So finally, we negotiated.

*You did the negotiating?*

Of course. I'm very good at negotiating. It was already my seventh year as a political organizer in various ways. I negotiated with the Klan to let them give me back my life in Mississippi, so . . . ! You get them in a situation where it's going to be an embarrassment for them to keep you out. They said, "Hippies are not allowed in." So I said, "Well, look, we're Jewish. You don't let Jews into the Stock Exchange?" The press was there. So I turned around to the press and I said, "They won't let Jews in the Stock Exchange!" "Oh no no no. That isn't what we said. Now wait a minute . . ." They got red-faced. So you can get in. Once they decided to let us in, though, they said that press are not allowed in the gallery, so the press had to back off and wait on the street. They already sensed what we were going to do. People were flashing money, they were starting to eat it and everything. They were clowning around.

*Making a show for the press?*

No. For each other. I relate to media that way. We're just going to create a little story and a lot of people are going to be hearing about it. Now if somebody brings a camera or something, well, that makes the job easier, but I'm not doing it for them. It's an important distinction. We had no concept of a "media event." The idea of manipulating the media was ridiculous. The people who own the media manipulate it, we just had some tricks up our sleeves. We knew that we were talking to a society that was postliterate. Either post or pre. It was now in a phase where it wanted to watch and listen, it didn't want to read. So for watching or listening, you've got to paint some pictures. You've got to have some images.

*Can you remember any of the things that influenced you in this direction?*
McLuhan, I was influenced by his writings. Andy Warhol, he was an influence. But all of us were thinking about this. Every person that left their community and came to the Lower East Side, who resisted the draft, who went for an alternative lifestyle, they had to do some thinking about it. It's called getting an education. You had to rebel, because it was not going to be handed to you right there in school, in the local church, or the local draft board center. The local newspaper wasn't going to tell you that this is a good thing to do. Of course, everyone gave some thought to it. I was just a leader among people who gave thought to it, that's all.

*Getting back to the story, what happened after they let you into the Stock Exchange?*
The press was not allowed to continue in the snake line, but they let us into the gallery. So we sat there with all the other tourists. We hugged and kissed a lot and everything. We were hippies. We were clowning, funnin'. Of course, we were all stoned. Sure, we were having a good time. Also, for part of the tour they tell you how the Stock Exchange was started. No one in the group had been on the tour before. Like many people who live in New York, they don't go to see the symbols, the tourist sights. So, you know, Carnegie made money, Ford made money, and everyone made money down there. It's like the lottery on a big scale.

And they explain what the ticker tape is all about. Everyone asked some silly questions, or some meaningful ones. Some just got interested, like real tourists. You can be a tourist and a hippie, too. But once we got into the gallery and we were all spread out, I passed out the money, and people had their own money they kicked in. You know, it was communal money. And at one moment, when they were all busy down there in the pit, ticker tape going like crazy, we gave the signal, and ran to the railing. Even though there were a couple of guards positioned on the gallery, there was no way to stop eighteen of us coming from different directions, all with money, handfuls of money, going "Take the money! Here's the real shit!" throwing it over the railing, and screaming and yelling while we're doing it! So, imagine . . . they looked up, I mean all these brokers, and they start booing, cheering. A lot more boos than cheers. And the ticker tape had stopped. I read that the ticker tape had stopped six minutes. I couldn't tell that at the time, but the normal hubbub of buying and selling stopped. They didn't know what to do. Then pandemonium broke out, and they started yelling "Money, money!" And they start running, they were all over on their hands and knees, gobbling. . . . After we threw the money, the guards were stunned. They didn't know what to do, we had them outnumbered. They had to send for reinforcements. The guards were saying things like, "You can't do that, you're not allowed to do that. That's illegal, we're going to get the police." "What do you mean? People throw away money all the time here! This is the way you do it, isn't it?" I mean, it's just a panic having to argue with me in real life. In a situation like that . . . because I'm fearless. I don't care if they pick me up and throw me in the Stock Exchange. Throw me in the pit. I'll be all right. I'm ready!

*Did the guards actually manhandle you?*
Sure, the guards shoved us around and everything. We pushed back. We were kind of pacifist then, so we weren't ready to punch out a guard. We already made our point. The money was out there, gone. The ticker tape

had stopped. They all were groveling around on their knees, tracing down these real bills. We were there a few more minutes, and we just left. They said get the hell out, we got out. So everyone's out, everybody's jumping up and down, laughing, giggling, hugging, big fun, and we're out on the sidewalk and then there was a press conference. There were reporters all over the place, blocking the streets. Because they had waited, they couldn't come in and see it. So there's no photos of what I'm telling you. That's what makes it a great myth, because every newspaper account was different. And interviewing me was like interviewing a hurricane. "Hi, I'm Cardinal Spellman," "Where'd you get your money?" "I said I'm Cardinal Spellman! You don't ask Cardinal Spellman where he gets his money!" "What kind of talk is that?" "How much money was it?" "I don't know. Thousands! We threw away all the money we had!" So accounts of it had to vary a great deal.

*It was a spontaneous scene with the press?*
Very. We burned money in front of the press. That was illegal then, by the way, to burn money. I hadn't done that before, but I had gone into a bank and just thrown money out. Or I'd sit there and play a flute, in the corner of the bank, dress up like an electronic Indian or something.

*Had you ever dealt with the press like that before?*
Of course I'd dealt with the press as an organizer. We'd already been on *The David Susskind Show*, which had been kind of a wild drama. "How do you eat?" We opened a box of food and started feeding the whole audience. "What's a hippie?" We opened a box and a duck flew out with the word *hippie* around its neck. And Susskind went crazy! You see, we were trying to destroy the whole Q & A, intellectual TV kind of Q & A. All of a sudden: What's a hippie? Well, here's one. It's a duck with the word *hippie* on it flying in the audience. You want to get under their skin, these cruel, levelheaded intellectuals with makeup on, being very liberal, analytical and everything. You want to bust through that. In

other words, more show, give people something more to hear and watch. It isn't a very big story to say that these people were on TV and said this. So what? It's what they did. We thought of these acts as public happenings that jolted the kind of collective fantasy world that we live in through TV, essentially. The national fantasy world. So it would be natural that later there would be hippie invasions of Disney World, and other sacred tombs. Surrounding the Pentagon with witches so that it would rise into the air. Also, we wanted to get people to do what they were saying. That was kind of a problem with liberalism at the time, because it was saying things, but it wasn't doing anything. We were very action-oriented. We were called "action freaks."

*Who called you action freaks?*
We called ourselves action freaks, and we'd say that was a compliment, because you acted on your ideas. In fact, Dwight McDonald, who was a friend of mine, an older man, intellectual, a critic of American foreign policy, once remarked to me a few years later, "Whatever gave you people the idea that you had to act on your ideas? That's anti-intellectual. It's against the whole tradition of Western intellectual thought." Of course, that's not true. The abolitionists were acting on their ideas. And Thoreau. We lived by the ideology of the deed.

*So what you were doing also had political significance?*
Of course. It's a lot different than giving your money to Santa Claus standing on the corner. That's a political act, too, by the way. I think they're all political acts. There's no such thing as interacting in society without it being a political act, the most fearsome of which is war. But all other acts are political, too. Even if you say, "I don't believe in politics," you've just acted. You've acted for the status quo. How many times have you heard people say, "I don't get involved in politics?" Well, the rulers of the society, the Powers That Be, that's exactly what they want the populace to say, because that gives them three more votes. In a sense,

one of the things we were saying at the Stock Exchange was that the people down on the floor weren't really engaged in capitalism, because they had it all rigged. I mean, they were all making money, they all represented people who are making money. It's the poor that feel the effects of capitalism. They've got to go out and work hard, protect their bicycles from being stolen, kill or be killed. I mean, they're in the dog race of capitalism as we know it. But the rich, they have socialism.

*But when you were dealing with the press . . .*
A put-on. I think they call it a put-on.

*Did you give your name to the press?*
No. That was just a thing of the times. Lots of those leaflets, even *Revolution for the Hell of It,* I signed "Free," even though people knew who it was, ultimately. Part of the purity of this moment was that people were doing acts without the ego gratification of seeing your name in lights. But after a while it became pointless. It didn't matter if I said I was Robin Hood, they printed Abbie Hoffman.

*So what was the press coverage like after the Wall Street invasion?*
It was hysterical. "Hippies went to the Stock Exchange, showered thousands of dollars onto the floor of the Exchange. The ticker tape stopped. The chairman of the board of the Stock Exchange says it will never happen again. We'll take measures to prevent this from ever happening." Blah blah blah. They get very serious and straight-faced. The broadcasters are giggling a little, and they're showing footage of the press conference on the street, so people can make those bridges in myth-making.

*Were you influenced by pop-culture phenomena, like the Beatles' press conferences, things like that?*
Of course. And Dylan. Dylan had a way of mocking the press as he was talking to the press. And the Beatles, of course, were great at it. Oh yes,

the Beatles were an enormous influence, as they later told us, we were on them.

*What other ways did the Beatles influence you?*
The Beatles were the complete artist, complete vision, designed the whole package. The songs, the words, sang it, lived it. And there were four of them, and they were all very different, so it was a collective experience, communal art. That was important, and their playful attitude about whatever they did. We liked the idea of collapsing dichotomies between work and play, between what the straight Left would call serious struggle for social change, and play. If you're fighting for liberation, why shouldn't you enjoy it? If you crack some barriers made by the imprinting system of the acculturation process, it's sort of like removing the shades of bullshit that have been layered over your head. And it's a good feeling. So, in a way, the Beatles were messengers of a kind of truth. A new truth. A new way that we could all relate together.

*Would you say that they embodied the counterculture?*
Definitely. Oh, yes. It was such a truism that Sgt. Pepper had an amazing impact on us, and on people all over the world, really, except for the Chinese, they were kind of shut off. When it first came out, it was like walking in and being one of the first people to see the Sistine Chapel, or seeing Shakespeare live, see him stand up and explain what he's going to do with his play, *Twelfth Night*. It was just incredible. Because up till then, and this is important in understanding the counterculture, long-haired music meant opera, it meant classical music, and it was meant for a very rich, elite, highly educated bunch of people. That was called long-haired music. Symphony music. Classical music.

*Why was it called long-hair music?*
Just because long hair through the thirties, forties, and fifties had become identified with the professorial, elite, irrelevant academic kind of

rich type. So that was long-hair music. But because of the Beatles and the whole movement, long hair was popular. You could get the Sgt. Pepper album literally in Woolworths. So you had one of those rare moments in history where the best and the most popular were the same. That's called a Renaissance. That was a Renaissance aspect to a decade which was Civil War. A decade that marked a whole century. No doubt in my mind it marked the century. No doubt who won.

*You?*

We. Someone gotta win someone gotta lose. I know we won because, see, I can sit here with you in this deli and I've got long hair and I'm talking to you. Before then the cops could have come right in and taken me out—suspicion. Now it's illegal. We had to fight for it. And that's one of the things. And we abolished legal segregation. Whatever president comes, we can't go back. We can't go back to slavery because of the Civil War the century before. We can't go back living under King George because of the Civil War the century before that. So every century has like a war that marks it, and no matter what happens after that, you can't go back. Obviously, they weren't complete revolutions, or we wouldn't have homeless people, we wouldn't have poor people. We've got one more Civil War to go in this country. One more to go. We've got a big class struggle, it's about economics. We didn't touch that in the sixties. I mean, we touched it the way that we did, by throwing out money at the Stock Exchange. You see, I couldn't do that act today, because it would be an insult to people that are poor and homeless. But then it was affluence. There was a general ethos and perception in the country that we were all doing well, that we were living on easy street, more or less.

*But in the sixties, many of the hippie kids associated with flower power and Timothy Leary weren't thinking so much about politics.*

This act was a crossover between the hippies and the more political people. I would be the link between that kind of consciousness and Dave Dellinger or A. J. Muste, Cora Weiss. Primary in my mind going to the Stock Exchange—or even the first guerrilla communications act that we did, when we surrounded Con Edison's office with big signs saying "Breathing is hazardous to your health. . . ."

*Tell me about this.*

We ran and put soot bombs inside the offices, the elevators, and everything. We all dressed up in black and looked sooty, which looked wild on TV, it was amazing. But let me say that, about all these actions, foremost in my mind was stopping the war in Vietnam. We tried to invent different ways which would break people away from the mainstream kind of thinking which got them to salute without thinking, my country right or wrong, whatever it says. If it says "go kill," then go kill. If it says "study," then study. If it says, "pay your bill," then pay your bill. People would hear about us or see excerpts on television, read about it in the papers. They would identify with it, get ideas of their own, and start doing it all over the place. "Ideology of the deed" implies that the act is going to be reproduced in various forms in various ways by others in a kind of spontaneous generation. That doesn't mean that we didn't have any structure of communications of our own, or leadership. We had all that, too. It was just that these kinds of events were moving faster along the communication belt than a leaflet.

*You were always thinking about the way things would look when they were photographed.*

Always. When I got up and dressed. I mean, that's the point. If I made a leaflet or a button I was aware of how it was going to communicate. Television was a little more tricky, as was the press, because you don't have the final say, so it's all distorted and everything. But ultimately I learned that that was okay, it didn't matter.

*Why was that?*

Because mythology is always distorting everything. The basic idea to get across is that someone went somewhere and tried to disrupt something. They tried to disrupt Con Edison, say. It doesn't matter what the media says about it, because some kind of emotional time bomb is stuck in the place.

*And how did that make it mythology?*

It was mythology the way I am a myth. The way people come up to me and say, weren't you a leader of the Klan in the sixties? Aren't you a woman? You're taller. Are you still on Wall Street? Didn't you play with the Grateful Dead? One of my favorites is that I invented long hair. I told him it wasn't true. He said, oh no, you made it legal in America. I said, now you're right! At the trial in Chicago, outside the courthouse on the opening day I did a front flip, full in the air, and landed on my feet. It was great that I could do it, it was about fifty-fifty at that age. But later, as that story got told, I heard I did it right in front of the judge, seventeen stories up. "Wow, he did a somersault right in front of the judge." So myth brings closure. For example, people said we were banging on the walls of the Democratic convention in 1968, but we didn't get within seven miles of the building. We couldn't get out of Lincoln Park. So the numbers increase, the closeness of the symbols increases. That's myth.

*Myth was a way to communicate critical messages through the media.*

But there were lots of positive things, too. We were giving out free food and had free concerts. One day a bunch of us said we were going to clean a street all across New York. It was Seventh Street, and we said we were going to clean the street from river to river. We put out leaflets and we got thousands of people. Certain things done around Liberty Week, or Hands Across America, most definitely, were bastardizations of a kind of public art that we brought to the modern era. Let's say we brought it with a political edge, and they took the political edge away.

*Your approach to the media was a lot different than the Old Left or the SDS.*
Oh sure, because the Old Left and SDS were drawing from the academic tradition and the religious tradition. They're not even that interested in winning.

*What do you mean by that?*
The academic tradition teaches you how to present a problem, and the religious tradition shows you how to be on the right side of the angels, and maybe even go down in martyrdom. But it's not exactly like the Super Bowl, where you've got another team to beat. It's a game, but hell you're playing the game as hard as you can. I play those games as hard as I can. That's why when they say, oh, you're just acting and everything, I say, yeah, well, three dislocated vertebrae, four broken noses. It's real blood. It is a little shocking, but this is, after all, real life that we're talking about. We're taking real risks.

*You were very involved with the new culture, the poetry, the rock music . . .*
The whole idea was to try and hyphenate the two political cultures. But, you know, now when I talk to people about reprinting my early books, they say, "Don't tell them they're political books, just say 'culture' and the publishers will say okay. Maybe we can get them through as art, but not as politics." Unfortunately, as the story gets told, you pick up a new book on the sixties, it is written by a college professor, so it's analytical, academic, and it slightly misses the point, the flavor of it all. Go and look at the underground newspapers of the time. The prettiest one was the *San Francisco Oracle*, they had twelve issues, and some small press is putting it out now as a limited edition. It'll go right away. Like I say, if I had all those poems, even if I had manuscripts,

early things that I wrote, they're worth much more than stuff I could write today.

*That's for collectors.*
Universities. But I don't have anything, I don't collect it. It's all out there in the gutter. A lot of the films, too. We had alternative newsreels. We had people with early video equipment, early cameras, filming all these events. But a lot of it is simply rotting away. The videotape then simply wasn't the quality it is today, so it's rotting away. Very hard to find a lot of good footage of me, for example.

*That's funny. I'm surprised.*
Well, maybe after I'm dead they'll dredge it up, but I haven't seen stuff that I thought was particularly good. One good shot of one good speech in May 1970, but the rest of the stuff is, you know, minor. And people like it, too, when they see it. But I'm telling you, the best stuff's lost. That's the thing about all this. You had to have been there. I'm telling you we surrounded a five-sided figure which symbolizes evil in many religions with a circle to demystify it, and the building rose—the Pentagon rose in the air. But you had to be there to see it! You ask anyone who was there, and they'll tell you, yeah, sure it turned orange and it rose, it went right up!

*In* Revolution for the Hell of It, *you said "Understanding is the first step to control, and control is the secret to our extinction."*
Right. As I said at one point, chaos is mightier than the sword. Of course, I wouldn't be alive if this wasn't true. I can't tell you how many times I've been . . . four times attacked by mobs of five hundred to a thousand people, or more, or small groups. And they never laid a glove on me.

*Quick reflexes?*
Peripheral vision. What looks like a rioting mob with a lot of movement seems to slow down. It's the same with athletes. If you talk to them,

they'll tell you that even though the game might look very fast, it doesn't seem that way to them. They've trained themselves to slow it down. It has something to do with the way you stay calm. When people are rioting they are out of control, they are not aiming. It's not like a cop. If three cops are coming after you, they've had a lot of practice. But a riot of a thousand people, they're just angry. They throw their babies at you, they throw their jewelry at you, they start punching their friends. You know, they're a frenzied mob. As long as they don't have a rope, you know . . . Also I've had situations where at least one hundred police have pulled guns on me, maybe three or four times that's happened. I got scared in Mississippi . . . I've always felt that dying for what you believe in is an honor, so that brings a certain madness to the situation, a certain confusion, and in the cop's mind, he doesn't know how to deal with this. This is something new. They haven't seen this. Of course, if I pull out a gun, they're used to that. If you pull out a gun they all know what to do. Mostly I would just try to use the fact that I had some presence. "You're sure you want to do this? You know who I am? You know who my uncle is? You'll be pounding the beat in Staten Island." Every police force has a place where cops get punished without getting kicked off the force. So you know that, you know cop talk. And they know you know their cop talk, and the only way you'd know that they don't want to pound the beat in Staten Island is if you have some pull. They think you know the inner ways of the power structure, so they back off. They get nervous about that. It's something that they haven't seen with your standard, run-of-the-mill suspect.

*Another quote from* **Revolution for the Hell of It:** *"Theater is involving for those who are ready for it, while it's dismissed as nonthreatening by those who could potentially wreck the stage."*

Those who would get it, would get it, and those that won't, they won't. It took a strange person to get it and be very threatened by it. There were some people who thought we were too sneaky and very dangerous, and when they understood that, then we were in deep shit. So we took risks. People risked a lot more than their career and marriage plans. I mean, it's tough. I'll go to a group now that wants to fight a toxic waste dump or a nuclear power plant, and someone will say "Well, my lawyer says I can get sued." Sued? I'm coming from where you could get hung! See, by '68 they were passing hordes of laws so that we couldn't even move across state lines, we were banned from speaking in certain states. The Interstate Riot Act. You couldn't wear a shirt that looked like the flag. They were going after hippie garb, etc. That was the period when the very strict marijuana-possession laws came in. They were catching on that the cultural thing mattered. Anyone looking at Freedom of Information Act files could see that. It was around this period they hired a psychologist to analyze me, and Jerry Rubin, too. I met the person later. They couldn't figure out the chaos, the confusion, they couldn't figure the motive. Why would they throw their money out at the Stock Exchange? These are white, smart kids. They could go work for IBM and everything. Why are they running around in slums getting their heads cracked by cops. You see, they couldn't figure it out. So as long as they couldn't figure it out, you were winning. Later on they did. It was the mid-'70s when you get the rise of the Right. They figured out how TV is used, the use of modern technology, especially computers. And you see antiabortion people out there doing civil disobedience, saying this is the civil-rights movement of the eighties. The way they mix up culture and religion. When I went to Pat Robertson's 700 Club as a fugitive in 1976, I covered it as an underground writer—I was really underground!—I was saying, hey, I'm watching the counterrevolution to the sixties, right here. They're using the same techniques, plus they've got plenty of money, and they're wrapped in the flag, and in the Bible. My God, it's going to be no contest. Organizers on the Right would tell you that they picked our methods apart. They didn't like our goals, but they liked our methods. They studied our methods and gave it back to us. Wouldn't you? Somebody had to study this. I mean, the U.S. didn't get away with a war against a little country. Something went wrong. Something happened.

*So this method of symbolic action had a direct political impact?*
You know, within a month they spent twenty thousand dollars building a bulletproof wall around the Stock Exchange gallery. In fact I'm told that if you go on the tour that they will say that this is where the hippies ran up and threw the money off the railing. It's become part of the tour. Symbolic warfare is close to the real thing. Disrupt the fantasy world, memory bank, all these images—you can show that they're so vulnerable and fragile. Their reaction is going to be, well, next week they're not going to be throwing money, they'll be throwing bullets, it'll be violent. In a way the disruptive thing is violent, even though it's very peaceful what we did and everything. To people in power, it makes fun of their precious symbol, Wall Street. It made fools out of them. Just a handful of hippies brought the thing to a stop. Changed the whole world of commerce in an instant. They don't like that. I mean later, just about everybody's going to be giggling about it. Ten, fifteen, twenty years later. But that's one of the neat little tricks. That's how you get away with it. That's why I'm alive, and that's why I'm fifty-two.

# VI

# COMMUNITY

# TRANSITION TOWN:
# A TONIC FOR THE PEAK OIL BLUES

*Alex Munslow*

The term *Peak Oil* warns of the end of cheap and plentiful energy. An expanding world population of 6.5 billion suggests a limit for growth will eventually be reached (if it hasn't been already) and no combination of current alternative energy sources will sustain the world's accelerating thirst for power. As oil production inevitably declines and resources become scarce, the world faces a turbulent descent. We depend on a globalized economy that is completely reliant on ready supplies of this nonrenewable resource. But envisioning a life without the luxuries afforded by abundant oil can quickly lead one to denial. It's much easier to absolve our responsibility to some higher authority—the government, the oil companies, technology, God.

The exact tipping point in world oil production cannot be plotted until a clear decline can be seen, by which time it will be too late. Experts analyzing this situation are divided between "early tippers" and "late tippers"—those who think world oil production has already peaked, or is about to peak in the next few years, and those who believe there are decades left. The Hirsch Report, a U.S. Energy Department study into the effects of Peak Oil, claims that without at least a decade of preparation, the world economic, social, and political cost would be "unprecedented." Without this "timely mitigation," confronting the effects of Peak Oil and climate change will be like trying to put up a new tent in the dark. If government reports warn us that at least a ten-year transition period is required if we are to survive the energy descent, the burning question is: When do we begin the transition?

In the UK we have seen the emergence of the Transition Town as a preparation for the coming oil crisis. Like most good ideas, it doesn't seem like a new one so much as an idea remembered. Its origins lie in the raised beds of Permaculture, the Australian agricultural design system pioneered by David Holmgrem and Bill Mollison. Inspired by the ideas of author Richard Heinberg and Dr. Colin Campbell of ASPO, a Peak Oil awareness organization, the first Transition Town began in Kinsale, Ireland, in 2004. Imagining a sustainable arrangement for life in the post-oil future, permaculturalist teacher Rob Hopkins and students from his Sustainability course collaborated on a town-planning strategy called the "Kinsale Energy Descent Action Plan." Hopkins and his team presented their plan in a time line of achievable steps taken over several years. At the heart of their strategy was the idea to turn the obstacles of the energy crisis into opportunities for building local resilience and revitalizing the community. Encouraged by great enthusiasm for the idea, Hopkins took the Transition Town vision to Totnes in Devon.

The Transition strategy begins with the formation of a small steering group (designed with its own demise from the beginning). In the early stages, local awareness is generated by a series of lectures, film viewings, and meetings. Compelling Peak Oil documentaries such as The End of Suburbia and The Power of Community serve as tools of mass tribal initiation at these gatherings, awakening people to the challenges of the coming crisis. After the town hall screenings, local audiences are encouraged to discuss the issues raised by the films and suggest ideas and solutions to their own community's oil dependency.

Existing local environmental and community organizations are invited to jointly organize events that respond to these issues, with smaller groups assigned to specific concerns such as food security, waste and recycling, education, housing, transport, and local economy. By a combination of serendipity and synchronicity, these roles are generally filled by the appropriate people at the required time. The momentum behind the project builds up over a period of months until the official "Unleashing" event finally launches the plan to the general public.

In order to assist communities working toward these goals, the Transition Network was set up by activist Ben Brangwyn to support and train town leaders as they adopt Transition Initiatives. Through its work across the UK, the Transition Network aims to "unleash the collective genius" within communities, leading to a more resilient and fulfilling lifestyle. Last September there were only two Transition Towns in the UK; inspired by the successes of Kinsale and Totnes, there are already around ninety towns now at various stages of transition, from "mulling it over" to fully "unleashed."

The Transition Town strategy avoids an "us and them" mentality, building bridges between community members and local government. The approach developed to relocalize the Totnes economy was endorsed by the Town Council, and a new local currency called the "Totnes Pound" is accepted by many local businesses and shops. Strategies like this may one day stop the flow of money out of local communities, providing a protective buffer between a healthy local economy and fluctuations in the national currency.

A general objective of Transition Towns is to preserve or reintroduce the importance of farming within a community, working toward local food production with less reliance on transport and chemicals. The benefits to this shift are obvious: Local food production sustains the local economy and bolsters the overall well-being of a community. "Seed swaps" are an excellent means of strengthening local farming and working toward sustainability. At these events, heirloom seed varieties are freely exchanged in an effort to revitalize the genetic diversity of crops while bypassing legislations written to protect corporate monopolies. According to UK law, seeds cannot be sold legally unless they appear on the EU National Seed List. Registration is expensive, so only a few seeds make it on, and these are generally owned by a handful of companies who have dominated the commercial market with hybridized seeds. These genetically modified seeds are designed to produce sterile plants, forcing farmers to buy a renewed supply each season and resulting in the extinction of many seed varieties. Seed swaps side step the corporate seed industry and thus play a crucial role in reclaiming control of local food production.

Transition Town meetings often employ the self-organizing method of "open space." According to this arrangement, attendees are invited to create the agenda and host their own discussion groups, within which participants freely move about. Whoever shows up to the meeting are the right people; whenever it starts is the right time; and when it's over, it's over. Those who attend have chosen to be there and are willing to contribute. Each group records the conversations, and at the end of the day, the full group reconvenes for feedback and comments, which are then made available via an Internet wiki.

Transition Towns provide training and courses to facilitate what has become known as "The Great Re-Skilling." This begins by interviewing the elders of the community. To return to a lower-energy future, it is necessary to engage with those who directly remember a lower-energy society and relearn skills that their generation took for granted. To instigate change, it is important to first understand the psychological barriers to transformation. The Transition Town model offers a set of creative tools for communities to engage with the dual problems of both Peak Oil and climate change. It deals practically with the physical manifestation of the problem and can be conveyed very simply to a large number of people at once.

Cheap oil has allowed Western societies to cut through the intricate web of beneficial relationships that once held communities together. Transition Town is a grassroots movement of people learning to relate to one another again. Behind the descent plan is the belief that with creativity and imagination, and under a well-designed strategy, the future without oil could be preferable to the present.

# BECOME AN URBAN HOMESTEADER

## Homegrown Evolution

Prompted over the past few years by oil wars, global warming, ecological collapse, natural disasters, and our psychotic federal government, we've made a few changes in the way we live.

Now the day begins when Erik gets up to let the chickens out of their henhouse. It's a structure so thoroughly secured against marauding raccoons that we've named it "Chicken Guantanamo." The hens have been patiently waiting for that door to swing open since first light. Next, while the coffee brews, Erik throws some flour and a cup of sourdough starter into the mixer. He bakes a loaf of artisanal sourdough bread for us every other day, and we rarely meet with any bread that tastes better.

I get up a little later than Erik and stagger into the garden first thing. I say hi to the hens, add some kitchen scraps to the compost pile, and turn on the drip irrigation systems that water our vegetable beds. As of this writing our garden is bearing tomatoes, cucumbers, fava beans, Swiss chard, figs, ground cherries, leeks, eggplants, assorted herbs, and a selection of cultivated weeds. I'm looking forward to the corn, avocado, and pomegranate harvest, all of which are a few months away.

For breakfast I enjoy homemade yogurt with raw honey or maybe a thick slice of the aforementioned sourdough, toasted and smeared with tangy homemade apricot butter. After breakfast I take three sheets of tomatoes down to the solar dehydrator so we'll have sun-dried tomatoes in the winter. Then I hang a load of laundry out on the line.

Where do Erik and I live? In the heart of urban Los Angeles, in a decaying bungalow on a small plot of land. We are urban homesteaders.

## WHAT IS AN URBAN HOMESTEADER?

An urban homesteader is someone who enjoys living in the city but doesn't see why that should stop her from engaging directly with nature, growing her own food, and striving for self-sufficiency.

We don't wish to retreat to the countryside and live like the Unabomber in a plywood shack. We believe that people are best off living in cities and cooperating with other like-minded folks. Instead of hoarding ammo and MREs, we're building the skills and forming the conditions and networks that sustain us, our friends, and our neighbors, now and into the future.

Urban homesteading is about preparedness, but we don't like that term very much. It connotes stockpiling things that you hope will keep your ass alive. Survivalism in general is about the fear of death. Urban homesteading is about life—it is a way of life founded on pleasure, not fear. Our preparedness comes not so much through what we have, but what we know. We are recollecting the almost-lost knowledge of our great-grandparents, those most essential of human skill sets: How to tend to plants, how to tend to animals, and how to tend ourselves.

Over the last couple of generations we've given up these skills in exchange for a self-destructive addiction to "convenience," becoming, as a friend of ours likes to say, the only animal that cannot feed itself. We do not make anything anymore, we just consume—we are "consumers," defined solely by our appetites, and empowered only in how we spend a dollar. We figured it was time to become producers again.

That is what we are trying to do here on our little urban farm: produce food, hack our house to generate power and recycle water, plot revolution, and build community. Changing what and how we eat is at the heart of everything, though. Homegrown food is mind-blowingly fresh and flavorful, 100 percent organic, untainted by disease, blood, or oil, and alive. Trust us, once you discover that lettuce actually has a distinct flavor, or you eat a sweet tomato still warm from the sun, or an orange-yolked egg from your own hen, you will never be satisfied with the prepackaged and the factory-farmed again. The next step after growing fresh food is using the old home arts to preserve it: pickling, fermenting, drying, and brewing.

Over and over again we've discovered that anything we figure out how to do ourselves tastes better than what the market offers us. If it wasn't, we probably wouldn't keep doing this. Yes, it is a "green" way to live, it is a prepared way to live, it has many virtues, but frankly, it is pleasure that inspires us to do more and more. Get into this a little, and you'll realize that all of your life you've been cheated. Urban homesteading is not about deprivation or suffering, it is about reclaiming your heritage, and your right to real food and real experience.

## MAKE THE SHIFT

We are not alone, and we didn't invent this idea. Urban homesteading is a movement, a quiet movement of sensible people making the smart choice of disconnecting ourselves in healthy ways from an increasingly untenable reality and creating our own culture from the ground up. We live better, we eat better, we're saving the planet. What's not to love?

Anyone can be an urban homesteader, even if you live in an apartment. You can grow more food than you think in a small space: on a balcony, a roof, a side yard. Do you live in a windowless hole? Then use a community garden plot, or claim land and become a pirate gardener. Opportunity abounds even for those of us in the dense metropolitan core. We've met a guy who keeps bees on his roof and harvests hundreds of pounds of honey each year in the middle of Brooklyn.

Most American cities sprawl. They possess tremendous amounts of wasted space. Once you take the red pill and open your eyes, all of that space begs to be cultivated. It is an offense on the level of sin for good land to sit unappreciated and unused under lawn and concrete. The single family dwelling with its defensive swath of front lawn and hidden backyard—the basic unit of the American dream—happens to be the perfect mini-farm. We have a vision of cities greened not by lawns, but by crops, thousands of city gardens collectively forming vast tracts of urban acreage. We each can start with our own patch of land and in doing so inspire others. Since we planted our parkway (that useless space between the sidewalk and the street that is technically city property) with vegetables, several of our neighbors have planted their own victory gardens.

Urban homesteaders are forming organic networks to share knowledge and know-how. What our ancestors took for granted, we have to reinvent. It is hard to figure all this out alone, so we have to help one another. Erik and I have been documenting our homesteading experiences on our own blog, Homegrown Revolution, for over a year. Now we are going to be the in-house urban homesteaders at *Reality Sandwich*. Over the coming months our posts here will cover the homesteading basics. Not by ranting, as we have today, but through step-by-step projects and practical advice that will make a homesteader out of you in no time.

## START YOUR GUERRILLA GARDEN

When we first encountered Taylor Arneson, he was bringing back to life the dead, sunbaked soil of an abandoned lot just off Sunset Boulevard in the rapidly gentrifying southern extreme of Los Angeles' Silver Lake district. A nearly featherless rooster, rescued from the streets of Hollywood, pecked at the compost Arneson and a couple of accomplices were spreading. Despite the shabby surroundings we were in the midst of some of the most expensive real estate in the country, on a lot that has stood vacant for many years. Arneson and his crew did not have permission to plant this lot—they are guerrilla farmers, repurposing the landscape by planting food.

To the landless urban farmer, every vacant lot, parkway, office building planter, and apartment courtyard is a potential cornfield, orchard, or vegetable patch. The guerrilla farmer is an opportunist, squeezing growing space into the disused cracks of our overpriced and poorly designed urban landscape—those precious interstitial spaces, patches of soil that for one reason or another have been abandoned by absentee landlords, negligent cities, or are caught in some sort of legal purgatory. A pirate of old would always prefer to target a fat, unarmed merchantman over a guarded flotilla. In the same way, a pirate gardener picks the easy targets and avoids the big battles.

To irrigate his guerrilla gardens Arneson taps into the nearest waterline. As he says, "Who it's owned by is a minor issue because tap water is so cheap that you can do a large garden for a few dollars a month, especially if you're growing things that are appropriate for the region and you use the water sparingly." Arneson does not go out of his way to contact the owners, but neither does he avoid them. "There's a lot of benefits for both parties. They get their space to look better, so they don't have as many complaints from the neighbors, and I'm building soil for them for when they go to do landscaping in the future." So far his biggest coup is a 15-by-150-foot strip in a disused planter along west Los Angeles' busy Bundy Boulevard where, last summer, he planted peppers, corn, squash, beans, fig trees, and a mulberry tree.

Nance Klehm, a professional landscaper and artist in Chicago, has done a number of clever appropriations of disused urban land for the purpose of growing food. Her "Neighborhood Orchard" project began several years ago when her neighbor, Trevino, refused to take any money for fixing her furnace. Klehm proposed an exchange, planting an apple tree in his yard in lieu of cash. Trevino responded enthusiastically and several years worth of similar bartering has resulted in what Klehm describes as a loosely organized agglomeration of plantings in her low-income, mostly Latino neighborhood on the south side of Chicago.

Neighborhood Orchard is simple and opportunistic, in the best meaning of that word. There's no big mission statement, no nonprofit 501c3, no board of directors, merely a set of informal relationships. Klehm does most of the start-up work for Neighborhood Orchard, which takes place in backyard gardens, and plants more than the host family can use so that there will be a surplus crop meant for sharing. "Neighborhood Orchard is not organized, we don't have meetings or an end of the year BBQ. People just know that they can go in different yards and pick from them."

The effort has had residual benefits, "It's kind of broken the barriers between our yards," says Klehm. "We borrow tools back and forth. We borrow trucks. So there's other things that have come out of this because we're in other people's yards and spaces and lives in a different way."

For Homegrown Evolution's first foray into piratical gardening, we hijacked the parkway in front of our house, that bit of dirt between the sidewalk and the street that technically belongs to the city, but is the responsibility of the homeowner to maintain. It's yet another space, like the vast asphalt hell of parking lots, garages, freeways, car lots, auto repair shops, and junkyards in our car-obsessed city dedicated to the needs of the personal automobile.

We decided to flaunt the city's strict rules about this space, which dictates the kind of things that can be planted (basically nothing that would inhibit someone from getting out of their Hummer), and planted a vegetable garden instead. Our neighborhood's interstercial qualities have worked to our advantage: It's the kind of neighborhood where city bureaucrats tend to look the other way.

For our parkway garden we built two six-by-six-foot raised beds, filled them with quality garden soil, and stuck in two matching wire obelisks for growing beans and tomatoes, and also as a nod to aesthetic concerns, since this is a public space. Much to our surprise it has been a big success. The first winter we had a bumper crop of carrots, beans, turnips, garlic, onions, and beets in the winter and the next summer a never-ending crop of cherry tomatoes.

We've encouraged neighbors to help themselves to vegetables from the parkway garden, though few have. Theft is a much smaller problem in public garden spaces then most would imagine. What has been nice has been the conversations we've had with neighbors while watering and tending the space. Several neighbors have said that it encouraged them to plant their own vegetables. Just before Halloween this year, as the corn we planted earlier in the summer neared harvest, we found an elderly neighbor standing and staring at the tall cornstalks. On the verge of tears, she told us that the corn reminded her of life on her family's farm in Cuba before the revolution. Our micro-field of corn was bringing up memories of her father and her life in Cuba some fifty years ago. Ironically, Cuba in recent years has become a leader in exactly this sort of interstercial urban agriculture after the fall of the Soviet Union ended oil subsidies that made large-scale industrial farms unworkable. Just to survive, Cubans have had to do exactly the sort of small-scale urban plantings that Arneson, Klehm, and Homegrown Evolution have been experimenting with.

In part, guerrilla gardening is a reaction to the criminally wasteful nonuse of land exemplified by vacant lots, parkways, and freeway medians. In Sir Thomas More's *Utopia,* he says of its residents that they, "account it a very just cause of war, for a nation to hinder others from possessing a part of that soil of which they make no use, but which is suffered to lie idle and uncultivated; since every man has by the law of nature a right to such a waste portion of the earth as is necessary for his subsistence."

Such a war was fought here in Los Angeles in the summer of 2006 over the South Central Farm, a community garden turned guerrilla garden cut out of a fourteen-acre swath of concrete and asphalt just south of downtown. South Central Farm began as an official community garden after protests by the community over the city's plans to build a trash incinerator on the site. Unfortunately the land reverted back to the developer nine years later, after a closed door City Council session. Despite the city's cowardly return of the land to the developer, the South Central Farmers squatted and continued their urban farming experiment. A long and complex tug-of-war between the owner, the developer, the city government ensued, and the South Central Farm ended in the early-morning hours of June 13, 2006, with the farmer's forced eviction by an army of Los Angeles County Sheriff Department officers. A month later this lush oasis of edible and medicinal plants and trees was bulldozed and the land is, once again, a barren vacant lot.

Perhaps the lesson with South Central Farm is the futility of direct confrontation with the moneyed and politically connected powers that conspire to make our urban spaces "idle and uncultivated." As Arneson and Klehm prove, the best strategy may be to look between the cracks, to cultivate our food in the margins, to abandon the big ideas and mission statements and simply pick up a shovel and plant wherever and whenever we can.

Tips for starting your own pirate garden:

1. Look for disused space near where you live or work. Vegetable gardening is intensive and you'll need to keep an eye on the plants.
2. Is the space weed-whacked on a regular basis? If so find an overgrown space where your plants won't get cut down.
3. Look for easy access to water. Unless you live in a rainy region, that will be key. Consider mixing pirate vegetables in with existing plantings to take advantage of automated watering systems. Just be sure that your food doesn't get sprayed with pesticides.
4. If you don't like the uncertainty of going completely guerrilla, ask neighbors, friends, and family, and your place of work if you can garden on their land. You get space, they get a tended yard, and you all get

fresh food. Or approach the owner of an abandoned lot and offer to maintain the lot in return for allowing you to plant a garden.

5. Make seed bombs. Seed bombs are balls of compost, clay, and native plant seeds that can be thrown into vacant lots to germinate wildflowers.

# SUMERIAN ECONOMICS

*Peter Lamborn Wilson*

Public secret: Everyone knows but no one speaks. Another kind of public secret: The fact is published but no one pays attention.

A cuneiform tablet called *The Sumerian King List* states that "kingship first descended from heaven in the city of Eridu," in the south of Sumer. Mesopotamians believed Eridu was the oldest city in the world, and modern archaeology confirms the myth. Eridu was founded about 5000 BC and disappeared under the sand around the time of Christ.

Eridu's god Ea or Enki (a kind of Neptune and Hermes combined) had a ziggurat where fish were sacrificed. He owned the *ME*, the fifty-one principles of Civilization. The first king, named "Staghorn," probably ruled as Enki's high priest. After some centuries came the Flood, and kingship had to descend from heaven again, this time in Uruk and Ur. Gilgamesh now appears on the list. The flood actually occurred; Sir Leonard Wooley saw the thick layer of silt at Ur between two inhabited strata.

Bishop Ushher once calculated according to the Bible that the world was created on October 19, 4004 BC at 9 o'clock in the morning. This makes no Darwinian sense, but provides a good date for the founding of the Sumerian state, which certainly created a new world. Abraham came from Ur of the Chaldees; Genesis owes much to the Enuma Elish (Mesopotamian Creation Myth). Our only text is late Babylonian but obviously based in a lost Sumerian original. Marduk the war god of Babylon has apparently been pasted over a series of earlier figures beginning with Enki.

Before the creation of the world as we know it a family of deities held sway. Chief among them at the time, Tiamat (a typical avatar of the universal Neolithic earth goddess) described by the text as a dragon or serpent, rules a brood of monsters and dallies with her "Consort" (high priest) Kingu, an effeminate Tammuz/Adonis prototype. The youngest gods are dissatisfied with her reign; they are "noisy," and Tiamat (the text claims) wants to destroy them because their noise disturbs her slothful slumber. In truth the young gods are simply fed up with doing all the shitwork themselves because there are no "humans" yet. The gods want Progress. They elect Marduk their king and declare war on Tiamat.

A gruesome battle ensues. Marduk triumphs. He kills Tiamut and slices her body lengthwise in two. He separates the halves with a mighty ripping heave. One half becomes sky above, the other earth below.

Then he kills Kingu and chops his body up into gobs and gobbets. The gods mix the bloody mess with mud and mold little figurines. Thus humans are created as robots for the gods. The poem ends with a triumphalist paean to Marduk, the new king of heaven.

Clearly the Neolithic is over. City god, war god, metal god vs. country goddess, lazy goddess, garden goddess. The creation of the world equals the creation of civilization, separation, hierarchy, masters and slaves, above and below. Ziggurat and pyramid symbolizes the new shape of life.

Combining *Enuma elish* and the *King List* we get an explosive secret document about the origin of civilization not as gradual evolution toward inevitable future, but as violent coup, conspiratorial overthrow of primordial rough-egalitarian Stone Age society by a crew of black magic cult cannibals. (Human sacrifice first appears in the archaeological record at Ur III. Similar grisly phenomena in the first few Egyptian dynasties.)

About 3100, writing was invented at Uruk. Apparently you can witness the moment in the strata: one layer no writing, next layer writing.

Of course writing has a prehistory (like the State). From ancient times a system of accounting had grown up based on little clay counters in the shapes of commodities (hides, jars of oil, bars of metal, etc.). Also glyptic seals had been invented with images used heraldically to designate the seals' owners. Counters and seals were pressed into slabs of wet clay and the records were held in Temple archives—probably records of debts owed to the Temple. (In the Neolithic Age the temples no doubt served as redistribution centers. In the Bronze Age they began to function as banks.)

As I picture it, the invention of real writing took place within a singly brilliant family of temple archivists over three or four generations, say a century. The counters were discarded and a reed stylus was used to impress signs in clay, based on the shapes of the old counters, and with further pictograms imitated from the seals. Numbering was easily compacted from rows of counters to number-signs. The real breakthrough came with the flash that certain pictographs could be used for their sound divorced from their meaning and recombined to "spell" other words (especially abstractions). Integrating the two systems proved cumbersome, but maybe the sly scribes considered this an advantage. Writing needed to be difficult because it was a mystery revealed by gods and a monopoly of the New Class of scribes. Aristocrats rarely learned to read and write—a matter for mere bureaucrats. But writing provided the key to state expansion by separating sound from meaning, speaker from hearer, and sight from other senses. Writing as separation both mirrors and reinforces separation as "written," as fate. Action-at-a-distance (including distance of time) constitutes the magic of the state, the nervous system of control. Writing both *is* and *represents* the new "Creation" ideology. It wipes out the oral tradition of the Stone Age and erases the collective memory of a time before hierarchy. In the text we have always been slaves.

By combining image and word in single memes or hieroglyphs the scribes of Uruk (and a few years later the predynastic scribes of Egypt) created a magical system. According to a late syncretistic Greco-Egyptian myth, when Hermes-Toth invents writing he boasts to his father Zeus that humans never need forget anything ever again. Zeus replies, "On the contrary my son, now they'll forget *everything*." Zeus discerned the occult purpose of the text, the forgetfulness of the oral/aural, the false memory of the text, indeed the *lost* text. He sensed a void where others saw only a plenum of information. But this void is the *telos* of writing.

Writing begins as a method of controlling debt owed to the Temple, debt as yet another form of absence. When full-blown economic texts appear a few strata later we find ourselves already immersed in a complex economic world based on debt, interest, compound interest, debt peonage as well as outright slavery, rents, leases, private and public forms of property, long-distance trade, craft monopolies, police, and even a "money-lenders bazaar." Not money as we understand it yet, but commodity currencies (usually barley and silver), often loaned for as much as $33^1/_3$ percent per year. The Jubilee or periodic forgiveness of debts (as known in the Bible) already existed in Sumer, which would have otherwise collapsed under the load of debt.

Sooner or later the bank (i.e., the temple) would solve this problem by obtaining the monopoly on money. By lending at interest ten or more times its actual assets, the modern bank simultaneously creates debt and the money to pay debt. *Fiat,* "let it be." But even in Sumer the indebtedness of the king (the state) to the temple (the bank) had already begun.

The problem with commodity currencies is that no one can have a monopoly on cows or wheat. Their materiality limits them. A cow might calve, and barley might grow, but not at rates demanded by usury. Silver doesn't grow at all.

So, the next brilliant move, by King Croesus of Lydia (Asia Minor, seventh century BC), was the invention of the coin, a refinement of money just as the Greek alphabet (also seventh century) was a refinement of writing. Originally a temple token or souvenir signifying one's "due portion" of the communal sacrifice, a lump of metal impressed with a royal or temple seal (often a sacrificial animal such as the bull), the coin begins its career with *mana*, something supernatural, something more (or less) than the weight of the metal. Stage two, coins showing two faces, one with image, the other with writing. You can never see both at once, suggesting the metaphysical slipperiness of the object, but together they constitute a hieroglyph, a word/image expressed in metal as a single meme of value.

Coins might "really" be worth only their weight in metal but the temple says they're worth more and the king is ready to enforce the decree. The object and its value are separated; the value floats free, the object circulates. Money works the way it works because of an absence not a presence. In fact money largely consists of absent wealth—debt—your debt to king and temple. Moreover, free of its anchor in the messy materiality of commodity currencies, money can now compound unto eternity, far beyond mere cows and jars of beer, beyond all worldly things, even unto heaven. "Money begets money," Ben Franklin gloated. But money is dead. Coins are inanimate objects. Then money must be the sexuality of the dead.

The whole of Greco-Egyptian-Sumerian economics compacts itself neatly into the hieroglyphic text of the Yankee dollar bill, the most popular publication in the history of History. The own of Athena, one of the earliest coin images, perches microscopically on the face of the bill in the upper left corner of the upper right shield (you'll need a magnifying glass), and the Pyramid of Cheops is topped with the all-seeing eye of Horus or the panopticonical eye of ideology. The Washington family coat of arms (stars and stripes) combined with imperial eagle and fasces of arrows, etc.; a portrait of Washington as Masonic Grand Master; and even an admission that the bill is nothing but tender for debt, public or private. Since 1971 the bill is not even "backed" by gold, and thus has become pure textuality.

Hieroglyph as magic focus of desire deflects psyche from object to representation. It enchains imagination and defines consciousness. In this sense money constitutes the great triumph of writing, its proof of magic power. Image wields power over desire but no control. Control is added when the image is semanticized (or "alienated") by logos. The *emblem* (picture plus caption) gives desire or emotion an ideological frame and thus directs its force. Hieroglyph equals picture plus word, or picture as word ("rebus"), hence hieroglyph's power and control over both conscious and unconscious—or in other words, its magic.

# MUTUAL AID REVISITED

*Anya Kamenetz*

When Hurricane Katrina struck New Orleans, the city where I went to high school and where my parents still live, I was a continent away in San Francisco. It was impossible to get any clear picture of what was happening from the news media. They depicted full societal breakdown, the war of all against all: looting, arson, withdrawal-crazed addicts roaming the streets. The chief of police was forced to step down after he went on national television and repeated hysterical, unfounded, and since-debunked rumors of small children being raped inside the Superdome.

There couldn't be a bigger contrast with the stories I got later from those who were actually there. While mayhem and fear certainly existed, so did an amazing collective will toward cooperation. An acquaintance told of the excitement and camaraderie among a group of friends and neighbors stranded by floodwaters on the second floor of an apartment complex. They rescued dogs and made sorties by makeshift raft to local supermarkets to bring food, water, medicine, and diapers to people awaiting rescue. "It was the best days of my life," he told me with no irony.

In the two years since the storm, recovery has been agonizingly slow. The failures of government are endless. The strength of people banding together to help one another, however, has been the one bright spot. I have seen it in the city's seventy-odd neighborhoods, where dozens of new neighborhood organizations have started up—people helping one another with rebuilding, planning, and expressing their political voice. I've seen it in the efforts of hundreds of newcomers—dubbed Young Urban Rebuilding Professionals—who have come or returned South to clean up, educate, feed, offer health care, create job opportunities, and organize people to help themselves. And I've seen it on the block where my parents live, where neighbors have become friends.

Community is a neutered word nowadays. In the stale intellectual landscape of contemporary politics, there are two opposing loci of control from which large-scale solutions to social problems are thought to flow. Liberals idolize the government; conservatives, individual interest (as pursued through the market). Neither side has much to say about cooperative power beyond the utterly platitudinous.

But human societies have always nurtured, and been nurtured by, a third type of institution. In New Orleans, for over a hundred years they have called them Social Aid and Pleasure Clubs. These are the neighborhood meeting places, burial societies, and musical marching clubs that strut their stuff on Mardi Gras, St. Joseph's Day, and whenever it's time for a party.

Whether guild or labor union, religious or ethnic society, producer or consumer cooperative, crew or brotherhood or club, these are the people's bastions of power. Over the past three decades they've played a vanishing role in the life of the average American. Now is the time for that to change.

Mutual aid societies prefigure most functions of the modern state. They're at least as old as armies, but their mission is life, not death. For millennia, people have banded together to provide one another with health care, pensions, unemployment aid, investment capital, buying power, aid to the poor, disaster relief, old age care, child care, culture, entertainment, political efficacy, education, food, shelter, and livelihoods. They have also leveraged their numbers to elicit some of these same benefits from those other two institutions, business and the government. Mutual aid extends the bonds of kinship and makes individuals into citizens.

Beginning in southern India around AD 800, a network of merchants' societies known as the Ayyavole 500 spread as far as Sri Lanka, Burma, and Sumatra. The merchants agreed to cooperate and abide by a dharma, or code of conduct, ensuring honor both within the group and with outsiders. They sponsored trade fairs and maintained good relations with their local communities through philanthropic activities and tribute. The Ayyavole name was adopted far and wide for over 500 years; it became a "brand" associated with high-quality products and fair dealings.

In the 1891 history *Two Thousand Years of Gild Life,* the social reformer Rev. Joseph Malet Lambert described the rules of guilds in ancient Rome, Anglo-Saxon England, and medieval Persia. Many of these societies united people by livelihood, some were religious cults, and others were locality based, but they had common characteristics: regular contributions by members; bonds of fellowship confirmed by an oath or promise and reinforced by regular feasts and drinking parties; rules for preserving courtesy and order; and interestingly, most often, burial assistance. Beyond these basic attributes, the "gilds" were flexible, allowing for "the application of the fellowship or association to the most pressing need of the society of the day, whether mutual insurance against theft or fire, facilitation of trade, or in an imperfectly organized society, for purposes of police."

In American society, these ultimately flexible institutions found a new place and purpose. The rise of America's unprecedented multicultural democracy, middle class, and global economic power is directly tied to the rise of intermediary institutions, most famously but not only the labor union. The first labor action in America was a strike among Maine fishermen in 1636. In Northeastern cities during colonial times, master craftsmen and journeymen of many different trades formed "friendly societies," which became politically active in the fight for independence. During the Jeffersonian era these organizations grew and provided a full range of social benefits to their members, including death benefits to widows, assistance to the ill and unemployed, loans and credits, and libraries. They also helped establish a high standard of craftsmanship, a minimum wage for their work, and settle disputes among members.

As America industrialized and urbanized, mutual aid helped maintain our humanity. Historian Richard Morris writes, "Workers created a wide variety of institutions, all of them infused with a spirit of mutuality. Through their fraternal orders, cooperatives, reform clubs, political parties, and trade unions, American workers shaped a collectivist counterculture in the midst of the growing factory system."

The phrase "labor history" invokes sepia-toned images of the late nineteenth and early twentieth centuries—sitdown strikes, the Triangle Shirtwaist Factory fire, and the successful fights against child labor and for the eight-hour day. If we hold up a vanished past as the paragon of what can be accomplished by mutual aid institutions, it will prevent us from seeing what is possible in the future. In fact, the heroic image is true to a point, but the facts are far from an unbroken march to victory. Three separate times in the nineteenth century, national unions built hundreds of thousands of members only to be quashed by economic panics and political repression. Two of the most significant national organizations, the Knights of Labor (which claimed as many members as all of America's churches in the 1880s) and the Industrial Workers of the World, were put down with the help of federal action. Just as they are today, the haves were always ready to scorn the "levellers, mob, dirty-shirt party, tag, rag, and bobtail, and ringstreaked speckled rabble."

Ironically, the collectivist counterculture met its match for good in the New Deal. The leaders of the biggest unions, representing mainly skilled, industrial, white, native-born, male workers, agreed to establishment status in exchange for pulling up the ladder for all who came after them. The "tuxedo unionist" was born along with the corrupt image that dogs unions to this day. More fundamentally, the New Deal transferred many large social functions from the old mutual aid institutions to the federal government, usurping power from the grassroots. The War on Poverty with the creation of Medicare in the 1960s accelerated the process, the closest that America has ever come to a true social welfare state. Overnight, America's workers, poor and elderly received more money and assistance, but in exchange they became clients of the government rather than true agents of their own and their fellows' destinies.

For a variety of well-documented reasons, participation in mutual social institutions of all types has been in a slide since the 1960s, and union memberships' slide has been uninterrupted. However, it was not until the Reagan years that labor began to be methodically forced away from the policy table. By no means coincidentally, our social safety net has also disintegrated since then. The health care system and private pensions; Social Security and Medicare; K-12 and higher education; even infrastructure and credit; if it's a social benefit it's in an economic and political crisis right now. With the collapse of labor as a wielder of meaningful power, our economy has reverted to a model not seen since the Gilded Age. The only type of mutual benefit association currently enjoying decided government favor, the corporation, is the winner that takes all.

Clearly, the time is ripe to restore the power of intermediaries to create social good. What's been less recognized even among self-professed radicals is how much of the power is in our own hands to do so. The idea is not to turn our backs on government, nor even the market, for what they can do to supply human needs, but to ask what we can also contribute as people cooperating together.

By many measures today, we are living in a golden age of collective energy and power thanks to the Internet. The values of association, fellowship, and participation are all flourishing here online. Livelihoods are generated collectively on the Internet, too: eBay is the second-largest employer in the country, with nearly a million people making their living as independent online merchants.

The cutting edge of New Economy business theory is all about how companies can capture this awesome power of collective participation for their own profit. Networks of people acting over the Internet for no reason other than to express themselves, amuse themselves, or connect with others create value as an emergent property. As consultant Don Tapscott, a top advisor to Fortune 50 companies, describes in his recent book *Wikinomics: How Mass Collaboration Changes Everything*, "social media" are becoming a crucial source of innovation, new products, and improved services for a whole range of companies; indeed, he says, every company needs a strategy for harnessing this kind of human capital power.

But the value of online networks have only rarely been tapped in a similar way by individuals themselves for the exchange of practical, immediate benefits—other than the very valuable and important one of information.

Similarly, the social entrepreneurship movement offers a new avenue for social change by conceiving organizations that are run as efficiently and innovatively as businesses, perhaps at a profit, but with social missions. Some social entrepreneurship organizations, like the Nobel Peace Prize–winning microlending program the Grameen Bank, fit the model of mutual aid societies and have found success as a result. But too many are conceived like welfare programs, run on a client-based, not member-participation, model from the top down. So they fail to empower people beyond their own employees.

For the past year I have been working with an organization that points the way toward a new future of mutual benefit. Sara Horowitz was raised in the traditional left—her grandfather was vice president of the International Ladies' Garment Workers Union, and she and her father were both labor lawyers. But she grew impatient with the old categories and old ways of thinking. In 1995 she founded Working Today, now known as the Freelancers Union. She won a 1999 MacArthur Genius Grant for her work with the organization, which was conceived as the first step toward a "New New Deal," or new social safety net, that fits the way Americans live and work today. They currently have 52,000 members and provide health care at group rates to 17,000 freelancers in New York City. Freelancers Union members are also eligible for life, dental, and disability insurance, discounts, and connect online to exchange referrals, tricks of the trade, and job opportunities. They are beginning to have meet-ups nationwide to encourage political participation and the all-important value of fellowship. Currently the Freelancers Union is expanding health insurance to members in 30 states. Plans for providing more benefits like unemployment and retirement are under way.

Right now a turn of the political wheel gives us an opening to grow and strengthen a new type of institution: networks formed by social entrepreneurs and maintained by members, using technology, for mutual aid. The Freelancers Union example shows what's already possible. Long term, Horowitz and I envision a new social safety net to replace the one that is disintegrating, delivered by a new breed of intermediaries. New unions or other types of nonprofit affinity groups can band together to deliver services such as pensions, unemployment insurance, and group health insurance. Unlike employers, membership-supported nonprofits have a bigger chance of having a long-term stake in their members' well-being—and 30 percent of the workforce and growing doesn't have a traditional employer relationship anyway. These new groups will have some characteristics of the old institutions, but will be more flexible and adapted to our less rooted way of life. They may unite people by type of work, neighborhood, heritage, or family status. They have a chance to move beyond old political debates and strengthen democracy by channeling people's energy into participation and efficacy.

What should the government's role be? Encouraging the growth of these institutions requires halting the political war on organizing and organizers fomented by business conservatives and waged through the courts. Financially, the investment would be modest: perhaps a program of tax breaks and incentives for providing benefits similar to that now given to corporations, as well as access to low-cost capital for organizations providing a social benefit. Mutual aid is not a political cure-all or even a policy program—it's a means of delivering solutions.

For individuals, the benefits are much richer, and they can start today. If you read the *Reality Sandwich* site, you probably already participate in some form of mutual aid, like a Dumpster-dived salvaged food potluck, a benefit party to help a friend with a health care expense, a clothing swap, or a community-supported agriculture program. A growing movement of people are getting together to provide themselves with space and resources to work and make art. They are lending money to one another at mutually agreed upon rates, rather than use banks. They are forming educational and fun business networks. The Burning Man community in many cities provides a form of the old Social Aid and Pleasure club. You don't need to wait for political action; you can work within or outside the existing system, just like Indian merchants or Roman craftsmen a thousand years ago.

The idea of fostering the growth of mutual aid satisfies many political and cultural yearnings at once. Conservatives have sought to strengthen churches as social institutions, and centers of worship do have an important place in the panoply of mutual aid societies. But they don't satisfy the full range of needs for organization and political efficacy in a multicultural, nontheocratic democracy. Liberals are very vocal about the need to foster community, but too often we form organizations under duress around political grievance or "resistance," and we don't sustain them. Without rewarding self-interest through providing benefits, long-term continuity goes missing. And with a charity-based model of simply delivering benefits across class lines, populism is an empty, not an empowering, message.

Unlike the prescription of government welfare benefits, which Americans seem to be hardwired against anyway and which seem further out of reach than ever in the current atmosphere of fear and scarcity, mutual aid fosters competition, and strengthens democracy by building civic involvement and political constituencies. Unlike winner-take-all capitalism, labor market intermediaries create more winners than before. The old solutions are dead, and we have a chance to get it right this time if we join together.

# RADICAL INTERDEPENDENCE AND ONLINE TELEPATHY: HOW TWITTER HELPS US FIND ONE ANOTHER

*Jennifer Palmer*

It's springtime in New Orleans after two and a half years of winter. A rebirth has begun—new flowers are blooming along the sides of streets that were once underwater. I was there for a sunshine-filled week in April during French Quarter fest. Musicians played out on the streets in their fedoras and shades and none of the clubs charged a cover. I'd never been to the city before and felt welcomed by its chilled-out vibe and music at every corner. I also responded to its open, at times jarring displays of pain and lonesomeness—some somber, some festive, and some that were both at once. This lack of pretense sets the stage for a liberated yet melancholic scene: The blues that made the city famous have themselves been beaten a deep, steel-drum azure to match the nighttime skies over the levees. All that's left is to play it—to bang on the stars and let the world know that this mythical place is rising again.

I went to check it out and saw firsthand the *new* New Orleans that I'd been reading about in colorful dispatches *not* found in the national news—which had long since stopped chronicling the city's grim struggle. These came in the form of the triumphantly poetical "tweets" of a woman named Evelyn Rodriguez, or "eve11" as she calls herself on Twitter, the microblogging social network where I hang out online. A Twitter user publishes "tweets," or tiny posts of 140 characters about whatever it is they're doing—however banal or inadvertently poetical—"everything from what they had for lunch, or what airport they're stuck in . . . to profound declarations of revolutionary activism and links to emerging tech tools."[1] These messages are read by a group of followers who have added the writer to the list of people from whom they want to receive tweets. These can be people they already know in real life or online, or they can be total strangers that they find through Twitter itself or a Twitter search engine such as Summize.

Even's tweets herald a Southern hipster/zydeco punk peer-to-peer renaissance that was a citywide version of the kind of awakening that I was experiencing on a personal level. Her messages of hope and resiliency came at just the right time, in just the right way, and were the ticker tape proof that the profound change that I felt in my own life was happening all around the world. And I didn't want to keep quiet about it anymore.

That isn't quite the right way to put it—as Evelyn would surely agree. It's hard to express enlightenment through words, but here goes: I realized that there is a speeding up in the rate of exchange between our thoughts and desires on the so-called inside and what actually happens on the so-called outside. This speeding up is demonstrating that any strict distinction between "inside" and "outside" is arbitrary. Twitter helps make this realization possible. It is the most fluid of the popular online social networks, such as Facebook and MySpace. When I'm on Twitter, rather than interacting as a member of a criteria-based group, I'm tuning into "collective life streams." I have more freedom to be myself, and I feel embraced by a perpetual flow.

Twitter can be used by text messaging via cell phones. This mobility provides new possibilities for making the most of "between" moments. Many people "tweet" as they travel between the places where groups meet—in other words, when they are outside of the group, defined only by their individuality. This in turn raises the possibility that they will discover new groups from far-flung places on the social graph. Tweets take place in taxi cabs and in airports, while waiting for trams and waiting for a concert to start. A group could be formed around people who are fans of a movie—or around passengers stranded together at an airport who use Twitter to craft a "real time" letter of complaint to an airline CEO.

Twitter is about being untethered from the world of long e-mails, heavy buildings, offices, and the computer screen—while participating in a flow that keeps you aware and informed. The more people you follow on Twitter, the wider a net you cast with which to gather information. I follow fewer people than many, but still I hear first about most breaking international, national, and citywide news from someone on Twitter.

Twitter is a great tool for DIY, self-organizing "un-groups," such as the stranded airline passengers mentioned above. As the name would imply, an un-group doesn't have a membership policy or an explicit set of rules and hierarchies. Un-groups aren't meant to be solemn brother- or sisterhoods that you swear an oath to uphold. They are the result of practical, quick, and simple collaborative efforts to solve any of a number of problems. They can appear as needed, then disband the moment a mission is complete. Un-groups make it possible for you to express, and act on, different parts of yourself, each in a distinct context. Perhaps you work as an executive for evil Phillip Morris trying to sell more cigarettes to teens, but you also coordinate your neighborhood's toxic waste cleanup near a high school. Twitter helps you do both.

We live in a moment that can accommodate such contradictions. For most people, societal transformation is not (yet) about abandoning all aspects of their familiar lives. Rather, they're trying to fit the change that's under way within the lives they currently have. Luckily, the revolution/ evolution only needs as much time and resources as you can give to it. Not everyone is ready to leave every vestige of the old ways behind—nor is that necessarily required. Enlightenment isn't about becoming some-one else, but becoming more uniquely *you*. As Evelyn put it:

> There's a myth that awakening and the ever-unfolding enlightening is only for saints, Buddhists, someone holier than thou, someone special, someone-anyone-else. (Ha! I'm totally busting the saint archetype—my imperfections have never been more glaringly obvious and wholly okay.) We think we'd become something Other, maybe we'll morph into Mother Teresa or Jesus or Buddha or Joan of Arc or god knows. That's not it—we become more nakedly ourselves, without the burden of maintaining an awkward and cumbersome image of ourselves (we most certainly do not become anyone else).[2]

The old structures are cracking under the weight of their own over-head. As we enter the new paradigm, change is being propelled by people across the globe who realize that they can connect with one another and organize in far more fluid ways than had been possible before. And they do it outside of the traditional hierarchies, such as corporations, the church, or governments. As Internet analyst Clay Shirky explains:

> The increase in the power of both individuals and groups, outside tradi-tional organizational structures, is unprecedented. Many institutions we rely on today will not survive this change without significant alteration and the more an institution or industry relies on information as its core product, the greater and more complete the change will be. The linking of symmetrical participation and amateur production makes this period of change remarkable. Symmetrical participation means that once peo-ple have the capacity to receive information, they have the capability to send it as well. Owning a television does not give you the ability to make TV shows, but owning a computer means that you can create as well as receive many kinds of content, from the written word through sound and images. Amateur production, the result of all this new capability,

means that the category of "consumer" is now a temporary behavior rather than a permanent identity.[3]

It turns out that we don't need to spend time and energy inside highly structured groups with large overhead costs and time-sucking bureaucracies. Nonmanaged, highly motivated un-groups can be an effective and efficient way to do things. Wikipedia is a great example. The online, user-generated encyclopedia is the product of over 100 million hours of unmanaged, unpaid, un-group effort.

Evelyn's tweets made me realize that an important crossover had happened: This new way of self-organizing had spread offline. It's common knowledge that most of New Orleans was left to drown after Katrina—a botched and tardy response by all responsible governmental agencies went largely unpunished. Many poorer residents who survived were given one-way tickets out of the city, in some cases as far away as Utah, and offered no viable way to return home. Some remain afraid to come back, hearing reports of increased crime and levees that still aren't repaired. But if there was ever a place where a brand-new way of living could take root in America, this is it. By following eveii's tweets, I've seen a new America being dreamed into being:

eveii: OH, an hour ago: "This is so New Orleans, I love it." Ref'ing Casey's Cozmic Drum Cage Interplanetary Rhythm" installation.

eveii: Couldn't describe half these hacked diginstruments at NoizeFest. Music may not be entirely my scene, but I love backyard roadshows anyhow.

eveii: Chaz Fest is quintessentially New Orleans. DIY, hand-drawn signs, live local bands, homecooked (yum crawfish dumplings) in funky backyard.

eveii: Musing aloud of a New Orleans neo-renaissance BarCamp-style unconference for grassroots folks to dream, ignite, share. Maybe at XO Studios.

I became addicted to these "verbal snapshots." Healers, activists, and social entrepreneurs were moving into the frontier land of the still decimated, flood-ravaged neighborhoods and turning garbage into gold. Evelyn likened it to a start-up at the neighborhood level. She tweeted about barter galleries and the organization "Food Not Bombs" offering weekly free meals made from food rescued from grocery store Dumpsters. She posted about the politicized messages and murals that the city's graffiti artists put up. She chronicled, through tweets, the artists' ongoing war against the "Gray Ghost," an angry ex-marine waging his one-man war against graffiti. He covers it up wherever he finds it (including historic buildings or street signs) with a coat of gray paint that in many cases is more unwanted than the original graffiti. Despite his vigilante efforts, the artists persist, tagging walls with slogans such as "Disobedience is progress" and "We have a lot of ♥ work to do."

There were art shows on front lawns and inside old multifamily "shotgun" houses (so named because of their long, barrel-like design). Entire abandoned homes were turned into pieces of art—like the one the flood filled with dirt is now literally blooming flowers from its windows, nooks, and crevices. One friend of Evelyn's owned two houses—one destroyed by Katrina, another by a fire. She tweeted about how he rebuilt the first and tore down the second to turn the lot into a communal, shamanic garden. Across New Orleans, nongroups keep emerging—online and offline—around one project after another, people coming together to make things happen out of a shared need to create community.

Several years ago ("in another lifetime," as she puts it) Evelyn was a social media consultant living in the Bay Area. A series of dramatic events—including her experience as an injured survivor of the 2004 tsunami, and her return a year later to the Thai beach where it happened—led her to give up her career and participate full time in the global awakening that she saw going on. She made art and helped others to make art as well. She "rolled into action" to help the needy, not out of obligation but simply because it felt right.

Since deciding to follow her heart, Evelyn has still had hard times, but it was during these periods that she was inspired to help create new ways of being. On her blog she writes about being broke and hungry in San Francisco and feeling like an outcast from the world of restaurants and people feasting happily on food that would be thrown away if not finished. During her darkest moment she took a walk and discovered a row of fruit trees in her neighborhood she'd never noticed before— branch after branch laden with ripe, succulent fruit. This fruit became her main source of sustenance for weeks, and inspired in her a vision of a future in which fresh and whole locally grown foods are available free for everyone. This vision, which she calls Pan Mesa, calls for you to celebrate the fact that you have food by sharing it with as many people as possible:

> Divide, and conquer. A very, very ancient tactic to breed war and conflict—and maintain the illusion of control and power over others. So, if we want to reclaim our power, sometimes the simplest of things to do, start by meeting me at the table. We'll see where things go from there. Stretch me, why don't you?
>
> I believe that everyone brings something to the table. That we as human beings have more common interests than separate. If only we would sit down together, share some bread and tea, and converse.

The Pan Mesa[4] philosophy is based in part upon the new, collaborative world of the Internet, where open-source software makes it cheap and easy to have your own website, and the things you post on your blog are meant to be shared as widely as possible.

Some critics claim that the Internet has cut people off from each other, leaving them isolated in front of yet another glowing screen. But it's becoming increasingly clear that the Internet is having the opposite effect, fostering a new version of friendship, one that is more open, more fluid, more diverse, and less determined by the social politics of the groupings you belong to (i.e., where you work, where you go to school, where you live). Net connections often ignore traditional social prejudices, and are based more on shared interests. A Pan Mesa vision of friendship is one that creates a feeling of connectedness through gift-giving and making things for others. Pan Mesa brings something from the most ancient aspect of human civilization—the communal meal—together with the new occurrence of the quick, flexible, and easy to form un-group.

Last year, a few days before the anniversary of 9/11, a Twitter friend mused:

> What would happen if everyone except health and emerg services took next Tuesday "off"? No business, no driving. Just self-reflection.
>
> And then: Maybe even cook a meal at home? From scratch?
>
> What if we invited our neighbors over too?
>
> **Not Just Another Day in the Neighborhood, Let's Gather the Neighborhood to Cultivate Peace**
>
> . . . is the subtitle for the *Make Tea, Not War Communi-teas* I'm kicking off Sunday and Tuesday.

But why only Tuesday? Why not the following Wednesday? Why not every spur of the moment thereafter? Rotate homes. Use Twitter and SMS to broadcast to your friends and neighbors spontaneous get-togethers like these from Evelyn:

> Paul brought home tons of heirlooms, twitter or text back if you'd like to come over at 6.

Or:

> Masala chai brewing. With goat cheese and figs from Saratoga farmer's market. Ready in hour. Come over to Bev's.

Twitter's "rushing river of brevities"—as web usability analyst (and anarchist noise musician) Vaspers the Grate describes them—is well suited for brainstorming new possibilities. The juxtapositions of a series of tweets can have a Beat-like quality to them, with connections startling enough to suggest unprecedented ideas. Reading a series of tweets can have the effect of a William Burroughs cutup; the immediacy of one tweet following another can take precedence over the actual content of individual messages. Burroughs gives his recipe for finding what he referred to as "intersection points" in his essay "In Present Time":

> Now try this take a walk a bus a taxi do a few errands sit down somewhere drink a coffee watch tv look through the papers now return to your place and write what you have just seen heard felt thought with particular attention to precise intersection points.

These instructions sound a lot like the transcript from a typical afternoon's worth of tweets. Except that with Twitter the number of intersection points increase, because the technology interweaves the "present time" of other people with your own.

It's amazing how Twitter quickens the feedback loop between our interior selves and the universe outside us. What we send out through Twitter often returns to us in unexpected ways, as if perfectly synchronized by an invisible hand. I don't know how it works exactly, but it's similar to the way a DJ reads the vibe of a crowd and responds with *the* track that manages to hit each individual like a deliciously distorted echo of his or her own voice, saying everything that needed to be heard. "How could the DJ *know* that's what I was feeling?" you wonder. Twitter "telepathy" creates the same complicated connections between members of un-groups, which makes it seem like magic.

In the case of eveɪɪ the telepathy happens with uncanny frequency. I'll be sitting around, thinking hard about something when my mobile will buzz and it will be eveɪɪ tweeting my exact thoughts. It happened so often, I began to wonder if there might be some mind reading involved. When I met her in person, at Flora's café in NOLA, she was relaxed, smiling, yet also serious and steady. Like Flora's, she struck me as deeply welcoming yet slightly sad. After a few minutes I realized it had never been clear to me why I felt compelled to meet with her. It had something to do with Twitter, it was related to the major transformations happening in the world and in my life—and how I was having a harder and harder time keeping that sense of change to myself. We talked about writing and Twitter and not drinking and her former professional life. Locals and national guardsmen stopped in for coffees to go.

As we finished our iced teas and got ready to leave, she told me that the week before she read *A Wrinkle in Time* for the first time, in one sitting. She'd then went on to read one of the sequels, *A Swiftly Tilting Planet*. She particularly liked the part in *A Wrinkle in Time* when Calvin feels compelled to walk out to the haunted house in the woods, where he runs into Meg and her younger brother, Charles. They ask him what he's doing there and he can't tell them. There was no other reason—no deeper explanation—just a compulsion to be at a certain place.

"I really like that," Evelyn said, and smiled as the barista walked around behind her, snapping off the café lights one by one.

"I like that, too," I said, my heart pounding in my ears. *A Wrinkle in Time* was my favorite book when I was a little girl. Out of the blue, a month or so prior, I'd ordered a first edition from Amazon. Oddly enough, I'd never read the subsequent books in the series.

"You should," Evelyn said, her eyes sparkling. "In *A Swiftly Tilting Planet* she writes about kything, a wordless one-to-one kind of telepathy. It's a way of being present with one another across time and space."

"Really? Well, I'll definitely have to read it," I said. Then I reached for my bag and pulled out my copy of *A Wrinkle in Time*. Evelyn, smiling, looked only slightly surprised to see it.

NOTES

1. http://www.pluperfecter.blogspot.com/.
2. http://evelynrodriguez.typepad.com/crossroads_dispatches/2008/04/
   enlightenment.html.
3. Clay Shirky, *Here Comes Everybody: The Power of Organizing without Organizations* (New York: Penguin Press, 2008), pp. 107–108.
4. http://panmesa.tumblr.com/.

# WRITING SOURCE CODE
# FOR DEMOCRACY

*Ken Jordan*

In September 2000, I was invited to a unique gathering that brought together high-level Internet engineers with environmental activists and
media professionals to strategize about the future of the Internet and the
fate of the planet. In a beautiful retreat center surrounded by tall redwoods and northern California mountains, we spent an intensive weekend discussing how new kinds of information technology could be used,
not to make money, but to make our society more equitable and sustainable. Though you might think this sort of brainstorming session was
common during the dot-com boom years, that wasn't the case. Activists
and indie media pros rarely had direct access to top technologists. Since
most funding for software development comes from big corporations,
nonprofit organizations and other social initiatives ended up using low-
rent versions of tools built for business purposes. But for this gathering,
we gave ourselves the freedom to ask if a different type of technology—
created with social, rather than business, goals in mind—might incite a
much deeper level of societal transformation. The conversation we
started that weekend changed the direction of my life.

This possibility had inspired a tiny organization called Planetwork,
which held a conference the previous May on the theme "Global Ecol-

ogy and Information Technology." At the time, these two subjects were an unlikely pairing. Few people saw a connection between the organic complexity of the natural world and the cold, corporate character of the military innovation called the Internet. But when I heard about the conference, I was thrilled that someone had made this linkage.

But then I always saw the Net differently than my dot-com colleagues. During my twenties and early thirties I'd lived in New York's East Village, splitting my time between community activism for peace groups and the homeless, and the downtown arts scene, hanging out with avant-gardists like Allen Ginsberg, Bernadette Mayer, and Richard Foreman. My day job was in book publishing, which was the family business. I got involved with the Web early on because of the opportunities it offered to create independent media, free from the control of global conglomerates, and led the launch of the Web's first multimedia music zine, SonicNet.com, which in its early days was devoted to alternative rock and edge culture. My curiosity about the origins of digital media—"Where did hyperlinks come from?" "What was the first online community?"—led to my collaboration on an anthology that traces the history of computers as an expressive medium. From that research, I understood that the Internet's potential went far beyond the basic combo of websites and e-mail. But I didn't realize how profoundly the tools we use to communicate can effect how society operates, how people organize collaborative efforts, and how power is distributed among citizens. The meeting in the redwoods opened my eyes to opportunities for a dramatic societal shift.

Following the Planetwork conference, some of the organizers and participants convened about two dozen people for two days of blue sky conjecture, and I was invited.[1] Upon arrival, our hosts handed out a thought-provoking proposal that encouraged us to think outside the box. Consider this: There are easily 10 million Americans who feel strongly about the environment and want to do something that will make a difference. Is it possible to gather these people into a "green AOL" (at the time AOL was the largest online community), aggregate their purchasing power, and catalyze a network of green consumers that could help shift the market toward sustainable practices? Imagine what would happen if a coordinated green buying block was there to develop and support new green and fair labor products and services, alternatives to the standard stuff offered by the market.

This kind of scenario was rarely, if ever, presented to high-level IT pros, at least not by people from politics and media who might take their ideas seriously, and maybe even act upon them. Though quite a few engineers have progressive politics and sometimes—if they live in Berkeley—vote for the Green Party, their salaries come from industry or government clients who pay them to do engineering tasks that follow standard business models. They program systems that, in effect, support society as it is; they aren't asked to envision society as it could be.

But when presented with the "green AOL" scenario, the techies in the room grew visibly excited and proposed a slew of extraordinary possibilities. What the techies realized—and what eventually dawned upon the rest of us—was that when you design communications systems using digital network technology, you are actually designing the behavior of the people who use the system. Most business IT is geared to make the people who use it more efficient as workers or consumers. Why not design communications tools that made people better, more engaged citizens?

While most nontechies, and even many techies, rarely look at digital networks from this perspective, this potential was never lost on Douglas Engelbart, the visionary who invented interactive, collaborative computing in the 1960s. It was Engelbart's lab at the Stanford Research Institute that gave us most of the ingredients that make the Web possible: sophisticated text editing, hyperlinks, online publishing, networked community, video conferencing, and the mouse. Unlike the businessmen who later turned interactive computing into a billion-dollar industry, Englebart's motive wasn't to get rich (he didn't), but rather to create a system that helped people to collaborate to solve the increasingly complex problems facing society.[2] He expected that there would always be a deliberate effort to improve our digital network tools based on the way people use them, and that society's needs would be paramount in the development of these systems.[3]

After making amazing headway and launching a fully functioning prototype—which in some ways is still more advanced than today's World Wide Web—Engelbart was in for a shock when public funding for his research dried up in the seventies. The purpose of digital media shifted to automating offices, rather than enabling increasingly sophisticated forms of collective problem-solving. Tech innovation became driven by short-term market trends, and most people came to expect that high tech would always serve corporate and military interests.

But by that time, as Bill Gates and Steve Jobs were first appearing on the scene, the key ingredients of today's digital network were already baked into the system. Over the years, more and more people have noticed that the Web has certain democratic characteristics. They point to:

* How the Internet's meshlike, distributed architecture allows people to connect directly (peer-to-peer) rather than through centralized, hierarchical hubs;

* The way messages can flow in any direction, unlike the traditional "broadcast" model where information is sent to the masses from a centralized source;

* The fact that anyone anywhere can add a website to the network that can be seen by anyone else on the network at any time, and that each new website can potentially reach an international audience; and

* The way every digital file can be copied and replicated exactly, giving rise to the mantra "information wants to be free."

The fact is, the folks who designed this system—West Coast researchers like Engelbart and his team of grad students, many of whom took part in the sixties counterculture[4]—knew what they were doing. The democratic potential of the Net did not appear by accident. Rather, the system these engineers designed embodied values that prized sharing, collaboration, and transparency, and reflected a deep distrust of centralized, hierarchical authority. Military money may have paid for much of it, but the generals who signed the checks never fully grasped what they were funding.[5]

During our weekend retreat in the California redwoods, the techies—who aligned themselves with the Engelbart tradition—offered different approaches to mobilizing large numbers of people around shared objectives, and providing them with tools to coordinate their actions. The idea of a "green AOL," though useful to consider as a conversation starter, was quickly rejected because a couple of us had worked with massive online communities like AOL and Prodigy, and were aware of the huge infrastructure and personnel expense necessary to support a single website with 10 million members (although that cost has come down quite a bit in the years since).

We began to explore other ways of connecting 10 million people online. As it turned out, there were several. The Net's architects designed it that way. The techies brought up obscure, cutting-edge innovations that the rest of us had never heard of, but which have since become widespread, such as online social networking, Web page maps that displayed dynamic geospatial data, and personalized information delivery via online subscriptions. It took awhile for most of us to grasp what these bizarre gizmos do—actually, it took a series of meetings every two months for over a year—but since then these abstract concepts have been made concrete thanks to Friendster, Google Maps, and RSS.

What the world hasn't seen, however, are versions of these tools developed explicitly in the public interest to serve civil society. Imagine a Friendster (or, in today's parlance, a Facebook) that connects you to a network of green shoppers in your community so you can coordinate purchases of local produce. Imagine using Google Maps to find farms in your area, and by clicking on the farm you could see how its water use is affecting the local water table. Imagine subscribing to RSS updates about water usage in your region that get sent when there is a drastic fall in water-table level. And imagine being able to connect with all the other people in your community who have subscribed to that RSS update each time the water table drops to a danger point, so you can organize a community response to this environmental threat—and make sure to purchase produce only from farms that protect the water table.

This is a simplistic example, to be sure, but hopefully it makes a point: IT can be shaped to serve the public interest. We live in the era of databases. An extraordinary amount of information is already being captured on hard drives; every day it becomes easier and less expensive to do so. By linking computers to the Internet, that data becomes available to inform the public about how society manages its resources. It can also enable each of us to connect with others so we can self-organize into groups to take action.

These citizen action tools don't exist today, but that's not because of the engineering obstacles, which are relatively small. As the techies told us again and again at that redwoods summit, the challenge isn't technical, it's *social*. As a society, we simply do not make it a priority to design and deploy online systems that enable people to be more engaged in their communities.

### 2. FORMING GROUPS

Of course, the democratic potential built into the Internet is being tapped in many ways. Groups like MoveOn, TrueMajority, and Avaaz have waged many successful online campaigns, lobbying for legislation and changes in government policy, attracting millions of volunteers to their causes. Barack Obama stands on the threshold of becoming the next president of the United States, and if he does, his ability to attract donations over the Internet will be a big reason why.

But a more intriguing aspect of the Web's democratic potential is how it enables people with shared interests to spontaneously coalesce into groups of all sizes. In the subtitle of his book *Here Comes Everybody*, Internet analyst Clay Shirky calls it "the power of organizing without organizations." The book describes how effective the Net is at attracting people to a project or cause. Shirky offers many examples of how simple tools like e-mail, blogs, wikis, and popular social networking sites (like Facebook and Flickr) give someone on a mission the ability to kick off and coordinate campaigns that can grow exponentially, engaging many thousands of people in a matter of weeks or months. Unlike in the pre-Web days, these online efforts don't cost a dollar in printing or mailing expenses. All they require is someone's time.

Shirky tells how a Boston physician in 2002, after reading newspaper accounts of sex abuse by a Catholic priest, started a group in his basement called Voice of the Faithful (VOTF) to push for church reform. Nothing special about that. But within a few months, at its first convention, VOTF had 25,000 members. Thanks to the Internet the group was able to forward articles from *The Boston Globe*'s website to a steadily growing e-mail list. Some VOTF members had their own blog sites, where they reached even larger numbers of people, who in turn became VOTF members. As Shirky points out, it had always been possible to clip articles from the paper, xerox them, and send them by snail mail to a group. But, as he says, "what we are witnessing today is a difference in the degree of sharing so large that it becomes a difference in kind."[6] In addition, the low cost of aggregating information led to the formation of an activist website, BishopAccountability.org, which "collated accusations of abuse, giving a permanent home to what in the past would have been evanescent coverage." Online social tools like websites for membership and e-mail for communications, enabled VOTF to "become a powerful force, all while remaining loosely (and largely electronically) coordinated." A few years earlier, without the Internet, this would have been inconceivable.

Shirky is on the mark when he describes why digital networks have reduced obstacles to collective engagement:

> Technology didn't cause the [sex] abuse scandal that began in 2002. The scandal was caused by the actions of the church, and many factors affected the severity of reaction in 2002, including the exposure of more of the church's internal documents and the effectiveness of the *Globe's* coverage. That combination was going to lead to substantial reaction in any case. What technology did do was alter the spread, force, and especially duration of that reaction, by removing two obstacles—locality of information, and barriers to group reaction.[7]

Because of the Internet, people can circulate information more effectively, and gather more easily into group initiatives. But it would be a mistake to see the Internet as it currently exists as having fulfilled its potential. The obstacles that Shirky refers to may have been reduced, but they have not been removed. In the basic architecture of the Internet itself lie many untapped opportunities to extend its ability to support and amplify collective action. What we have today is pretty good, but it could be much better, exponentially so.

The fundamentals of the Internet encourage an open flow of information and connection, directly from one person to another (or to a group), without walls or intermediaries. But in practice, largely because of the online businesses that have been built upon the Net's foundation, information and group formation can and do bump into walls.

Some walls are built by governments, as in China, where citizens are denied access to certain information. Other walls are more subtle, such as the wall erected by mainstream media to a news story that falls outside its narrow worldview, even if that story generates considerable attention among an engaged group of bloggers and readers. Another wall could be imposed by the telecoms and cabal companies, if given their druthers to have a two-tier (or many-tiered) Internet that favors corporate product over independent voices. This threat has given rise to a "net neutrality" movement that has managed to protect the network to date, though future victories are not assured.

Another wall is the one that surrounds every online community, from MySpace to Twitter. When you join any of these sites, you fill out a profile from scratch. That profile information stays with the site, and you can't take it with you when you go somewhere else online. For instance, when you leave Facebook and log into MySpace, all the information accumulated in your Facebook profile stays behind. Even though you've said on Facebook that one of your interests is environmental advocacy to preserve redwoods in northern California, no one on MySpace would know, unless you go through the tedious process of typing that same info into your MySpace profile, which most folks don't. In fact, the profile you create on these sites isn't even owned by you. That information is the site's intellectual property. Their business models are based on the premise that they know what you want (thanks to your profile) so they can sell you things with laser-like efficiency. And they don't want you to take that data away from them. Usually, they won't even tell you what they plan to do with it.

But suppose that every time you joined a new online social network, without having to fill out yet another endless series of forms to describe yourself and your interests, people there automatically knew you were a rainforest activist (assuming you wanted them to know). Suppose that part of your "traveling profile" included testimonials from other activists you've worked with, so that people who meet you for the first time could see that among activists you have a good reputation. Imagine how much more effective that would make group formation for the environmental movement.

The technology to make this kind of "introduction" service exists today. In fact, there are a number of ways to do it. But don't expect Facebook or MySpace to spearhead its creation. It's just not part of their business model; their attention is elsewhere. In today's climate, if the financial allure of a new digital service isn't immediately apparent, it's nearly impossible to steer significant resources toward its development, especially if more than three people in a garage are needed to create a launchable product. The "introduction" service would take more work than that, but not hugely so. Still, this kind of public interest tech is not easy to build a business model around—as a result, it doesn't get done.

There's a strange assumption that if an online tool is any good, it ought to make someone rich, even though history tells us otherwise: Many of the key ingredients of our digital communications stew were developed in research labs by engineers who never profited from their innovations. For quite some time, though, digital research has been driven by the computer, telecommunications, and entertainment industries (which are increasingly blurring into the same, multiheaded hydra), helping them to advance their existing business practices. Meanwhile, few resources are available for innovating online social tools that make it easier for people to connect to information and one another so they can contribute to a sustainable future.

### 3. DIGITAL IDENTITY

Let's return to that September 2000, blue sky brainstorming session in the California redwoods. That weekend was so highly charged with possibility that the group reconvened every two or three months for a year and a half, switching back and forth between the Bay Area and New York, percolating a new worldview based on the opportunities offered to civil society by applied IT innovation. Eventually the group was formally constituted as the Link Tank ("think tank" with a geek twist), though among ourselves we half-jokingly called it the Web Cabal. Some fifty people ultimately took part in these sessions, contributing to a radical vision of an egalitarian, sustainable society made possible by networked digital communications.

What made these summits special was having professional political activists and media makers in detailed discussion with senior engineers who really knew their stuff. These techies were architects of large IT systems that had scaled up to meet the needs of millions of users. Engineers like to solve problems. Usually, engineers are presented with problems like, "How can I protect my intellectual property, so that each time someone downloads my digital thingy, I get paid?" As you would expect, the engineer will then design a system meant to meet that objective. But the Link Tank asked its engineers a different kind of question, such as, "How can millions of people who care about the environment join collectively to take actions that will drive the marketplace to support more sustainable practices?"

As we discussed different scenarios, it became apparent that any system meant to connect one person to another because of their shared interests hinges on the personal "profile" of each participant. Your profile needs to say that you're an environmental activist in order for other environmental activists to find you and make a connection. So how does that profile get created, and—most importantly—how much control do you have over it once it exists? After all, if your profile only sits on Facebook, and it isn't even your property but rather is owned by Facebook, its utility is pretty limited. But if you could carry your profile with you across the Internet, like a kind of flag that you wave as you enter a website, and if you could control who has access to your profile information based on criteria that you set (for instance, if you only want to reveal your environmental activism to certified members of Greenpeace), that would greatly increase your opportunity to link with others.

After all, that's basically how it works in meat space (or, as some refer to it, real life). You don't leave your identity at the door when you go from one social milieu to another. If you walk into a work meeting and run into a cute girl you met at a Greenpeace rally, you don't have to tell everyone present that you're a Greenpeace member. You always carry experiences from different parts of your life with you, and you can be selective about what aspects of your self that you reveal under different circumstances. Why should online be different? Especially since the underlying structure of the Internet allows for this kind of flexibility.

As we got deeper into it, during these Link Tank discussions we came to realize that digital identity may be the central issue facing civil society in the Internet age. It not only affects how people are able to connect to one another and form groups. It also has implications for how we link to news and information, how we access products and services, how we behave as consumers, and how we participate in our communities as citizens. Once your profile says certain things about you—for instance, that you are interested in green news stories, want to buy locally grown food, and want to participate in zoning efforts that protect the local water table—then it becomes possible to match you to those who feel similarly, as well as to information and services you can use. For some, this kind of personally targeted online experience is increasingly seen as the pinnacle of what the Internet has to offer.

At the same time, digital identity raises issues about privacy protection: Who has information about you, what can they do with it, and what options are there to control what they do? What happens if some of the companies you do business with—like Amazon, Disney, and Google—combine the profile data they have about you into a shared file, and use it for purposes you don't agree with, without your consent? Of even greater concern, what happens if the government gets hold of that information, what privacy protection do we have?

It turns out that identity is the one key ingredient that Engelbart and the other Internet architects didn't cook into the system. Because so few people used those early networks, they simply didn't have to worry about it then. If you were on the Internet when it launched in the 1970s, everyone knew who you were. Profiles weren't necessary, and if you acted in a dishonest way or did something to piss others off, they could always find you; they knew where you lived. It was only when the system scaled up to serve millions of people that the identity issue presented itself.

The vision that grew out of the Link Tank was captured in a paper I cowrote with Jan Hauser and Steven Foster in 2003 called "The Augmented Social Network: Building Identity and Trust into the Next Generation Internet."[8] We presented these ideas at a number of conferences, and in certain circles (geek utopian, to be sure) this paper got a lot of play. We figured that the next step was to raise funds for an initiative to nurture this vision and develop some prototypes. But it turned out that the progressive funding world (foundations, NGOs, liberal donors, university research initiatives) wasn't ready to evaluate cutting-edge tech apps, let alone one based on the idea that the right kind of tech can propagate egalitarian and sustainable values in society. To many people, to this day, communications infrastructure is mistakenly viewed as "values agnostic."

Nonetheless, a half dozen initiatives did get under way, led by idealistic programmers (and their friends), often at considerable personal and financial sacrifice since support from civil society was fitful at best. Diligently, with their eyes on the prize, they developed different aspects of what became known as "user-centric digital identity." Privacy specialists made sure this system was secure: You have total control over your personal information, and no one else—including the government—can access it without your permission.

An organization called Identity Commons[9] was established to evangelize this vision, and to provide a venue for coordination. New technologies with arcane names like XDI,[10] Higgins,[11] i-names,[12] Information Cards,[13] and OpenID[14] began to get some traction, and a few prototypes—pieces of the whole user-centric digital identity puzzle—were completed. By 2006, these achievements, in turn, attracted the attention of major players with deep pockets.

Who showed up? Microsoft, IBM, Oracle, Novell, and other technology firms that came to realize how a trusted, user-based identity system is necessary if the Internet is going to support a wide range of next-generation products and services.

Fingers crossed, a truly visionary digital identity system will be produced by these efforts, and the intentions of the tech utopians who shepherded this vision over the years will be present in the final version. But without the direct involvement of civil society, which has such a great stake in the outcome, it's hard to say what will happen. It should come as no surprise, however, that the first application of user-centric digital identity will be to enhance your online-shopping experience, connecting you more efficiently to stuff you might want to buy—albeit in a less intrusive manner that gives you control over your personal data.

## 4. DECISION-MAKING AT THE EDGES

People often say: Society's problems will not be solved by technology. This implies that you can somehow separate how society operates from the technology we use. It doesn't recognize that society is shaped by the technology available to us.

In his book *The Creation of the Media,* Paul Starr offers an example everyone should know of the influence that technical innovation has on social organization. He traces how the emergence of newspapers in the North American colonies in the eighteenth century, coupled with the creation of a reliable postal service, provided the communications backbone that gave birth to modern representative democracy. Breakthroughs in printing led to the publication of journals, pamphlets, and papers in larger numbers, at a lower cost. The postal service distributed these publications in a timely way, so readers across the colonies knew about recent events, removing the "locality of information" obstacle that Clay Shirky referred to. Post offices also encouraged group formation—

removing Shirky's second obstacle: They became social hubs where people read newspapers out loud. Custom held that new papers could be read by anyone who happened by the post office, which mirrors the attitude toward content sharing on today's Net. In fact, a town's printing press was often located beside the post office, and items from papers that arrived by post were copied verbatim by printers into their publications, an analog version of e-mail forwarding. In its way, eighteenth-century communications tech offered an early version of the Internet's barrier-reducing capabilities.

Armed with information about current affairs, and able to congregate into groups to discuss what they knew, some people in the colonies (white men with property, of course) felt strongly that they should be involved in the decisions made by government that effected their lives. So they chose representatives and sent them by coach to assemble with other representatives in formally constituted bodies to vote on decisions that affected their communities. They used the best technology for group assembly and decision-making then available: horse and buggy, face-to-face dialog in public places, the circulation of printed materials to support claims and proposals, roll call votes or paper ballots, and the publication of decisions made so they could be read by other citizens. The result was a form of representative government, practiced in towns and cities across the colonies, that offered the most accountability between governors and the governed that a state had yet managed to achieve.

Today we're still living with a government that, in its basics, is a product of cutting-edge eighteenth-century technology. Of course, much has been layered on top of it. But dig deep enough and eventually you hit underlying, archaic assumptions that have gone unchallenged for centuries. Here are a few:

* *Regional assemblies.* Representative assemblies should be organized on the basis of where people live, rather than by specialized issue or project.

* *Generalist representatives.* Elected representatives are expected to have sound judgment about all subjects, and are empowered to make decisions even on subjects they know nothing about.

* *Centralized information.* For good decisions to be made, pertinent information must be gathered in a central location, so a small group of people with access to that information can propose a decision to the larger representative body, which votes on it. Widespread public access to that information, so it might be challenged or amended, is not essential to the process.

* *Permanent bodies.* Governing bodies composed of elected representatives—such as the Senate, Congress, state assemblies, city councils, etc.—should never be dissolved.

These assumptions are the product of the limitations of eighteenth-century technology. The framers of the Constitution took them for granted, which is no surprise, since no practical alternatives were available. But they also didn't anticipate the long-term consequences—government institutions that have become staggeringly bureaucratic, slow, obscure in their operations, unresponsive to citizen needs, and controlled by corporate interests.

The early democratic philosophers assumed that citizens would personally know, or at least have a passing acquaintance with, their elected leaders—there would always be a direct connection between the government and the people. Until the early twentieth century, the White House doors were open to unannounced guests who stopped by to meet the president. But the number of seats in Congress today is the same as it was one hundred years ago. It's physically impossible for a U.S. Representative to press the flesh with even a fraction of his constituents, let alone have a meaningful chat with them. Government has become a TV spectacle, reduced to a sports contest that repeats every four years, like the World Cup, while the problems facing society—the environmental crisis, global food shortages, peak oil—are so complex that only specialists can begin to untangle them. Our elected representatives are ill-matched to the tasks before them, and the current system leaves most citizens feeling disconnected, untrusting, and with the overwhelming sense that their actions make no difference.

As a techie might put it, our form of representative democracy doesn't scale well.

At the Link Tank sessions, two dozen of us would gather in conference rooms in either the Bay Area or New York, exploring ways that digital networks enable connection between participants in group actions. We drew network diagrams on blackboards or white sheets, mapping various ways that people could link to one another. We kept returning to structures that allocated tasks and decisions to clusters at the edge of the network, where expertise was concentrated or an action's effect was most likely to be felt, rather than bringing all important decisions back to a single, super-powerful hub at the center.

The intention behind these exercises was to find ways of empowering those with the most at stake—who usually have the greatest motivation to act, as well as the most relevant knowledge—so they can participate in making solutions to common problems. With digital networks, group formation can be far more fluid, transparent, and nonhierarchical. This opens up new possibilities for collaboration, new types of decision making structures, and the freeing up of creativity where it hadn't been present before.

It's an approach that hinges on the development of user-centric digital identity. With the right kind of personal profile, identifying expertise in a community becomes much simpler, as does linking people so they can collaborate.

Collaboration can take many forms. It can include: a loosely joined network of homeowners doing renovations who cooperatively purchase sustainable construction materials; a county zoning board tasked with protecting the water table; a car pooling initiative that connects people to drivers heading to the same destinations; or even an entire township that, following the Transition Town model, seeks to collectively lower its ecological footprint by instituting new sustainable practices. Digital networks present us with the opportunity to innovate new forms of collaboration for achieving shared objectives that could be far more effective than the tools we currently have at our disposal.

Try looking with fresh eyes at the decisions facing our communities and our nation, taking into account the tools we have to share information and convene groups to take action. If we rewrote the Constitution from scratch, would our current type of representative democracy be the optimum choice for governing ourselves? Or would we use a different model more appropriate for our time?

Consider a county in northern New York State that wants to contribute to sustainability by reducing its ecological footprint. Suppose it tried an alternative approach to government, one based on assumptions quite different than the ones that hailed from the eighteenth century, discussed above—new possibilities suggested by the capabilities of the Internet. It might include:

* *Issue assemblies.* Representative assemblies would be convened to focus on separate issues that impact sustainability, such as transportation; energy; toxic clean ups; and local organic agriculture. Some assemblies—such as transportation and energy—might have the standing of government bodies, while others—like local organic agriculture—might be groups of consumers loosely organized into buying clubs to support local farmers.

* *Expert representatives.* Elected representatives to the issue assemblies should be recognized experts with professional experience in their area of specialty.

* *Distributed information.* The information introduced into assembly discussions should be made available online, so everyone can see and comment upon it, allowing outside experts to participate in the decision-making process.

* *Temporary bodies.* Once a particular issue is addressed—for example, implementing a new transportation plan for the county, or evaluating alternative energy sources to generate power for the region—the assembly is dissolved, keeping the group from calcifying into yet another sclerotic bureaucracy.

The social tools we have today—e-mail, websites, wikis, blogs, etc.—aren't adequate for the complexities this kind of system demands. But shouldn't we be experimenting with new tools, testing different kinds of systems, to see what really might be possible?

One such experiment, called Smartocracy, was spearheaded by Link Tank member Brad deGraf in 2006. It uses digital networks to explore an alternative approach to democratic decision-making, one that might prove more effective, though just as egalitarian, than the notion of "one person/one vote." The concept is explained on the Smartocracy website: Collect $20 donations from one thousand participants, and then use the Smartocracy system to collaboratively decide which deserving projects or institutions should receive grants from the pooled sum of $20,000. The site goes on to say:

Democracy has a fundamental problem, namely that "one-person/one-vote" guarantees that the wisest among us will be devalued, in favor of the least-informed. Here [on Smartocracy], participants have equal weight, not in voting, but in deciding who to give their votes to. Instead of "one person/one vote," it's "one person/ten votes to give away." . . . Each participant gets an equal number of votes (initially 10) for each decision to be made, to be exercised not by them but by their proxies. That simple change, from voting to delegating your vote, creates meritocracy in an equitable, natural way. The most highly respected participants are by definition on more people's lists.[15]

Instead of each participant casting a single vote, you get ten votes to distribute to proxies who you trust. You might give three votes to one and seven to another. By doing so, you authorize these proxies to make decisions on your behalf. But by distributing your votes among several experts, rather than authorizing a single proxy to cast all your ballots, you help set the context for a conversation between several trusted experts, a team that is empowered to act in the interest of the entire group. Smartocracy is an ingenious approach to democratic collaboration. At the same time, it's a logical extension of what digital networks have to offer.

In the years leading up to the Constitutional Convention, many flavors of representative government were tried, each growing out of local conditions and customs. Some were successful, others failed. From those experiments came the experience that guided the founders as they laid the foundation of American representative government. Today we need similar experiments.[16]

It's worth mentioning that one outcome of this approach might be entirely new economic models that don't rely on money to motivate people's actions. Rather than receiving cash, participants in a collaboration could be rewarded in other ways. Online systems are particularly good at tracking a person's contributions to a group effort, and at calculating appropriate compensation—which might be a service offered by another person in the network. This means that networks can be convened to meet shared objectives without having to raise massive funds to pay for it; if there's enough will to get a project going, the group can find plenty of ways to reward participants other than with cash. (Not to linger on doomsday scenarios, but considering the questionable state of the global economic order, and the possibility that a series of environmental and resource crises could trigger a sudden collapse, this visionary approach to collaboration becomes even more relevant.)

Back in the days of the Link Tank, only a few seemed to grasp that the digital infrastructure carries implicit values about sharing and collaboration. But every day, this awareness dawns on more people. A generation has grown up with the Internet as part of the atmosphere it breathes. Through the Net, we viscerally experience our interconnection with others, each of us individual nodes in an intricate, interdependent network. At the same time, the environmental crisis calls us to become more conscious of our interdependence with all life on Earth—yet another network we are part of. The intricate collaborations of nature become models for our own behavior. The most beautiful ecosystems are the sum of many moving parts, working together in collaboration. We have much to learn from them.

NOTES

1. The group of twenty-three was initially convened in Ben Lomand, California, in September 2000 by Brad deGraf and Neil Sieling, with the Planetwork organizers Elizabeth Thompson and Jim Fournier. Also there were: Debra Amador, Juliette Beck, Bruce Cahan, Bonnie DeVarco, Andres Edwards, Steve Foster, Chris Gallagher, Lev Gonick, Jan Hauser, James Hung, Allen Hunt-Badiner, Michael Litz, Christie Rothenberg, Greg Steltenpohl, Hardin Tibbs, Michael Tolson, Amie Weinberg, and Nate Zelnick. Ultimately, an additional two dozen people took part in the process, either by attending meetings or engaging in online discussions. Among them were: Jeffrey Axelrod, Jack Bradin, Owen Davis, Gerald de Jong, Tom Laskawy, Tom Munnecke, Robin Mudge, Ellen Pearlman, Jonathan Peizer, Richard Perl, Richard White, and Duncan Work.

2. See http://www.bootstrap.org/chronicle/chronicle.html (accessed July 10, 2008).

3. See http://www.bootstrap.org/augdocs/augment-81010.htm (accessed July 10, 2008).

4. As described by John Markoff in *What the Dormouse Said* (New York: Viking, 2005).

5. To fully appreciate the culture that gave rise to the networked personal computer, check out hypermedia pioneer Ted Nelson's remarkable book *Computer Lib/Dream Machines*, published by Hugo's Book Service in 1975, now unfortunately out of print.

6. Clay Shirky, *Here Comes Everybody: The Power of Organizing without Organizations* (New York: Penguin Press, 2008). The quotes in this paragraph are taken from pages 149–152.

7. Ibid., p. 153.

8. The ASN paper was first presented at the Planetwork conference in San Francisco in May 2003 and appeared in *First Monday* in the August 2003 issue, accessible at http://www.firstmonday.org/Issues/issue8_8/jordan.

9. Visit the Identity Commons at http://www.idcommons.org.

10. Wikipedia defines XDI as: "XDI (XRI Data Interchange) is a generalized, extensible service for sharing, linking, and synchronizing data over the Internet and other data networks using XML documents and XRIs (Extensible Resource Identifiers)." For more information, visit http://www.xdi.org (accessed July 10, 2008).

11. The Higgins home page on the Eclipse website says "Higgins is a framework that enables users and applications to integrate identity, profile, and relationship information across multiple data sources and protocols. End-users can experience Higgins through the UI metaphor of Information Cards." For more information, visit http://www.eclipse.org/higgins (accessed July 10, 2008).

12. The i-names website explains: "URLs are for connecting web pages. Now get the address for connecting people and businesses in rich, long-lasting digital relationships: i-names. Whether you are an individual looking for a safe, lifetime personal address or a business seeking long-term, opt-in customer relationships, there's an i-name for you." For more information, visit http://www.inames.net (accessed July 10, 2008).

13. The Information Card Foundation website explains: "You already know how to use cards in your wallet to present ID, to purchase things, to show you are a member of a club, or that you have a relationship with a merchant like Best Buy. Now what if it was just as easy to login or do business on-line as it is to present a card in the rest of your life? No more typing. No more filling in forms. And that is just the beginning. Just as media became a lot more flexible and useful in the digital world, now your cards can manage more things for you!" For more, visit the Information Card Foundation at http://www.informationcard.net (accessed July 10, 2008).

14. On the OpenID website it says: "OpenID eliminates the need for multiple usernames across different websites, simplifying your online experience. You get to choose the OpenID Provider that best meets your needs and most importantly that you trust. At the same time, your OpenID can stay with you, no matter which Provider you move to. And best of all, the OpenID technology is not proprietary and is completely free." For more information, visit http://openid.net (accessed July 10, 2008).

15. Though the Smartocracy system has been taken off line, information about it can be found here: http://smartocracy.net/ovrvw.html (accessed July 10, 2008).

16. For more ideas about how digital networks could be used to revolutionize democratic practices, see the anthology *Rebooting America: Ideas for Redesigning American Democracy for the Internet Age*, edited by Allison Fine, Micah Sifry, Andrew Rasiej, and Joshua Levy, and available as a free download at http://rebooting.personaldemocracy.com.

# ACKNOWLEDGMENTS

This book offers a small slice of the vibrant discourse that can be found on the *Reality Sandwich* website, where we publish new articles daily. Please visit us at http://www.realitysandwich.com, and become part of the ever-expanding conversation.

*Reality Sandwich* is a group effort, and we've been amazed by the extraordinary team that has come together around this project since its inception; it was launched without financing and has been bootstrapped largely by volunteer labor. The editors would like to express our deep appreciation for our cofounding partners, Michael Robinson and Jonathan Phillips, whose inspired insights and fierce dedication have been critical to the site's success. Without the expertise of our technical director, Dan Robinson, the site would have never launched; he's driven our technology efforts using Drupal, the open-source publishing system, leading a group of excellent engineers from the Bay Area consultancy Civic-Actions; we'd like to extend a special thanks to Alex Scott, Doug Green, Fen Labalme, and Gregory Heller. We are deeply greatful to our friends Ronald Johnson and Brandie Hardman, who first joined us as investors, and then became full team members, organizing events and helping us to expand our operations to include two new websites—the social network Evolver.net and the e-marketplace Evolver Exchange—both of which should be live by the time this book sees print. If you haven't been to Evolver.net yet, please check it out and join a growing global community of people collaborating to make real change. In addition, a tip of the hat to David Latimer, Jill Ettinger, Bob Solomon, Salma Shamy, Elke Dehner, Kevin Balktick, Craig Reuter, Kelly Heresy, Maya Lemberg, and Jon Claffey for all the energy and enthusiasm they've brought to the nuts and bolts of *Reality Sandwich*, including the areas of advertising sales, licensing, legal work, event production, and online marketing. Travis Kyle did a wonderful logo animation for our online videos. We're also grateful to our interns: Caroline Contillo, Zahra Stavis, Alex Ratner, and Renee Verdier. And how could we not thank the world's most entertaining CFO, Howie Seligman?

We've been blessed by a remarkable group of editors who share our vision of transformation, and who have contributed their intelligence and enthusiasm to the site. Senior Editor Steven Taylor keeps *Reality Sandwich* fresh with new features each day. He also took on the Herculean challenge of preparing the text of this volume for publication on a four-week deadline, and managed multiple tasks and three dozen correspondence threads with characteristic graciousness and a conscientious eye for detail. Many of the articles in this volume were prepared for the site by our contributing editors; we salute them all: ST Frequency, Jennifer Palmer, Lisa Webster, Ruhiya Kristine Seward, Charles Shaw, Adam Elenbaas, Tristan Gulliford, and Jon Leon Torn. In addition, *Reality Sandwich* wouldn't be nearly as rewarding to visit without the short posts written by our news writers: Bill Machon, Erin Shaw, Morgan Maher, Kal Cobalt, sati, Jennifer Flynn, Stephen Hershey, William McGillis, wanderlust, Bridget Algiere, and Melinda Wenner.

As inferred above, this book came together in record time, thanks to the interest and efforts of our editors at Tarcher, Mitch Horowitz and Gabrielle Moss, as well as our agent, Eric Simonoff. Another important collaborator has been Carlos Menjivar, with whom we've produced a series of inspirational discussions, workshops, and parties at Jivamukti Yoga School; we look forward to many more. And a shout out to our compadres at Post Modern Times, João Amorim and Nikos Katsaounis, who are pursuing with video the same nexus of ideas and culture that are found on *Reality Sandwich*. Please stop by their website at http://www.postmoderntimes.com.

Lastly, Ken would like to acknowledge the extraordinary support that his wife, Carmel Kooros, has given to *Reality Sandwich* (thank you, sweetie).

# ABOUT THE CONTRIBUTORS

Poet **Michael Brownstein** is also the author of three novels: *Country Cousins, Self-Reliance,* and *The Touch.* He has read widely from *World on Fire,* a prophetic antiglobalization call to arms. His latest novel, *Must Not Sleep,* is available as a free audio download at Podiobooks.com, as well as in print form on the Web at *Reality Sandwich.* Politically, Michael understands that simple protest won't change what is basically a demonic intrusion into our lives. The crazed behavior afflicting us worldwide has to be dealt with magically as well. His shamanic work is reflected in the CD *Healing Dick,* where he drums and sings to heal Dick Cheney's heart (www.healingdick.com).

Born in a remote Oregon town, **Kal Cobalt** has written stories since the age of six. At eighteen, K.C. published stories in the (now-defunct) Internet zine *All In Your Mind* and the international print zine *T.H.F.* In the ensuing ten years, K.C. has published numerous short stories online, in magazines, and in anthologies. In 2007, K.C. was published in *Velvet Mafia* for the third time in their "Young Punks Rule" issue celebrating authors under thirty-five. K.C.'s work will also be seen in numerous "best-of" annual anthologies in the fall. This year has also seen K.C.'s relocation to Portland, Oregon. Currently, K.C. is at work on a novel and a number of nonfiction projects as well as the usual reams of short stories.

**Erik Davis** is an author, award-winning journalist, and independent scholar based in San Francisco. He is the author, most recently, of *The Visionary State:*

*A Journey Through California's Spiritual Landscape.* He also wrote *Led Zeppelin IV* and *TechGnosis: Myth, Magic, and Mysticism in the Age of Information,* the latter a cult classic of visionary media studies that has been translated into five languages. His essays on art, music, technoculture, and contemporary spirituality have appeared in over a dozen books, including *AfterBurn: Reflections on Burning Man, Zig Zag Zen, Book of Lies, 01010I: Art in Technological Times* (SFMOMA), and *Prefiguring Cyberculture.* Davis has contributed articles and essays to a variety of publications, including *Bookforum, Slate, Salon, Blender,* the *LA Weekly,* and the *Village Voice.* For many years he was a contributing writer at *Wired.* He has given talks at universities, media art conferences, and festivals around the world, and much of his work is available at www.techgnosis.com.

**Stephen Duncombe** is an associate professor at New York University's Gallatin School and a lifelong political activist. Stephen Duncombe's new book, from which his essay is drawn, is called *Dream: Re-Imagining Progressive Politics in an Age of Fantasy.*

**Charles Eisenstein** is a writer, speaker, and the author of *The Ascent of Humanity* and other books. His work focuses on the revolution in human civilization and its relationship to the planet, as well as a parallel, spiritual revolution: a shift in the human sense of self. Born in 1967, he graduated from Yale University with a degree in mathematics and philosophy and spent most of his twenties in Taiwan as a Chinese-English translator. Later he taught at Penn State for four years before leaving to devote his time to speaking and writing. His passion and dedication is, in his words, "to the more beautiful world our hearts tell us is possible." A large body of his writings and recordings are available for free on the Internet.

Originally from Minneapolis/St. Paul, **Adam Elenbaas** holds a B.A. in philosophy and theology, an M.A. in English language and literature, and an M.F.A. in creative writing. A recovering Christian fundamentalist, Elenbaas is currently working toward the publication of his book, *Fishers of Men,* an experimental-memoir based upon his recent years of recovery work with shamanism in the Peruvian Amazon. Adam is a contributing editor at *Reality Sandwich*.

**Jill Ettinger** is a respected figure in the natural products industry, enhancing community outreach through creative marketing, copywriting, and event coordination in her work with companies Traditional Medicinals and Sambazon. As well, she is the program director for the organic and natural product industry's Socially Responsible Business Awards. She furthers her community involvement as a curator and contributing writer for RealitySandwich.com, and writes regularly for other publications including *Global Rhythm* magazine and Rethos. com. Documenting and evolving the natural products and global music industry as part of the critical move toward a holistic future, Jill cofounded Inner-Continental.org in 2007. Bridging the history and future of our food sources and our cultural expressions, like music, is an important move in ensuring diversity continues to enrich our world family.

**ST Frequency** is the alias most associated with Atlanta-based writer and musician S. Corey Thomas. As part of the artist collective Kids with Codenames, ST has organized electronic music events and is currently working on a new full-length album. He holds a B.A. in English from Georgia State University and has studied British and American culture at the University of Northumbria at Newcastle. During this time overseas, he developed a chronic wanderlust that flares up every twelve months or so. His most recent travel adventure was a jaunt through China and Thailand, where feral Buddhist monkeys scaled his torso for photo-ops. ST Frequency is a contributing editor at *Reality Sandwich*.

**Sharon Gannon** is a cofounder and codirector of the Jivamukti Yoga Center in New York City, one of the nation's most popular yoga centers. A student of Brahmananda Saraswati, Swami Nirmalananda, and Pattabhi Jois, she brings a highly disciplined asana and meditation practice to her teaching yoga as a spiritual practice, relating the ancient teachings of yoga to the modern world. She is coauthor of *Jivamukti Yoga: Practices for Liberating Body and Soul* (Ballantine

Books, 2002) Her recently published book, *Cats and Dogs Are People Too!*, offers optimistic measures to improve our relationship to animals.

**Stanislav Grof**, M.D., Ph.D., is a psychiatrist with over forty years experience of research into nonordinary states of consciousness and is one of the founders and chief theoreticians of transpersonal psychology. Dr. Grof's early research in the clinical uses of psychedelic substances was conducted at the Psychiatric Research Institute in Prague, where he was principal investigator of a program systematically exploring the heuristic and therapeutic potential of LSD and other psychedelic substances. In 1967, he accepted a two-year Clinical and Research fellowship at Johns Hopkins University, Baltimore, Maryland, after which he continued as chief of psychiatric research at the Maryland Psychiatric Research Center and as assistant professor of psychiatry at the Henry Phipps Clinic of Johns Hopkins University. From 1973 to 1987, Dr. Grof was scholar-in-residence at the Esalen Institute in Big Sur, California, giving seminars, lecturing, and developing Holotropic Breathwork with his wife, Christina Grof. He also served on the board of trustees of the Esalen Institute. He is the founder of the International Transpersonal Association (ITA) and its past and current president. In this role, he has organized large international conferences in the United States, the former Czechoslovakia, India, Australia, and Brazil. At present, he lives in Mill Valley, California, conducting training seminars for professionals in Holotropic Breathwork and transpersonal psychology and writing books. He is also professor of psychology at the California Institute of Integral Studies (CIIS) in San Francisco and at the Pacifica Graduate School in Santa Barbara and gives lectures and seminars worldwide. He has published over 140 articles in professional journals, as well as many books, which have been translated into German, French, Italian, Spanish, Portuguese, Dutch, Swedish, Danish, Russian, Czech, Polish, Bulgarian, Greek, Turkish, Japanese, and Chinese.

**John Major Jenkins'** pioneering work to reconstruct ancient Mayan cosmology began with his early books, *Journey to the Mayan Underworld* (1989), *Mirror in the Sky* (1991), *Tzolkin: Visionary Perspectives and Calendar Studies* (1992/1994),

*Mayan Sacred Science* (1994/2000), *The Center of Mayan Time* (1995), and *Izapa Cosmos* (1996), and culminated in his groundbreaking book *Maya Cosmogenesis 2012* (1998). He is also the author of *Galactic Alignment* (2002), coauthor of *Pyramid of Fire* (2004), and has a three-CD audio program with Sounds True called *Unlocking the Secrets of 2012: Galactic Wisdom from the Ancient Skywatchers*.

**Ken Jordan** is publisher of *Reality Sandwich* and Evolver.net. He has been an online pioneer since leading the 1995 launch of the award-winning SonicNet.com, the Web's first multimedia music zine and digital music store, which later became a property of MTV. In 1999 he cofounded the first online media issues portal, MediaChannel.org, in partnership with Globalvision and OneWorld.net. As a consult to WITNESS in 2006, he conceived the group's human rights video Hub. He is coauthor of the influential white paper "The Augmented Social Network: Building Identity and Trust into the Next-Generation Internet" (published in *First Monday,* August 2003), and is coeditor of *Multimedia: From Wagner to Virtual Reality* (W.W. Norton, 2001), an anthology of seminal articles that trace the development of the computer as an expressive, interactive medium. In the days before the Web, he was a community organizer, worked in book publishing, and collaborated with the legendary playwright and director Richard Foreman on *Unbalancing Acts: Foundations for a Theater* (Pantheon, 1992). He has written for *Wired, Paris Review,* and *Index,* among other publications, and has consulted with many start-ups, NGOs, and foundations.

**Anya Kamenetz** is a journalist, blogger, and author of the 2006 book *Generation Debt*. She is a staff writer for *Fast Company* magazine and a columnist for Yahoo!. Her work has appeared in *The New York Times, The Nation, New York Magazine,* the *Village Voice, Penthouse,* and many other publications. She blogs at The Narrow Bridge: anyakamenetz.blogspot.com.

**Homegrown Evolution's Erik Knutzen and Kelly Coyne**, authors of *The Urban Homestead,* have become increasingly interested in the concept of urban sustainability since moving to Los Angeles in 1998. In the that time, they've slowly converted their 1920 hilltop bungalow into a mini-farm, and along the way have explored the traditional home arts of baking, pickling, bicycling, and brewing, chronicling all their activities on their blog Homegrown Evolution (www.homegrownevolution.com).

In 1981, **Paul Levy** had a life-changing spiritual awakening that almost killed him. In the early stages of his awakening he was thrown in mental hospitals a number of times and (mis)diagnosed with manic-depressive disorder. Little did the psychiatrists realize that Paul had gotten drafted into a higher-dimensional shamanic initiation process which mimicked psychosis but was an experience of a far different order. A healer, Paul is in private practice helping others who are also spiritually awakening. He is writing a book about his abuse at the hands of the psychiatric community called *Psychiatry Almost Drove Me Crazy*. Due to his ordeal, Paul has unique insight into the crazy and "crazy-making" aspect of both psychiatry and our world. In a dream come true, Paul now has psychiatrists study and consult with him and send him clients. He is in the book *Saints and Madmen: Psychiatry Opens Its Doors to Religion*. Paul is the author of *The Madness of George W. Bush: A Reflection of Our Collective Psychosis* (which can be ordered on his website). Each week Paul facilitates a number of "Awakening in the Dream Groups," which are circles of people who are discovering how to help one another awaken to the dreamlike nature of reality. A visionary artist, Paul is creating an "Art-Happening Called Global Awakening." Please visit his website at www.awakeninthedream.com. Paul's e-mail is paul@awakeninthedream.com.

In the early eighties **Antonio Lopez** cofounded the seminal L.A. punk zine, *Ink Disease*. From there he traversed zine culture, professional journalism, and media literacy education. He has written for *Mondo 2000, High Times, Punk Planet, Tricycle, In These Times, Brooklyn Rail,* and scores of zines, newspapers, and magazines. His essays about media and culture have been featured in numerous anthologies, and he authored *Mediacology,* a book about media education and sustainability.

**Barbara Alice Mann**, a community-recognized Ohio Bear Clan Seneca, is a Ph.D. scholar specializing in Native American studies and early American literature, as well as international women's studies, as it intersects indigenous studies. In addition to eight scholarly books, with a ninth due out in 2009, she has published numerous chapters and articles, mostly on indigenous topics. She lives, writes, teaches, and works for indigenous causes in her homeland, the beautiful-river *Land of the Three Miamis* (the state of Ohio), where, like her ancestors, she stoutly resists being "Christianized and cilivized."

**Jean-François Martel** is a writer and filmmaker currently living in Montreal, Canada. He has written and directed several short films, and has worked as a screenwriter for the international new media studio Moment Factory. As a musician and songwriter, he plays in a band called The Other Nights (myspace.com/theothernights). A fateful encounter with a vagabond prophet in the midnineties, a childhood sighting of suspicious lights in the sky, and a handful of transformative psychedelic experiences lie at the root of his fascination with all things spiritual, esoteric, and magical.

**Jay Michaelson** is a writer and teacher whose work focuses on the intersections of sexuality, spirituality, Judaism, and law. He is a Ph.D. candidate in Jewish thought at Hebrew University, a visiting professor at Boston University Law School, and, outside the academy, a teacher who has taught Kabbalah, meditation, and spirituality for fifteen years, from Yale University to Burning Man, NPR to Elat Chayyim. Jay is the author of the books *God in Your Body: Kabbalah, Mindfulness and Embodied Spiritual Practice* (Jewish Lights, 2006) and *Another Word for Sky: Poems* (Lethe Press, 2007), a columnist for the *Forward* newspaper, the executive director of Nehirim: GLBT Jewish Culture and Spirituality, and the chief editor of *Zeek: A Jewish Journal of Thought and Culture* (http://www.zeek.net).

**Paul D. Miller** is a conceptual artist, writer, and musician working in New York. His writing has appeared in the *Village Voice*, *The Source*, *Artforum*, *Ray-*

*gun, Rap Pages, Paper Magazine,* and a host of other periodicals. His book *Rhythm Science* was published by MIT Press in 2004. *Sound Unbound,* an anthology of writings on sound art and multimedia by contemporary cultural theorists, followed in 2008. Miller's work as a media artist has appeared at the Whitney Biennial; The Venice Biennial for Architecture (2000); the Ludwig Museum in Cologne, Germany; Kunsthalle, Vienna; The Andy Warhol Museum in Pittsburgh, and many other museums and galleries. His live music/theater/film performance, DJ Spooky's *Rebirth of a Nation,* ran at the Lincoln Center Festival after premieres in Vienna and at Spoleto USA in Charleston, South Carolina. As DJ Spooky that Subliminal Kid, Miller has collaborated with musicians and composers such as Iannis Xenakis, Ryuichi Sakamoto, Butch Morris, Kool Keith aka Doctor Octagon, Pierre Boulez, Killa Priest from Wu-Tang Clan, Steve Reich, Yoko Ono, and Thurston Moore. His recent albums include *Optometry* (2002), a jazz project featuring Matthew Shipp, William Parker, Joe Mcphee, Carl Hancock Rux, Daniel Bernard Roumain, and High Priest from Anti-Pop Consortium, and *Dubtometry* (2003), a dub remix of the same, featuring Lee "Scratch" Perry and Mad Professor. Miller's latest collaborative release, *Drums of Death,* features Dave Lombardo of *Slayer,* Chuck D of *Public Enemy*, Vernon Reid of *Living Colour,* and Jack Dangers of *Meat Beat Manifesto.*

**Alex Munslow** is an independent video producer based in Brighton, UK.

**Stella Osorojos** is a freelance writer and diplomate in Oriental medicine. Her stories have appeared in *Condé Nast Traveler, Travel & Leisure, InStyle,* and more. Her private practice, focused on energy medicine, is based in Santa Fe.

**Padmani** is a lawyer, yoga teacher, and spiritual seeker. She lives with her partner in Toronto, Canada.

**Jennifer Palmer** is a writer, DJ, and philosopher who goes by the name TRUE out on the internets. Her blog, BRANDTRUEBOY (http://trueboy.blogspot

.com), started as an art experiment in 2002, in which she posted as three fictitious characters that she passed off as "real" people who e-mailed, commented, and chatted with other bloggers. Her current projects include writing a novel, honing her text message poetry skills, and building the dopest vinyl-based beat library in New York City.

**Jonathan Phillips** grew up in the Colorado Rockies. He has worked for The September 11th Fund, served as a columnist for Music for America, and spearheaded the street theater/media group Greene Dragon. After experiencing a number of mystical experiences, kundalini awakenings, and "miraculous" encounters, Jonathan turned his focus toward spirituality. He currently serves as *Reality Sandwich*'s community director, doing "The Electric Jesus" and "Sex and Spirit" podcasts. He is also executive editor of the NYC events newsletter, Souldish.com, and organizes the NYC Gnostics. He is a Reiki master practitioner and leads Sacred Warrior and Electric Jesus workshops, using energy work to bring out the divine.

**Daniel Pinchbeck** is the author of *2012: The Return of Quetzalcoatl* (Tarcher/Penguin, 2006) and *Breaking Open the Head* (Broadway Books, 2002). He is editorial director of *Reality Sandwich*.

**Michael Robinson** is educator, visual artist, and director of the acclaimed New York design studio Nowhere. Recent clients include Alicia Keys, Courtney Love, Levi Strauss, and Coca-Cola. He led the global rebranding of the Ramada Hotels and Kmart. He is currently at work on the first monograph of his Universus project, which will feature twenty-two meditations for people who use alphabets in their day-to-day communications. He is the creative director of *Reality Sandwich*.

**David Rothenberg** is author of *Why Birds Sing* (Basic Books, 2005) and *Thousand Mile Song: Whale Music in a Sea of Sound* (Basic Books, 2008).

**Diana Reed Slattery** is a practicing writer, VJ, and Xenolinguist. She is currently working on her Ph.D. with the Planetary Collegium. Topic: Communicating the Unspeakable: Linguistic Phenomena in the Psychedelic Sphere. She is the author of a novel, *The Maze Game*.

**Steven Taylor** is the author of *False Prophet: Field Notes from the Punk Underground* (Wesleyan University Press, 2003). His articles, reviews, essays, and poems have appeared in various anthologies and zines. From 1976 to 1996 he collaborated on music and poetry works with Allen Ginsberg, and has been a member of the seminal underground rock band The Fugs since 1984. He teaches at the Jack Kerouac School of Disembodied Poetics at Naropa University and is senior editor at *Reality Sandwich*.

**Alberto Villoldo**, Ph.D., is a medical anthropologist who has spent the last thirty years investigating the healing practices of the shamans of the Amazon and the Andes. He is the founder and director of the Four Winds Society, and author of *Shaman, Healer, Sage; Mending the Past and Healing the Future with Soul Retrieval; The Four Insights; Yoga, Power, and Spirit;* and *Courageous Dreaming*.

**Wahkeena Sitka Tidepool Ripple**, known as Sitka for short, is a mystic, artist, and gypsy seeking balance, wholeness, vibrancy, health, mental clarity, ecstatic passion, and peace in life. As an artist, she has explored polyrhythmic overtone singing, toning, and sound healing, photography, web design, graphic design, poetry, online journaling, songwriting, essay writing, jewelry making, and leather working. As a mystic, she has been surfing the zuvuya of consciousness for years studying Reiki, practicing Tantric and Thai bodywork, energetic and psychic awareness, dancing ecstatically, and exploring the cosmic psychedelic superconsciousness. Her perspectives and attitudes are influenced by personal, spiritual, physical, and psychological healing; visionary consciousness; full-body ecstatic experiences through dance and sexuality; and mindfulness presence meditation. She intends to contribute to the transformation of consciousness on Gaia, by embodying and reintegrating the Divine Feminine energy on this out-of-balance planet.

**Peter Lamborn Wilson** is a scholar of Sufism and Western Hermeticism and a well-known radical-anarchist social thinker. His books include *Sacred Drift: Essays on the Margins of Islam* (City Lights, 1993), *Escape from the Nineteenth Century and Other Essays* (Autonomedia, 1998) and, most recently, *Green Hermeticism: Alchemy and Ecology* (Lindisfarne, 2007).